John P. Murphy

Principles of English Grammar

Used by the Brothers of the Christian schools

John P. Murphy

Principles of English Grammar
Used by the Brothers of the Christian schools

ISBN/EAN: 9783337311360

Printed in Europe, USA, Canada, Australia, Japan

Cover: Foto ©Lupo / pixelio.de

More available books at **www.hansebooks.com**

PRINCIPLES

OF

ENGLISH GRAMMAR

USED BY THE

BROTHERS OF THE CHRISTIAN SCHOOLS.

———•———

NEW YORK
WILLIAM H. SADLIER
11 BARCLAY STREET

PREFACE.

THE present text-book attempts to combine theory with practice. It aims at putting English Grammar on a scientific basis. With this view, it has not lost sight of the Old English in which our language is rooted, and of the various stages through which our language has passed in the process of its growth and development.

We are too prone to forget that the English now spoken and written has come to us in its present form, with all its flexibility and power of expression, through many stages in which idioms and terms struggled for existence; that where one expression has survived, hundreds have been destroyed; that the present forms of words and phrases and idioms are intelligible to us only through their past history; and that it is only in a study of the nature and genius of our own language throughout the course of its growth and development that we can steer clear of foisting upon i rules and laws that are foreign to its whole spirit.

Grammar is profitable in proportion as it initiates the pupil into familiar acquaintance with the rules and principles governing the construction of the language. How may this be best effected?—The pupil begins by learning the nature and functions of the various classes of words that enter into a sentence. He next learns how to analyze and parse a sentence. He gradually becomes familiar with the forms that are of best usage in the present stage of the language. Parsing and the analysis of sentences are useful in so far as they help the pupil to acquire familiarity with correct forms, and no farther. Therefore, the most definite rule for the study of Grammar which we can lay down is this: Ground the pupil slowly, carefully, and thoroughly in the principles and rules regulating the classification, government, and relation of words, and then show him how admirably these principles and rules have been applied by the best models of pure English. Hand in hand with the grammar should go the spelling-book, the dictionary, and the reading-book, containing the best models, and furnishing the pupil with ideas which he should recast in his own words. The pupil should be accustomed to use correct grammatical expressions in his remarks and recitations, and to write correct grammatical sentences in his compositions. It is only by such practice, kept up during years of thoughtful study, that the pupil will be enabled to make profitable the study of Grammar as here given.

After the rules and principles of Grammar have been fairly mastered, it is of small avail to spend several hours a week in the merely mechanical drill-work of correcting false syntax and parsing sentences. For this reason, it has been deemed best not to overcrowd the pages of Syntax with exercises for parsing. The examples given under each rule will be found sufficient for the purpose. The pupils' time were far more profitably employed in constructing sentences according to models of good English.

In the following pages we have practically carried out our method as laid down in the *Management of Christian Schools* (Chapter ix., pp. 73–84).

June 29, 1890.

CONTENTS.

INTRODUCTION - - - - - - - - - - 7

PART I.—ORTHOGRAPHY.

CHAPTER   I. Letters: Their Origin and Formation - - 3
CHAPTER   II. Letters: Capitals - - - - - - 6
CHAPTER III. Letters: Italics - - - - - - 8
CHAPTER   IV. Words - - - - - - - - - 9

PART II.—ETYMOLOGY.

CHAPTER   I. The Parts of Speech Defined - - - - 12
CHAPTER   II. Parsing - - - - - - - - - 13
CHAPTER III. Nouns - - - - - - - - - 15
       I. Classes of Nouns - - - - - 15
        EXERCISES - - - - - - - 16
      II. Person - - - - - - - 18
     III. Number - - - - - - - 18
        EXERCISES - - - - - - - 22
     IV. Gender - - - - - - - 25
        1. Different Words - - - - - 26
        2. Suffixes - - - - - - 26
        3. Composition of Words - - - 27
        4. Personification - - - - - 27
        EXERCISES - - - - - - - 28
      V. Case - - - - - - - 28
     VI. Declension - - - - - - 31
        EXERCISES - - - - - - - 31
CHAPTER   IV. Articles - - - - - - - - 34
        EXERCISES - - - - - - - 35
CHAPTER   V. Adjectives - - - - - - - - 35
       I. Classes of Adjectives - - - - 35
        EXERCISES - - - - - - - 36

CONTENTS.

		PAGE
	II. Comparison of Adjectives	39
	III. Irregular Comparisons	40
	Exercises	42
Chapter VI.	Pronouns	43
	I. Personal Pronouns	43
	Declension of the Simple Personal Pronouns	44
	II. Relative Pronouns	45
	III. Demonstrative Pronouns	47
	IV. Interrogative Pronouns	47
	Exercises	48
Chapter VII.	Analysis of Sentences	51
	I. Classification of Sentences as to Meaning	51
	II. Principal Parts of Sentences	52
	III. Adjuncts	55
	IV. Phrases	56
	V. Principal Words and their Modifiers	58
	Exercises for Analysis	60
	1. Simple Sentences	60
	2. Secondary Modifiers	61
	3. Substantive Phrases	63
	4. Adjective Phrases	64
	5. Adverbial Phrases	64
	6. Explanatory and Independent Phrases	65
	7. Complex Phrases	65
	8. Compound Phrases	65
	9. Imperative, Interrogative, and Exclamatory Sentences	66
Chapter VIII.	Sentence-Building: Its Nature	67
	Exercises	69
Chapter IX.	Verbs	74
	I. Classification of Verbs as to Form	75
	II. Classification of Verbs as to Meaning	76
	III. Modification of Verbs	77
	Voice	77
	Mood	78
	Tense	80
	Number and Person	81
	IV. Conjugation of Verbs	82
	Auxiliary Verbs	82
	Forms of Conjugation	83

CONTENTS.

		PAGE
V.	Conjugation of the Verb *Have*	85
VI.	Conjugation of the Verb *Be*	88
VII.	Conjugation of the Transitive Verb *Love*: Active Voice	90
VIII.	Conjugation of the Transitive Verb *Love*: Passive Voice	93
IX.	Progressive Form of the Verb *Study*	96
	Remarks on the Conjugations	98
	EXERCISES	100
X.	Irregular Verbs	107
	1. Verbs that vary in all three parts	108
	2. Verbs whose Imperfect Tense and Perfect Participle are alike	110
	3. Verbs both regular and irregular in their principal parts	112
XI.	Defective Verbs	114
	EXERCISES	117
XII.	Infinitives	119
	EXERCISES	120
XIII.	Participles	121
	EXERCISES	122

CHAPTER X. Adverbs - 123
    I. Classification of Adverbs - 124
    II. Modification of Adverbs - 127
    III. Functions of Adverbs - 129
    EXERCISES - 130

CHAPTER XI. Prepositions - 131
    List of Prepositions - 132
    EXERCISES - 135

CHAPTER XII. Conjunctions - 136
    EXERCISES - 139

CHAPTER XIII. Interjections - 140
    EXERCISES - 141

CHAPTER XIV. Words Used in Various Senses - 143

CHAPTER XV. Analysis of Complex Sentences - 151
    Classification of Sentences as to Form - 151
    Models for the Analyzing of Complex and Compound Sentences - 155
    EXERCISES - 156

CHAPTER XV' Sentence-Building: Rules - 158
    EXERCISES - 162

CONTENTS.

PART III.—SYNTAX.

Chapter	I.	Subject and Verb	166
Chapter	II.	The Verb	170
Chapter	III.	The Noun	179
Chapter	IV.	The Pronoun	182
Chapter	V.	The Article	193
Chapter	VI.	The Adjective	197
Chapter	VII.	The Adverb	204
Chapter	VIII.	The Preposition	209
Chapter	IX.	The Conjunction	212
Chapter	X.	The Interjection	214
Chapter	XI.	Idiom	215

PART IV.—PROSODY.

Chapter	I.	Definitions	224
Chapter	II.	Punctuation	228

    I. The Period - - - - - - - 228
    II. The Colon - - - - - - - 229
    III. The Semicolon - - - - - 230
    IV. The Comma - - - - - - 231
    V. The Interrogation and Exclamation Points - 233
    VI. Dash, Hyphen, Parenthesis, Brackets, Quotation Points - - - - - 233

Chapter	III.	Versification	236
Chapter	IV.	Rhythm in Prose	244

    Extracts for Rhythmic Analysis - - - 252

PRINCIPLES
OF
ENGLISH GRAMMAR.

INTRODUCTION.

1. **Grammar** is the science of the elementary forms of language and of their relations to one another.

2. The **elementary forms** of language are the various parts of speech, idioms, and phrases of which the language is composed.

3. **Language** is the expression of thought by means of words.

4. **Words** may be either spoken or written, and are subject to certain rules.

5. The rules relating to the combining of letters and sounds are known as **Orthography**.

6. The rules relating to the classifying and modifying of words are known as **Etymology**.

7. The rules relating to the agreement and government of words in a sentence are known as **Syntax**.

8. The rules relating to the rhythm and harmony of words in verse and prose are known as **Prosody**.

9. These four subjects—Orthography, Etymology, Syntax, and Prosody—constitute the four principal divisions of Grammar.

10. **English Grammar** is here treated in the order of these divisions. Under each heading are stated the principles and laws governing words, phrases, and idioms as used by the best writers.

"Grammar," says Cardinal Newman, "is the scientific analysis of language, and to be conversant with it, as regards a particular language, is to be able to understand the meaning and force of that language when thrown into sentences and paragraphs" (*Idea of a University*, p. 334). Grammar is a science rather than an art, because its object is to classify words and lay down rules and principles of speech.

The student must bear in mind that the English language has a history in which its growth and its variations are recorded. The forms of good English to-day were not the forms of good English three hundred years ago, nor will they be the same three hundred years hence. The grammarian has no voice in imposing these forms upon the language. He is powerless to change them if he would. His province is simply to arrange and classify them and to account for them as best he may.

PART I.
ORTHOGRAPHY.

CHAPTER I.
LETTERS: THEIR ORIGIN AND FORMATION.

1. **Orthography** treats of letters and sounds.
2. **Letters** are certain signs invented to represent certain vocal sounds.

Thoughts were first represented by pictures; from these pictures, as used in Egypt in the distant past, the letters of the English language have been derived.

3. **Vocal sounds** are produced by the organs of speech.
4. **The organs of speech** are the tongue, the throat, the palate, the teeth, the lips, and the nose.

   (1) Sounds formed by the throat are called **gutturals**. Such is the sound of g in *gain*, or k in *keep*.
   (2) Sounds formed by the tongue and palate are called **palatals**. Such is the sound of j in *join*.
   (3) Sounds formed by the tongue and teeth are called **dentals**. Such is the sound of d in *done*.
   (4) Sounds formed by the lips are called **labials**. Such is the sound of b in *bad*, or p in *paid*.
   (5) Sounds formed by causing the breath to pass through the nose are called **nasals**. Such is the sound of *ng* in *sing*.

(6) Hissing sounds formed by the tongue and teeth and the tongue and palate are called **sibilants**. Such are the sounds of z in *prize*, and s in *sure*.

5. Letters are divided according to the organs of speech employed in expressing their sounds.

6. In English there are twenty-six letters. These letters are divided into vowels and consonants.

7. A **vowel** is an open sound. It is formed by the act of breathing upon the vocal chords.

8. There are five vowels; namely, a, e, i, o, u. Of these, three are primary, and two are derived.

9. The three **primary vowels** are a as sounded in *far*, i as sounded in *bit*, and u as sounded in *full*.

10. The two **derived vowels** are e as sounded in *obey*, which is composed of the vowels *a* and *i*; and o as sounded in *note*, which is composed of the vowels *a* and *u*.

11. The union of two vowels representing a single sound is called a **diphthong**.

12. A **consonant** is a sound produced by direct contact of particular organs of speech.

13. There are nineteen consonants. These may be divided as follows:

(1) **Labials:** b, v, w, m, p, f. These six letters represent the elementary lip-sounds.

(2) **Dentals:** d, t, n. These three letters represent the elementary teeth-sounds.

(3) **Gutturals:** h, k, and g hard, as in the word *gain*. These three letters represent the elementary throat-sounds.

(4) **Linguals:** l, r. These two letters are sometimes called trill-sounds. They are formed by the tongue and palate.

(5) **Palatals:** j, y. These are also formed by the tongue and palate.

(6) **Sibilants:** s, z. These are formed by a hissing sound of the tongue and palate.

(7) The consonant **c** has the sound of *s* or *k*, **q** has the sound of *ku*, and **x** has the the sound of *ks*.

14. The letters **w** and **y** have consonant-sounds at the beginning of a word or syllable, and vowel-sounds at the end of a word or syllable; as, *we, ye; new, try.*

15. Words change in **form** with the growth of a language. This is due to a change in **sound**. Change in sound is carried on in every language according to certain fixed laws.

16. The general drift of language, through all stages of its growth, is to shorten words. Thus we say *none* for *no one, don't* for *do not, don* for *do on.*

17. The change in words effects a change in the letters composing the words. This change also is subject to a fixed law.

18. The most general law of change in letters is this: Letters pronounced by the same organs may be interchanged.

Thus the flat labial **b** may become the sharp labial **p**, as from *absorb* is derived *absorption;* the flat dental **d** may become the sharp dental **t**, as *clasped* is reduced to *claspt,* or *passed* to *past.*

19. Sometimes there is an interchange between letters formed by **different parts of the same organs**; for example, the guttural **k**, which is formed by the palate and tongue near the throat, may become the palatal **ch**, which is formed by the palate and tongue near the teeth.

Thus has the old English word *dic* become the modern English word *ditch,* and the old English *wicce* is now pronounced *witch.* So the guttural **g** in *brycg* has been softened in our word *bridge.* In Lowland Scotch the word is still called *bryg.*

20. Sometimes the change in sound is effected by the **transposition of letters.**

Thus the old English not only said *three*, but they derived from it the word *thrid*, which we now pronounce *third*, and their word *lipsed* has become our *lisped*.

21. Sometimes **letters are dropped** out of a word.

Thus the olden form *maked* has now come to be spelled *made;* and what was once *haves* has now become *has*. So *lad* in one stage of the language had for its feminine *lad-ess*, whence we derive the word *lass*.

22. Sometimes a **dental** becomes assimilated with, or absorbed into, a following **sibilant.**

Thus where the old English said *godspel* we say *gospel*, and our modern *Essex* was once spelled *Estsex*.

23. Sometimes the **sibilants s, z,** and the **liquid r** interchange.

Thus where we say *forlorn* the old English said *forlosen*, and where we say *frozen* they said *froren*. Milton uses the word *frore* for *frozen:*

—" The parching air
Burns *frore*, and cold performs th' effect of fire."—*Paradise Lost.*

CHAPTER II.

LETTERS: CAPITALS.

Letters are either **small** or **capital**. The body of a printed page is generally given in small uniform letters. As exceptions to this practice we find some words beginning with capital letters and some words written in italics. There are certain rules governing this arrangement. We will begin with **capitals:**

1. The first word of every **sentence** should begin with a capital letter.

2. The first word in every **line of poetry** should begin with a capital letter; as,

> That music breathes all through my spirit,
> As the breezes blow through a tree;
> And my soul gives light, as it quivers
> Like moons on a tremulous sea.—FABER.

3. The first word of a **direct quotation** should begin with a capital letter; as, *Dora said, "My uncle took the boy."*

4. The **personal pronoun** *I*, the **interjection** *O*, and **single letters** forming abbreviations of proper names, should be capital letters.

5. **Proper names** should always begin with capitals; as, *Alice, William, George Washington, The United States. Sweden.*

6. Under this rule fall the names of the **days** and of the **months**, which take capitals; but not those of the **seasons**, which take small letters.

7. Titles of **honor** and **distinction** should begin with capitals; as, *Dr. Johnson, Charles the Bold, Hon. W. E. Gladstone.*

8. **Names** of the **Deity** should begin with capitals; as, *The Father, the Son, the Holy Ghost, God, Providence, the Almighty.*

9. So also should pronouns referring to the **Deity** begin with capitals; as,

> Oh, make Thou us through centuries long,
> In peace secure, in justice strong.
> WHITTIER, *Centennial Hymn,* 1889.

Some authors would write all pronouns with small letters. But too great respect cannot be shown to the name of the Supreme Being, even in print.

10. Adjectives derived from **proper names** should begin with capitals; as, *American, Elizabethan English, Johnsonian style.*

11. Certain words, derived from proper names, have become part of the language as verbs or common nouns, and are written with small letters; such as *gerrymander, boycott, buncombe, lynch, burke, galvanism, mesmerism;* also the words *roman* and *italics,* applied to type.

12. **Personified objects** may begin with capitals; as,

"Come, gentle *Spring!* ethereal *Mildness,* come."—Thomson.

13. **Emphatic words** may begin with capitals; as,

"The evidence of History, I say, is invaluable in its place; but if it assumes to be the sole means of gaining Religious Truth, it goes beyond its place."—Card. Newman. Here the words *History* and *Religious Truth* are emphasized.

CHAPTER III.

LETTERS: ITALICS.

1. **Emphatic** words, phrases, and clauses are sometimes printed in italics.

(1) **Emphatic words:** as, "When *blows* have made me stay, I fled from *words.*"

(2) **Emphatic phrases:** as, "A mere *string of sentences* is not a composition."

(3) **Emphatic clauses:** as, "I could not have done it, *unless you had helped.*"

2. **Italics** help to make the sense of a sentence clear; but it is desirable that in composition the least possible number of words be italicized.

3. Words borrowed from **foreign languages** should be put in italics: as, "Venturing upon really *extempore* matter."

It is advisable to employ the fewest possible foreign words in English composition. What cannot be expressed in English words can scarcely find a responsive idea in the ordinary English-speaking mind.

4. The names of **books, newspapers, periodicals,** and **ships** are usually printed in italics; as,

Cardinal Wiseman wrote *Fabiola;* *The Catholic World* is a monthly magazine; John Hassard was literary critic for *The Tribune;* Robert sailed on the *City of Paris.*

5. Italicized words in the **Old Testament** and the **New** are words introduced by the translators to render the sense intelligible to the English reader. They are generally words having no equivalent in the original Greek or Hebrew.

CHAPTER IV.

WORDS.

1. **Words** are sounds possessing a distinct meaning. They may be of one or more syllables.

2. A **syllable** is one or more letters, one at least being a vowel, sounded in a single breath; as, *man, bad-ly.*

3. A word of one syllable is a **monosyllable**; a word of two, is a **dissyllable**; a word of three, is a **trisyllable**; a word of more than three, is a **polysyllable.**

4. **Words** are either primitive, derivative, or compound.

5. **A primitive** word is a root-word, or a primary sound representing an idea; as, *mind*. It is the last form to which a word may be traced.

6. **A derivative** word is a word derived from a root-word by the addition of one or more syllables; as, *mindful, unmindful.*

7. **A compound** word is a word formed by the union of two or more words. The words may be primitive, as, *hat-box; ill-will;* or they may be derivative, as, *poverty-stricken.*

8. From root-words other words may be formed by adding prefixes or suffixes.

9. The **prefix** is a syllable placed before the root-word; as, *re-mind.*

10. The **suffix** is a syllable placed after the root-word; as, *thought-ful.*

11. Both prefixes and suffixes may consist of more than one syllable.

12. Words of more than one syllable are accented.

13. **Accent** is the stress of voice placed upon a particular syllable in a word.

14. Correct accent is essential to correct pronunciation.

15. **Correct pronunciation** follows the usage of the best speakers. The dictionary is supposed to give the best usage, but sometimes custom prevails over the authority of the dictionary. Each age has its own mode of pronouncing words. For instance, in Pope's time our word *tea* was pronounced *tay.* Thus he writes:

Here thou, great Anna! whom three realms obey,
Dost sometimes counsel take—and sometimes tea.
—RAPE OF THE LOCK.

So was the word *sea* pronounced *say*. Thus Cowper wrote:

" I am monarch of all I survey,
My right there is none to dispute;
From the centre all round to the sea
I am lord of the fowl and the brute."
—ALEXANDER SELKIRK.

In Shakespeare's day the word *Rome* was pronounced *room*. Hence the line:

" Now is it Rome indeed and room enough."—JULIUS CÆSAR.

16. Words should also be correctly **spelled.**

Correct spelling is difficult in the English language, owing to the fact that the language contains forty-three primary sounds and only twenty-three available letters in which to express them. Still, correct spelling is an essential part of education.

Some rules for spelling may be laid down, but correct spelling is chiefly acquired by practice. For rules of spelling, see the Brothers' *Pronouncing Speller*, pp. 93-98.

PART II.
ETYMOLOGY.

1. **Etymology** in grammar treats of the classification and modification of words.

2. Words, in English, are divided into nine classes, called **parts of speech**; namely, the *noun*, the *article*, the *adjective*, the *pronoun*, the *verb*, the *adverb*, the *preposition*, the *conjunction*, and the *interjection*.

CHAPTER I.
THE PARTS OF SPEECH DEFINED.

1. A **noun** is a word used as a name; as, *James, horse, New York, school, water, soul.*

2. An **article** is a word used to determine the sense in which a noun is taken; as, *The school, a man, an eye.*

3. An **adjective** is a word used to qualify or describe a noun or pronoun; as, *A good apple; five diligent boys; unhappy me.*

4. A **pronoun** is a word that stands for a noun; as, *Frank loves his book, he has long lessons, and he learns them well.*

5. A **verb** is a word that expresses being, action, or the being acted upon; as, *God is; William spells a word; the wind blows; the general was wounded.*

6. An **adverb** is a word used to modify the meaning of a verb, an adjective, or another adverb; as, *Summer is here; quickly it comes, and as quickly goes.*

7. A **preposition** is a word used to express the relation between an object and a preceding name, state, or action, as, *He went from New York to Baltimore;—Henry has come for me.*

8. A **conjunction** is a word used to join sentences or the elements of a sentence; as, *He is patient and happy, because he is a good Christian.*

9. An **interjection** is a word used to express emotion; as *Oh! alas!*

CHAPTER II.

PARSING.

1. **Parsing** is the explaining of the functions and relations of words in a sentence, according to the rules and definitions of grammar.

2. A **sentence** is a combination of words expressing a complete thought.

3. The essential part of every sentence is the **verb**, expressed or understood.

4. A sentence may express:

(1) An **assertion**; as, God is love.—Thomas has not studied.
(2) An **interrogation**; as, Does history always reveal the truth?
(3) A **command**; as, Honor the Light Brigade.
(4) An **entreaty**; as, Lead, kindly light! ... Keep Thou my feet.

EXERCISES IN PARSING.

Example 1.—*The fire burns.*
Fire is a noun, because it is a name.
The is an article, because it determines the definite sense in which the noun *fire* is taken.
Burns is a verb, because it expresses action.

I.—*Name in the following sentences the noun, the article, and the verb, and parse each as in the example:*

1. Longfellow wrote *Evangeline.*—2. The flowers bloom.—3. The ship sailed.—4. The moon shines.—5. James studies history.—6. Andrew reads.—7. The boy told an untruth.—8. Birds build nests.—9. The horse is a quadruped.

Example 2.—*A good boy obeys his parents.*
Good is an adjective, because it expresses the quality of the noun *boy.*
His is a pronoun, because it stands for the noun *boy.*

II.—*Point out the noun, the article, the adjective, the pronoun, and the verb, in the following sentences, and parse each as in the first and second examples:*

1. Beaumont and Fletcher wrote plays conjointly.—2. Mary learns her lessons.—3. A cheerful temper is a great blessing.—4. They disregard their teachers.—5. Boys are heedless.—6. Shakespeare lived in the reign of Queen Elizabeth.—7. An idle scholar is no credit to his teacher.—8. A noble mind scorns a mean action.—9. Milton wrote *Paradise Lost.*—10. Washington was a true patriot.

Example 3.—*Alas! how we miss the kind words and the gentle touch of our dear mother!*
How is an adverb, because it modifies the verb *miss.*
Of is a preposition, because it expresses the relation of the object *mother* to the preceding nouns *touch* and *words.*
And is a conjunction, because it connects the nouns *words* and *touch.*
Alas is an interjection, because it expresses an emotion

III.—Distinguish the parts of speech in the following sentences, and parse each as in the first, second, and third examples:

1. Shakespeare is the greatest dramatic poet in the world.—2. The rose is a beautiful and fragrant flower.—3. The good scholar attends diligently and carefully to his lessons.—4. Candor, sincerity, and truth are amiable qualities.—5. Emerson was a great New England writer.—6. A peach, an apple, a pear, or an orange is very delicious.—7. Men live and die, but God lives forever.—8. Alas! how unfortunate he is!—9. Whittier is known as the Quaker Poet.

CHAPTER III.

NOUNS.

I.—CLASSES OF NOUNS.

1. A **noun** is a word used as a name.

2. A **name** may include many things of the same class, when it is called common; as, *man, boy, book*. These words are known as **common nouns**.

3. A name may refer to some particular person or place, when it is called proper; as, *John, Baltimore, Ireland, America*. These words are known as **proper nouns**.

4. Two or more words forming a proper name are treated as a single word; as, *John Henry Newman, Jersey City*. They are parsed as **compound proper nouns**.

5. **Common nouns** may be sub-divided as follows:

> (1) **The compound noun.**—This is a common name formed of two or more words joined together; as, *silversmith, spoonful, man-of-war, father-in-law*.

(2) **The collective noun.**—This is a common name denoting a collection of many individuals; as, *family, meeting, flock, swarm.*

(3) **The abstract noun.**—This is the common name of a quality, considered apart from its substance; as, *goodness, hardness.*

(4) **The participial noun.**—This is a common name derived from the verb, and retaining the participial form; as, *reading, writing.* Here the word *reading* is derived from the verb *to read,* and retains the form of the present participle, *reading.*

EXERCISES.

I. Indicate orally, or by means of the letters **pr., a., pl., th.,** *if the noun is the name of a person, an animal, a place, or a thing:*

1. grass t.	2. king pr.	3. tiger a.	4. Albany pl.
shepherd	hill	flag	fire
prairie	turf	wood	baker
lion	crown	huntsman	kiln
collar	Washington	lead	mouse

II. Tell whether the proper noun indicates the name of a person, or a place. Put **pr.** *for person,* **pl.** *for place:*

1. Venice pl.	2. Margaret pr.	3. Newark	4. Cork
St. Louis	Liverpool	Montreal	Francis
Andrew	Brooklyn	Edward	Teresa

III. Insert one or other of the following words before the most appropriate quality or attribute:

1. Wax, grass, glass, gold, yeast.
2. Cake, water, iron, steel, winter.
3. Apple, leather, rain, vinegar, poison.
4. Gas, copper, beef, silver, bronze.

NOUNS. 17

1. Wax is soft. —— is green. —— is brittle. —— is yellow. —— leavens dough.

2. —— is sweet. —— is liquid. —— is hard. —— is pliable. —— is cold.

3. —— are wholesome. —— is tough. —- is useful. —— is sour. —— is dangerous.

4. —— illumines. —— is malleable. —— is nourishing. —— is shining. —— is a metal.

IV. State to what particular class each of the following nouns belongs:

1. hardness, ab.	2. pailful, cd.	3. herd, col.	4. sister-in-law
body	iniquity	water	penmanship
society	singing	generosity	humility
soul	goldsmith	writing	riding
virtue	glassful	moon	congregation

V. Classify the nouns in the following sentences, stating to what general or particular class each of them belongs:

1. The Jews are scattered over the whole world.—2. Luke's family went to Boston last month.—3. Paris, the capital of France, is situated on the river Seine.—4. The convention was held at Chicago, a city in the State of Illinois.—5. Milton lived in the seventeenth century.—6. "O the blasting of the fever."—LONGFELLOW.

VI. Form abstract nouns from the following words:

broad, breadth; black——; bright——; clear——; rapid——; honest——; good——; high——; long——; true——; wide——; virtuous——.

VII. Write four sentences, each containing a COMMON *noun;—four, each containing a* PROPER *noun;—three, each containing a* COMPOUND *noun;—two, each containing a* COLLECTIVE *noun;—two, each containing an* ABSTRACT *noun;—two, each containing a* PARTICIPIAL *noun.*

VIII. Write three sentences bearing relation to one another, and containing the nouns MOTHER, LOVE, SON, HAPPINESS.

If the sentences so written contain a **central idea**; that is, if they all treat of a single subject, they are called a **composition**.

II.—PERSON.

6. To nouns belong person, number, gender, and case.

7. **Person** varies according as the noun is the name of the speaker or writer, the person or thing addressed, or the person or thing spoken of.

8. There are **three persons**; the first, the second, and the third.

9. The **first person** denotes the speaker or writer; as, *I, George, command it.*

10. The **second person** denotes the person or thing addressed; as, *Henry, will you come?—Wave your tops, ye pines.*

11. The **third person** denotes the person or thing spoken of; as, *John and Joseph are going to school.*

12. Every noun is by its nature in the third person. But a noun used to explain a pronoun, when it is said to be in apposition with the pronoun, takes the **person of the pronoun**. So also, a noun denoting a person or thing addressed, is said to be in the **second person**.

III.—NUMBER.

13. **Number** is a property of nouns, that distinguishes one thing from more than one.

14. There are **two numbers**, the singular and the plural.

15. The **singular number** denotes but one thing; as, *pen, fox.*

16. The **plural number** denotes more things than one; as, *pens, foxes.*

17. Most nouns form their plural number by adding **s** to the singular; as, *house, houses; book, books.*

18. Nouns ending in **ch** soft,[1] **o** preceded by a consonant[2] **s, sh, x,** or **z,** form their plural by adding **es** to the singular; as, *match, matches; tomato, tomatoes; cross, crosses; brush, brushes; box, boxes; waltz, waltzes.*

19. Nouns ending in **y** preceded by a consonant form their plural by changing **y** into **i** and adding **es**; as, *army, armies.*

20. Nouns ending in **y** preceded by a vowel follow the general rule of adding **s**; as, *chimney, chimneys; storey, storeys.*[3]

21. The following nouns ending in **f** change the **f** into **v** and add **es**:

Singular.	Plural.	Singular.	Plural.	Singular.	Plural.
calf	calves	loaf	loaves	thief	thieves
elf	elves	self	selves	wolf	wolves
half	halves	sheaf	sheaves	beef	beeves
leaf	leaves	shelf	shelves	staff	staves

The plural form *beeves* does not convey the same idea as the singular *beef*. The word *elf* also takes *elfs* in the plural, and the word *shelf* takes *shelfs*.

22. The following nouns ending in **fe** form their plural by changing **f** into **v** and adding **s**: *knife, knives; wife, wives; life, lives.*

---

[1] *Ch* soft, as in the word *church*; *ch* hard, as in the word *chemistry*.

[2] Some words ending in *o* preceded by a consonant add *s* only to form the plural: as, *piano, pianos; zero, zeros.*

[3] *Storey*, a stage or floor of a building, is generally written *story* in America; but in England the correct form is still retained.

23. Some nouns form their plural by the **change of vowels.** There are three orders of vowel-changes, as follows:

1. **a** is changed to **e.**		2. **oo** is changed to **ee.**		3. **ou** is changed to **i.**	
Singular.	*Plural.*	*Singular.*	*Plural.*	*Singular.*	*Plural.*
man	men	goose	geese	mouse	mice
woman	women	tooth	teeth	louse	lice
		foot	feet	cow	kine

These are remnants of older plural formations.

24. Some nouns form their plural by the addition of **en** or **ren**; as, *ox, oxen, child, children; brother, brethren.*

This mode of forming the plural is of comparatively recent date. The plural of *child* was formerly *childer.* Thus we read:

"The *childer* are pretty *childer.*"—BEAUMONT AND FLETCHER.
The Knight of the Burning Pestle, act i., sc. 2.

25. The names of things **weighed** or **measured** are generally used in the singular number only; as, *flour, ale, rye, barley, tea.*

In commercial language men speak of *teas* and *ales;* but it is better English to say *tea* and *ale of various qualities.*

26. Some nouns having a plural form are frequently treated as nouns in the **singular** number; as, *alms, mathematics, means, news, ethics, optics, amends, shambles.* The word *summons* has *summonses* in the plural.

27. Some nouns are used in the **plural** only. The most ordinary are: *annals, ashes, bellows, billiards, bowels, compasses, entrails, intestines, measles, oats, pincers, scissors, snuffers, thanks, tongs, trousers, vespers, wages.*

Shakespeare uses *bellows* in the singular:

"The *bellows blows*."—*Pericles*, i., 2.

His contemporaries, Beaumont and Fletcher, speak of "a *thanks*."
—Vol. i., p. 5.

28. **Foreign words** that have become naturalized form their plural in the ordinary English way; as, *index, indexes; memorandum, memorandums; focus, focuses; automaton, automatons; beau, beaus.*

We still say *radius, radii; datum, data; parenthesis, parentheses; axis, axes; phenomenon, phenomena; cherub, cherubim; seraph, seraphim*. But we may form the plural of *formula* by *formulæ* or *formulas*, and *bandit*, by *banditti* or *bandits*.

29. The plural of **compound nouns** is formed by making the principal word plural; as, *step-son, step-sons; brother-in-law, brothers-in-law*. But we say *attorney-generals* rather than *attorneys-general*.

30. Where **both parts** of the compound noun seem to have equal prominence, each, following the French idiom, takes the plural form in the plural number; as, *man-servant, men-servants; knight-templar, knights-templars; lord-justice, lords-justices.*

31. Compound nouns ending in **ful** follow the general rule of adding **s**; as, *mouthful, mouthfuls; spoonful, spoonfuls.*

32. Some nouns, originally neuter, are **alike** in the singular and the plural; as, *deer, sheep, swine, salmon.*

33. **Particles** used as substantives form their plural by adding 's, or **es**; as, the *ifs* and the *buts;* the *ayes* and the *noes;* the *O's* and the *Macs;* the *t's* and the *i's.*

EXERCISES.

I. Write the following nouns in the plural:

1. patron	patrons	2. fox	foxes	3. echo	echoes
citizen	——	fuss	——	grotto	——
cousin	——	tax	——	key	——
heir	——	lash	——	tomato	——
comrade	——	fish	——	potato	——
window	——	willow	——	throe	——

II. Write or spell the plurals of the nouns:

Day, *days;* navy, ——; key, ——; fly, ——; valley, ——; fancy, ——; duty, ——; balcony, ——; enemy, ——; monkey, ——; bay, ——; Henry, ——; Emily, ——; boy, ——; penny, ——; bounty, ——; journey, ——; sky, ——; study, ——; beauty, ——.

III. Give the plurals of the following nouns:

1. Wife, calf, knife, beef, loaf. 2. Muff, proof, handkerchief, half, fife. 3. Life, self, shelf, wharf. 4. Gulf, dwarf, wolf, safe, hoof, thief.

IV. Write or spell the words of this section in the singular:

1. Teeth, mice, pianos, geese, matches. 2. Children, women, ladies, potatoes, skies. 3. Oxen, horses, feet, moneys, armies. 4. Eyes, stomachs, peaches, folios, trenches.

V. Indicate orally, or by means of the letters s. *or* p., *whether the nouns of this section are used in the singular or in the plural:*

1. wages p.	2. rice s.	3. thanks p.	4. billiards p.
alms	sugar	scissors	tongs
barley	oats	wheat	news
riches	mathematics	potatoes	pincers
annals	measles	parsley	raisins
politics	means	pneumatics	acoustics

VI. Give the plurals of the following nouns :

1. Father-in-law, step-daughter, son-in-law, cousin-german, spoonful, woman-servant, glassful. 2. Deer, salmon, trout, cupful, major-general, daughter-in-law, account-book, lord-justice.

VII. Write the figure (1) after the nouns of the first, (2) after those of the second, and (3) after nouns of the third person:

I, your general, order you to the fort.—Charles, give me a book from the library.—John, you may go home.—George, buy me some postage stamps.—Archbishop Carroll was a friend of Washington.—Napoleon died on the Island of St. Helena.—Comrades, hasten to the battle.—Gentlemen, the hour so long expected has come.—Children, be obedient to your parents, and strive to grow in holiness.

VIII. Write in the plural the nouns in italics:

A *book*, a *pen*, a *pencil*, a *slate*, are used in the class-room.—A *stove*, a *knife*, a *fork*, a *table*, are used in the kitchen.—A *history*, a *geography*, a *novel*, are in the library.—A *horse*, a *wagon*, a *carriage*, are in the stable.—A *statue*, a *crucifix*, a *picture*, a *chair*, an *altar*, are in the sanctuary.—A *duck*, a *goose*, a *chicken*, a *rabbit*, are in the farm-yard.—A *boy*, a *girl*, a *woman*, a *man*, were in the lecture-hall.—Goldsmith played on the *flute*.

IX. Spell the plurals of the italicized nouns:

In reading *history* consult your *atlas*.—Have *Mass* said for the repose of his soul.—Virgil sat beneath the *beech*.—He prays in the *church*.—He has the *eye* of a *lynx*.—The ball broke the *sash* of the *window*.—The door was open, and the *boy* entered the room to get a *book*.—Has the *visitor* come with his *servant?*—Where are the *broom* and the *brush* that I gave you?—The *book-case* is empty.—The *arch* has a keystone.—He is without *spot* or *blemish*.—Have you seen the *princess?*—Mend the *shoe*.—The *nuncio* called on the cardinal.—Pope's *grotto* is in Twickenham.

X. Write in the plural the words in italics:

The *fly* alighted on a window.—The *lily* and the *morning-glory* were in bloom.—The *city* was noted for its large *chimney*.—The *index* is complete.—The *formula* of the *row* was written with much *difficulty*. —The *focus* did not suit his *eye*.—John praised the *beauty* of the *toy*.— The *view* is delightful.—Pope was the greatest English poet of the eighteenth *century*.

XI. Give the plurals of the italicized nouns:

The *plow* and the *rake* are in the barn.—With a *knife* the *loaf* was cut in halves.—Teach the *boy* to read.—Play the *piano*.—Her *mother-in-law* has gone home.—The *lesson* is recited.—The *woman* is sick.— The *bird* is on the tree.—The *flower* has faded.—The *man* is in business.—The *step-daughter* is here.—The *army* was defeated.—The *enemy* could not attain his purposes.

XII. Write in the singular the nouns in italics:

The house contains seven *storeys*.—The *brooks* are swollen.—Children delight in listening to interesting *stories*.—John received the *toys*. —The *men* are working well.—His *teeth* are aching.—The *mice* were caught.—The *stores* are all closed.—The *cakes* are broken.—The *pictures* were painted.—Has Henry the *pens* and *pencils?*—*Potatoes* and *tomatoes* are nutritious vegetables.—The *banditti* withdrew to the mountains.

XIII. Fill in the blank with such of the following words as will complete the sense:

Steel, iron, silver, lead, flour, sugar, wool, straw, clay, milk.

1. Swords are made of ——. Boilers are made of ——. Hats are made of ——. Pipes are made of ——. Cake is made of ——. Watches are made of ——. Candy is made of ——. Carpets are made of ——. Bells are made of ——. Books are made of ——. Shoes are made of ——. Cheese is made from ——.

XIV. Write two sentences, each containing a noun in the first person; three, each containing a noun in the second person; three, each containing one noun or more in the third person.

XV. Write three sentences, each containing one noun or more in the singular number; also three, each containing one noun or more in the plural. Write four short sentences on GOLD; *write four on* BREAD.

IV.—GENDER.

34. Gender, in English grammar, is a property of nouns, which expresses distinction in the names of living beings and of things without life.

Gender belongs only to the word, and not to the sex it may represent. Thus, the person *man* is of the male sex, while the word *man* is of the masculine gender.

35. There are **three genders,** the masculine, the feminine, and the neuter.

36. The **masculine gender** is that which denotes the names of male beings; as, *man, stag.*

37. The **feminine gender** is that which denotes the names of female beings; as, *woman, cow.*

38. The **neuter gender** is that which denotes the names of things that are neither male nor female; as, *stone, water.*

The word neuter means neither. It is simply a grammatical term applied to the *names* of things without life.

39. A noun that may be either masculine or feminine is said to be of the **common gender**; as, *parent,* which may be father or mother; *child,* which may be boy or girl.

40. The masculine and feminine of nouns are distinguished in three ways:

I.—By the use of different words.

Masculine.	Feminine.	Masculine.	Feminine.
bachelor	maid, spinster [1]	king	queen
		lad	lass
boar	sow	lord	lady
boy	girl	landlord	landlady
brother	sister	man	woman
buck	doe	master	mistress
bull	cow	nephew	niece
cock	hen	papa	mamma
colt	filly	ram, wether	ewe
drake	duck	sir	madam
father	mother	son	daughter
friar or monk	nun	stag, hart	hind
gander	goose	steer	heifer
gentleman	lady	uncle	aunt
stallion, gelding	mare	widower	widow
husband	wife	wizard	witch [2]

II.—By the use of suffixes.

Masculine.	Feminine.	Masculine.	Feminine.
abbot	abbess	marquis	marchioness
actor	actress	negro	negress
bridegroom	bride	patron	patroness
count	countess	prophet	prophetess
czar	czarina	protector	protectress
duke	duchess	prince	princess
emperor	empress	shepherd	shepherdess
hero	heroine	songster	songstress
heir	heiress	tailor	taileress
lion	lioness	tiger	tigress

The suffix **ess** comes to us from the Norman-French.

---

[1] In legal terms the word *spinster* is applied to every unmarried woman.

[2] *Witch*, until recently, was of the common gender; as, "Your honor is a *witch*."—Scott, *Fortunes of Nigel*, 2.

III.—By composition of words.

Masculine.	Feminine.	Masculine.	Feminine.
buck-rabbit	doe-rabbit	male-child	female-child
cock-sparrow	hen-sparrow	man-servant	maid-servant
he-goat	she-goat	male-descendants	female-descendants

41. When the sex is not apparent the **neuter** pronoun is sometimes used; as, "*It is a fine bird.*" Sometimes also preference is given to the **masculine** form of the pronoun; as, "*A parent should care for the education of his child.*"

The **gender** of nouns was differently determined by the old English people. It depended on both the form and the meaning of the word, as in the French and German languages. The present distinction came into general use during the fourteenth century, and was due in a great measure to the inability of the Norman-French lords to master the laws governing gender in the language of their English subjects.

PERSONIFICATION.

42. Things without life are said to be **personified** when they are spoken to, or spoken of, as persons or living beings; as, "*Charity seeketh not her own.*"

—A brave vessel,
Who had, no doubt, some noble creature in *her*,
Dashed all to pieces.

43. Personification endows a neuter noun with the attributes of sex; as,

"Fine old Christmas, with the snowy hair and ruddy face, had done *his* duty that year in the noblest fashion."—DICKENS.

"And Belgium's capital had gathered then
Her beauty and *her* chivalry."—BYRON.

EXERCISES.

I. State orally, or by means of the letters m., f., c., *or* n., *whether the noun is masculine, feminine, common, or neuter.*

1. king, m.	2. dressmaker, f.	3. horse, c.
queen	milliner	mistress
general	embroiderer	house
captain	lion	knowledge
nephew	hen	duck

II. Indicate the gender of the nouns by placing m., f., c., *or* n. *after each, in the following sentences:*

The orphan is deserving of care.—The child is father of the man.—The way was long, the wind was cold.—Labor conquers all things.—

"The children coming home from school
Look in at the open door."

LONGFELLOW, *The Village Blacksmith.*

III. Change into the feminine the nouns that are italicized:

The *shepherd* is dead.—Is the *lion* fierce?—Where is the *bridegroom* this morning?—The *tailor* has brought the coat.—The *widower* is very poor.—The *baron* is reading Newman's "Callista."—The *heir* has succeeded to the estate.

IV. Change the italicized nouns into the masculine:

The *lady* has gone to the library.—The *girl* is going to Boston.—The *patroness* of the children is dead.—The *princess* has married.—Her *aunt* is sick.—The *empress* has gone to Germany.—The *countess* is at the hotel.

V.—CASE.

44. Case is a mode of inflection showing the relation of a noun or pronoun to some other word in a sentence.

45. There are **three cases**; namely, the nominative, the possessive, and the objective.

46. These three cases admit only of **two forms** for nouns: the nominative and the possessive. The nominative and objective cases of nouns are always **the same** in form.

47. A noun or pronoun that is the subject of a verb, is said to be in the **nominative case**; as, *Reinhart sculptured the statue of Clytie.*

48. **How to find the nominative.**—The subject of a verb, when a noun or pronoun, is always in the nominative case.

The subject of a verb is that which answers to the question containing *who* or *what* before the verb: as, *Reinhart sculptured the statue of Clytie.* Who sculptured the statue of Clytie? *Reinhart.* Therefore the proper noun *Reinhart* is the subject. *The sunflower blooms.* What blooms? *The sunflower.* Therefore the common noun *sunflower* is the subject. *The table was struck.* What was struck? *The table.* Therefore the common noun *table* is the subject. All these subjects are in the **nominative case**.

49. The **possessive case** is that form of a noun or a pronoun that denotes the relation of possession; as, *The man's hat; my coat.*

The **possessive case** may express:

(1) **Ownership**; as, *John's* house.
(2) **Origin**; as, *Scott's* novels, *Singer's* sewing machine.
(3) **Kind**; as, *Boys'* clothing; *men's* hats.
(4) **State of being**; as, His *uncle's* death; his *father's* sickness.

50. The possessive case of nouns is formed, in the singular, by adding an **s** with an **apostrophe** to the nominative form; as, *The bird's feathers.*

51. When the nominative plural ends in **s**, the apostrophe alone is added to form the possessive; as, *The ladies' fans.*

52. When the nominative plural does not end in **s**, the possessive case is formed in the same manner as in the singular; as, *Children's toys are dear to them.*

53. The sign of the possessive is now used only in words expressing living beings. Thus we say, *The bird's nest, my grandfather's clock.*

Neuter nouns, when personified, take the possessive form.

It is incorrect to say *the house's roof*, as was formerly said; the proper form is, *the roof of the house.* Nouns of time, however, still retain the old form of the possessive; as, *A week's supply, a day's journey.*

54. The **'s** stands for **es**, the genitive singular of some masculine and neuter nouns in old English.

It is erroneous to consider the **'s** a contraction of the word *his.* Feminine nouns did not take the suffix **es** to form the possessive till the thirteenth century; hence it is that, while we say *Lord's Day*, we also use the expression *Lady-Day* instead of *Lady's Day.*

55. A noun or pronoun that is the object of a verb or of a preposition, is said to be in the **objective case**; as,

"I heard the ripple washing in the reeds."—TENNYSON.

56. How to find the objective.—The **object** of a verb or of a preposition answers to the question containing *whom* or *what* after the verb or the preposition; as, *I heard the ripple washing in the reeds.* I heard *what?* I heard the *ripple.* Washing in *what?* Washing in the *reeds.*— *Ripple* and *reeds* are in the **objective case.**

VI.—DECLENSION.

57. The **declension** of a noun is the naming of the noun according to all its cases in both numbers.

EXAMPLES OF DECLENSION.

Singular.	*Plural.*	*Singular.*	*Plural.*
Nom. Ox	Oxen	*Nom.* Sheep	Sheep
Poss. Ox's	Oxen's	*Poss.* Sheep's	Sheep's
Obj. Ox	Oxen	*Obj.* Sheep	Sheep
Nom. Man	Men	*Nom.* Lady	Ladies
Poss. Man's	Men's	*Poss.* Lady's	Ladies'
Obj. Man	Men	*Obj.* Lady	Ladies

EXERCISES.

I. Give the possessive form of the following nouns:

1. William, thief, woman, stomach, ox, army.
2. Echoes, Mary, women, buffaloes, torches, children.

II. Change the phrases in italics into nouns in the possessive case, as in the following example:

"*The history of a people* is the record of *the civilization of a people* = A *people's history* is the record of *a people's civilization.*"
The marbles of the boy are in the drawer.—He came to do *the will of his father.*—The quaker wife *of Robert of Lincoln.*—*The warbling of the bird* echoes through the hall.—I found in the street *the book belonging to Ann.*—*The tools of the carpenter* are in the tool-chest.—*The hat of the lady* is decked with an ostrich-feather.—*The merits of the historian* depend upon the earnestness with which he seeks to know the truth.—It is *the journey of a day* between the two towns.

*Why is it permitted to say a **day's journey**, and not a **chimney's top**?* (53.)

III. Write out the following exercise on slates or copybooks, drawing one line under the nominative case, and two lines under the objective case.

Grammar is an important study.—Wordsworth is the most careful writer among modern poets.—Her home is on the deep.—We left him alone with his glory.—Cardinal Newman writes classic English prose.—The end of government is the good of mankind.—Write your address on your slate.—Clytie was changed into a sunflower.

IV. Where the dash occurs, insert, in the proper case, a noun that will complete the sense.

Health, girl, patriot, day, George, work, Turk, children, evening, Indian.

Edward Everett was a celebrated orator.—Temperance promotes ——. The bright morning star, harbinger of ——. Isabel saw a tear starting in the —— eye.—The —— blood was spilled in a noble cause.—Bring me —— hat.—Great —— are wrought by prayer.—The —— was warm.—The —— was dreaming of the hour.—The —— were captured by the ——.

V. Where the dash occurs insert a noun that will complete the sense.

1. Bird, boy, clock, pony, soldier. 2. Musician, straw, knowledge, hope. 3. Snow, fire, squirrel, songs, philosopher.

The wind was bitterly cold.—How sweetly the —— sings.—Do —— like to skate?—The old —— spoke the truth.—The wooden —— is stopped.—The —— ran away.

2. The —— played on the harp.—We acquire —— by patient study.—While —— remains there can be no positive misery.—A —— will furnish an occasion when people are determined to quarrel.

3. The —— covered the ground.—The merry little —— sat quietly on the branch.—The —— burns cheerily.—He sang sweetly the old —— of his boyhood.—St. Anselm was a great —— as well as a distinguished churchman.

NOUNS.

VI. Parse the nouns in the sentences given below, as in the example.

Example.—William has found a bird's nest in the hedge.

William is a noun, because it is a name; it is a proper noun, because it is the name of a particular individual;—in the third person, because it is spoken of;—in the singular number, because it means but one;—of the masculine gender, because it denotes a person of the male sex;—in the nominative case, because it is the subject of the verb *has found*.

Bird's is a noun (*why?*);—it is a common noun (*why?*);—in the third person (*why?*);—in the singular number (*why?*);—in the masculine gender (*why?*);—in the possessive case, because it denotes the relation of possession.

Nest is a common noun, of the third person, singular number, neuter gender, because it denotes a thing that is neither male nor female, and in the objective case, because it is the object of the verb *has found*.

Hedge is a common noun, of the third person, singular number, neuter gender (*why?*);—and in the objective case, because it is the object of the preposition *in*.

1. The wreck was washed upon the shore.—2. A gloomy house stood by the roadside.—3. The eagle has a strong and piercing eye.—4. Bleak winds whistled through the pines around the cabin.—5. A wise man's anger is of short continuance.—6. Flakes of snow soon hid the ground from view.—7. St. Teresa of Jesus is one of the glories of Spain. Her writings are highly esteemed.

" It was morning on hill and stream and tree,
And morning in the young knight's heart."
LOWELL,—*Vision of Sir Launfal.*

VII. Write four sentences, each containing a noun in the nominative case; three, each containing a noun in the objective case; two, each containing a noun in the possessive case.

VIII. Write two sentences, each containing one noun in the nominative case, one in the objective case, and one in the possessive case.

IX. Write sentences, each containing one or more of the following words:

teacher	brother	sisters	house
field	rivers	fish	farmer's
boat	ship	disobedient	parents

X. Write five short sentences on the subject of your last reading-lesson.

XI. Put in your own words, and in not more than six sentences, what you think of the study of grammar.

CHAPTER IV.
ARTICLES.

1. An **article** is a word used to determine the sense in which a noun is taken; as, **the** *school,* **a** *man,* **an** *eye.*

Some grammarians give to the article the name of **adjective** because it always accompanies nouns.

A noun may be taken in a definite or in an indefinite sense.

2. There are **two articles,** the definite and the indefinite.

3. The **definite article is the.** It points out some particular object or objects and limits their sense; as, **the** *book,* **the** *history.*

4. The indefinite article is an or a. It does not point out any particular object; as, **a** *town,* **an** *engine.*

5. A is used before a **consonant** sound; as, *a swarm, a yearling, a well, a unit.*

6. An is used before a **vowel** sound; as, *an errand, an excuse, an urn, an hour.*

EXERCISES.

I. Supply the proper article in the following sentences:

1. Can you describe —— ostrich?—2. What kind of bird is —— eagle?—3. Bring —— knife and —— apple.—4. Romans placed —— ashes of —— dead in —— urn.—5. Crœsus was considered —— rich man.—6. The country possessed —— fertile soil, —— variety of scenery, —— abundance of game, and —— healthful climate.

II. Where the dash occurs insert one or other of the following words, preceded by a *or* an.

1. Youth, elm, hour, eagle. 2. Honorable, union, watch, yoke.

1. Be thankful for a *reward*. It is —— that you see flying. Come —— at ——, not later. He is —— that needs instruction. The woodman has cut down ——.

2. The four societies formed ——. The boys received a present of ——. The farmer has —— of oxen. That young man is occupying —— position.

CHAPTER V.

ADJECTIVES.

I.—CLASSES OF ADJECTIVES.

1. An **adjective** is a word used to qualify or describe a noun or pronoun; as, *a good school; five diligent boys; he is strong.*

2. Adjectives are divided into **five classes**: common, proper, numeral, pronominal, and participial.

3. **A common adjective** is a word that expresses quality, quantity, or place; as, *good, bad, little, much, eastern, outer.*

4. **A proper adjective** is an adjective derived from a proper name; as, *the **American** flag, the **Irish** cause, the **Canadian** people.*

5. **A numeral adjective** is an adjective that expresses number; as, *two pears, the **first** speaker, a **twofold** purpose.*

6. Numeral adjectives are of three kinds; cardinal, ordinal, and multiplicative.

> (1) The **cardinal adjective** tells *how many;* as, *one, two, three.*
> (2) The **ordinal adjective** tells *which one;* as, *first, second, third.*
> (3) The **multiplicative adjective** tells *how many fold;* as *single* or *alone, double* or *twofold, triple* or *threefold.*

7. **A pronominal adjective** is an adjective that performs the office of certain pronouns; that is, it may be used with a noun, or it may represent the noun; as, *Silver and gold I have **none**; **few** shall part where **many** meet.*

8. The principal pronominal adjectives are: *All, another, any; both, each, either, enough, every, few; former, latter; little, less, least; much, many, more, most; none, neither, one, other, same, several, some, such.*

9. **A participial adjective** is an adjective derived from a verb and having the form of a participle; as, *a **loving** mother; the **rising** sun.*

EXERCISES.

I. *Insert such of the following nouns as the adjectives given will qualify:*

1. Archway, man, shadow. 2. Beast, book, parent.
3. Student, girl, countenance.

1. A shattered ——. 2. A voracious ——. 3. An earnest ——
A venerable ——. An instructive ——. A dutiful ——. A fleeting
——. A devoted ——. A pleasing ——.

II. Write out the following sentences, underlining the articles and adjectives that occur:

His gifted pen transmutes everything into gold, and his own genial nature reflects its sunshine through his pages.

The gentle spirit of his father walked with him through life, a pure and virtuous monitor; and, in all the vicissitudes of his career, we find him ever more chastened in mind by the sweet and holy recollection of the home of his infancy.—IRVING,—*Life of Goldsmith.*

III. Indicate orally, or by means of the letters p. *or* c, *whether the adjective is proper or common:*

1. true	2. French	3. sweet	3. Alpine
dull	pleasant	small	wise
English	happy	British	Grecian

IV. Insert one or other of the following numeral or pronominal adjectives that will complete the sense in the following sentences:

Each, all, once, former, none, later, some, one, other, such, twenty

They had —— an apple.—He spoke —— after being struck.—The —— book has a large circulation, the —— has but little.—The —— went to the field, —— remained behind.—The boat is the —— that was used yesterday. —— of the men rode a gray horse, the —— a black one. The punishment was —— as he deserved.—The —— cows were in the barn.

V. Write out the following sentences, drawing one line under each numeral, and two lines under each pronominal adjective:

Every Catholic home should have a supply of Catholic books.—The first time I was on the ocean, I read a novel by Dickens.—Critics prefer Thackeray to all other English novelists.—I am reading his *Henry Esmond* for the fifth time.—Twenty large vessels sailed up the river in one day.—Several were late.—Few know how to be grateful.—Neither will come.—Gibbon wrote the first chapter of his great history for the seventh time before he became satisfied with it.—Many were studying Milton.—None should be unacquainted with Shakespeare.

VI. Write out the following adjectives, and indicate by means of **c., p., n., pro., part.,** *to which class each of them belongs.*

1. small, c.	2. German	3. Spanish	4. nut-brown
fourth	two	amusing	hard
interesting	tenth	rising	soft
some	Irish-American	beloved	many

VII. Parse the adjectives in the sentences here given according to the two following examples:

Example 1.—*All good books are interesting companions.*

All is a pronominal adjective, because it is used with the noun *books*, and it may also take the place of a noun.

Good is a common adjective, because it qualifies the noun *books*.

Interesting is a participial adjective, because it has the form of a participle, and qualifies the noun *companions*.

Example 2.—*Two of my schoolmates won prizes in the French language.*

Two is a numeral adjective, because it expresses number.

French is a proper adjective, because it is derived from a proper name.

1. The red squirrel is a blithe creature.—2. The same duties were expected of each.—3. Spenser is a great allegorical poet.—4. This gently flowing stream empties into a beautiful lake.—5.—Our three

friends walked across a plowed field, and soon came to a running stream.—6. We saw a merry yachting party of American and English gentlemen on Lake Ontario.

II.—COMPARISON OF ADJECTIVES.

10. **Comparison** is the change in the form of an adjective, to express different degrees of quality or quantity; as, *hard, harder, hardest; soft, softer, softest.*

11. The **degrees** of comparison are three in number: the positive, the comparative, and the superlative.

12. The **positive degree** is expressed by the adjective in its simple form; as, *wide, great.*

13. The **comparative degree** is expressed by adding -r or -er to the positive; as, *wider, greater.*

14. The comparative degree is used when **two** persons or things, or two sets or classes of persons or things, are compared.

15. The **superlative degree** is expressed by adding -st or -est to the positive; as, *widest, greatest.*

16. The superlative degree is used when a comparison is made between **more than two** persons or things.

17. **Regular comparison.**—The **comparative** of adjectives of one syllable is commonly formed by adding -er to the positive, and the **superlative** by adding -est; as, *great, greater, greatest.*

18. **Comparison by adverbs.**—Degrees of comparison may also be expressed by adding the adverbs **more** and **most** to the adjective; as, *gay, more gay, most gay.*

19. Adjectives of more than one syllable are generally compared by means of the adverbs **more** and **most**; as, *lovely, more lovely, most lovely.*

20. The degrees of diminution are expressed by the adverbs **less** and **least**; as, *noble, less noble, least noble*.

21. Those adjectives whose signification does not admit of different degrees cannot be compared; as, *two, all, infinite, exact, supreme, universal, eternal, certain*.

III.—IRREGULAR COMPARISONS.

22. Some adjectives are compared **irregularly**. A study of their nature, their origin, and their history will give greater insight into the construction of our language. For the purpose of this study, we shall divide them into two groups.

Group A.

Positive.	Comparative.	Superlative.
late	later or latter	latest or last
nigh	nigher (near)	nighest, next
near	nearer	nearest
old	older or elder	oldest or eldest

(1) **Late** has two comparatives and two superlatives: of these *latter* and *last* are the oldest. So also *near* has *next* and *nearest* for its superlatives, and *old* has *elder* and *eldest* as well as *older* and *oldest*.

(2) **Last** is a contraction of an old form *lat-st = latest*. The t is dropped out according to the law in Orthography, ch. i. 21. **Latter** and **last** refer to the order of things; as, "The *latter* group." "The *last* of the Saxons." **Later** and **latest** refer to time; as, "I shall see you *later*." "Tuesday is the *latest* day." This distinction is of recent origin.

(3) **Next** is a contraction of *nighest*. It is derived from the old English *nĕh-st*, in which the h was a sharp guttural, sounded as ch in *loch*. The process of the change may be represented thus: $h + s = k + s = x$. So also, at an earlier stage of the language, our word *highest* was sounded *hext*.

(4) **Near** we have placed in the comparative because it was itself once a comparative.

(5) **Elder, eldest** have vowel-change as well as inflexion.

Group B.

Positive.	Comparative.	Superlative.
good	better	best
bad, ill, evil	worse	worst
little	less	least
much, many	more	most

23. The comparatives and superlatives in this group are all formed from positives no longer in use. Let us examine them.

(1) **Better** comes from a root **bat** = good. This root may stil' be traced in our expression "*to boot*"—the vowel changing as we have seen it in the word elder.

(2) **Best** = bet-st = bet-est. Here, as in the word *last*, the t is dropped out, according to the law in Orthography, already referred to.

(3) **Worse** = *wor-se* comes from a root, *weor* = bad. The suffix -se is another form of the regular comparative ending, -er. We have seen how s and r are interchangeable (Orth., ch. i. 22). *Worst* is shortened from *worrest* (Orth., ch. i. 15). Chaucer sometimes uses *badder* for *worse*.

(4) **Less** is formed from a root **las**, meaning *weak, infirm.* **Less** = *les-s*, in which the suffix -s (= -se) is another form of the comparative -r (*Ibid*). Therefore *lesser*, like *nearer*, is a double comparative. Shakespeare uses the word *littlest* (*Hamlet*, iii. 2).

(5) **Much** once meant *large, great*. The root *mo* in *mo-re* and *mo-st* also means *great*. Shakespeare uses this root as a comparative in the form *moe*.

"Friends, I owe *moe* tears
To this dead man, than you shall see me pay."
—*Julius Cæsar*, v. iii.

EXERCISES.

I. Compare the following adjectives:

Positive.	Comparative.	Superlative.	Positive.	Comparative.	Superlative.
1. wise	——	——	2. warm	——	——
small	——	——	rude	——	——
soft	——	——	ripe	——	——

II. Insert one or other of the words here given, in the following sentences:

happy	wise	tall
cold	harder	noble
larger	healthy	greatest

1. He is older than you.—He is a —— boy.—William is not as —— as Mary.—George is a —— youth.—The flower is the —— I have seen.—This is a —— day.—This pair is —— than the one you gave me yesterday.—Jane is a —— girl.—I have the —— respect for his nephew.

III. Compare the following adjectives by adding -r *or* -er, *and* -st *or* -est.

Positive.	Comparative.	Superlative.	Positive.	Comparative.	Superlative.
wise	——	——	full	——	——
noble	——	——	long	——	——
gentle	——	——	round	——	——
lazy	——	——	strait	——	——
near	——	——	true	——	——
high	——	——	strict	——	——
simple	——	——	humble	——	——
ample	——	——	thick	——	——
ugly	——	——	serene	——	——
profound	——	——	remote	——	——

IV. Parse the adjectives in the following sentences, according to the example:

Example.—*Two honest men were they.*

Two is a numeral adjective (*why?*);—it cannot be compared; it limits the noun *men*.

Honest is a common adjective (*why?*);—it is compared (pos. *honest*, com. *more honest*, sup. *most honest*), and qualifies the noun *men*.

1. The burnt child dreads the fire. — 2. The surrounding country presents a charming prospect. — 3. Vicious people generally corrupt their companions.—4. A clear and upright conscience is something to be prized.—5. A beautiful eye makes silence eloquent.

V. Parse the nouns, articles, and adjectives in the following extract:

"She was dead. Dear, gentle, patient, noble Nell was dead. Her little bird—a poor, slight thing, the pressure of a finger would have crushed—was stirring nimbly in its cage; and the strong heart of its child-mistress was mute and motionless forever." — Dickens,—*Old Curiosity Shop.*

CHAPTER VI.

PRONOUNS.

1. A **pronoun** is a word that stands for a noun; as, *His slate; my hat; who is afraid?*

2. Pronouns are divided into **four classes**; namely, personal, relative, demonstrative, and interrogative.

I -PERSONAL PRONOUNS.

3. A **personal pronoun** is a pronoun that by its form marks person. It distinguishes the speaker, the person spoken to, and the person or thing spoken of.

4. Personal pronouns are divided into **two classes**; namely, simple and compound.

5. The **simple personal pronouns** are five: **I,** of the first person; **thou,** of the second; **he, she,** and **it,** of the third person.

6. The **compound personal pronouns** are also five: **myself,** of the first person; **thyself,** of the second person; **himself, herself, itself,** of the third person.

The compound personal pronouns are formed by the addition of the word **self** to the possessive case of the first and second persons, and the objective case of the third person.

In a previous stage of the language the word **self** was added to the objective case of the first and second persons, and men said, *meself, theeself.* In the thirteenth century the present custom of saying *myself* and *thyself* began to prevail.

7. The compound personal pronouns have no possessive case, and are alike in the nominative and objective. Their plural form is *ourselves, yourselves,* and *themselves.*

8. The word **self,** originally an adjective, has come to be considered a noun. The form **oneself** is of recent origin.

9. The functions of the compound personal pronouns are:

(1) **Reflexive;** as, *He* hurt *himself.*
(2) **Emphatic;** as, *I* shall do it *myself.*

In old forms of the language, *me* was used for *myself;* as, *I lay me down to sleep.*

10. Declension of the Simple Personal Pronouns.

	First Person.		Second Person.	
	Singular.	*Plural.*	*Singular.*	*Plural.*
Nom.	I	we	thou	ye, or you
Poss.	my, or mine	our, or ours	thy, or thine	your, or yours
Obj.	me	us	thee	you

PRONOUNS.

Third Person.

	Singular.			Plural.
	Mas.	*Fem.*	*Neuter.*	
Nom.	he	she	it	they
Poss.	his	her, or hers	its	their, or theirs
Obj.	him	her	it	them

11. Of the two possessive forms, **my, our, thy, your, her, their,** are used before the noun with which they express the relation of possession; as, *This is **my** hat;* and **mine, ours, thine, yours, hers, theirs,** are used when the governing noun is understood; as, *This hat is **mine;** these books are **yours.***

II.—RELATIVE PRONOUNS.

12. A **relative pronoun** is a pronoun that relates to a word or phrase going before; as, *The man **who** wishes to succeed must labor.* It also connects different clauses of a sentence; as, *I paid for the goods **which** were sent to me.*

13. The word, phrase, or clause to which the pronoun relates is called the **antecedent.**

14. The **simple relative pronouns** are **who, which, what,** and **that.** They do not vary in person and number.

15. **Who** is applied to persons, **which** to animals and inanimate things, **that** to persons and things, **what** to things.

16. A relative is of the **same** person, number, and gender as its **antecedent.**

17. **What** and **that** have no declension.

18.   DECLENSION OF **WHO.**

Singular and *Plural.* { *Nom.* who
                              { *Poss.* whose
                              { *Obj.* whom

19. Who is sometimes used for *he that;* as,

"*Who* steals my purse steals trash."—SHAKESPEARE,—*Othello,* iii. 3.

20. DECLENSION OF **WHICH.**

Singular and *Plural.* $\begin{cases} Nom. & \text{which} \\ Poss. & \text{whose} \\ Obj. & \text{which} \end{cases}$

21. Which formerly applied to persons as well as to neuter antecedents; thus, where we say, *Our Father who art in heaven,* men formerly said, *Our Father which art in heaven.*

Ben Jonson speaks of "our one relative *which.*" Addison, two centuries later, pleads for the use of *who* and *which,* as against the introduction of the relative *that.* He represents those pronouns as saying: "We are descended of ancient families, and kept up our dignity and honor many years, till the Jack Sprat *that* supplanted us."

22. What is sometimes used for *that which;* as, *What I do now, you shall know later on.*

It is needless to call *what* a compound or double relative. It is simply a relative pronoun.

23. The adverbs **where** and **there**, united with the prepositions **of, to, by, in, with,** are used instead of the relatives; as, *This is the book whereof I spoke,* instead of, *This is the book of which I spoke.*

Whereof = of which, of what. **Thereof** = of that.
Whereby = by which, by what. **Thereby** = by that.
Whereto = to which, to what. **Thereto** = to that.
Wherein = in which, in what. **Therein** = in that.
Wherewith = with which, with what. **Therewith** = with that.

24. The **compound relative pronouns** are formed by adding *ever* or *soever* to *who, which, what*. They are declined like the simple relatives.

III.—DEMONSTRATIVE PRONOUNS.

25. A **demonstrative pronoun** is a pronoun that points out the noun with which it is used; as, *He gave me this book.*

This is a demonstrative pronoun, pointing out the noun *book*.

26. The demonstrative pronouns are two: **this** and **that**, with their plurals, **these** and **those**.

27. The **function** of demonstrative pronouns is simply to name or point out.

Demonstrative pronouns do not qualify in any sense.

28. This is always demonstrative. **That** is used as a conjunction, a demonstrative, and a relative. In the following sentence the word *that* is employed in all its senses:

"I say, *that*[1] *that*[2] *that*[3] *that*[4] *that*[5] gentleman used, is correct."

That[1]=conjunction; *that*[2] and *that*[4]=demonstrative with noun; *that*[3]=noun; *that*[5]=relative.

IV.—INTERROGATIVE PRONOUNS.

29. An **interrogative pronoun** is a pronoun employed in asking questions.

30. Who, which, and **what,** when used in asking questions, are called **interrogative pronouns**; as, *Who did this? Which is the book? What do you want?*

31. The interrogatives **who** and **which** are declined like the corresponding relatives.

32. In old English, all the relatives, with the exception of **that**, were once interrogatives only.

33. **Who**, as an interrogative, is used of **persons** only, and may be masculine or feminine; as, *Who spoke to you?*

34. **What**, which was in old English the neuter of *who*, is singular and neuter when used without the noun; as, *What are you doing?*

35. When used with the noun, **what** may be singular or plural, and of any gender; as, *What book are you reading? What author wrote the book? What boys are going to play ball?*

36. **What**, used interrogatively in connection with persons, expresses:

> (1) The **nature** or **quality** of the person; as, *What is God?* God is a pure spirit. "Whence and *what* art thou, execrable shape?"—*Milton.*
>
> (2) The **state** of the person; as, *What is that man?* He is an auctioneer. "*What* is this woman, quoth I, so worthily attired?"—*Langland.*

37. **Which**, as an interrogative, is **selective**; that is, it implies that there is a certain number of persons or things from which selection is to be made; as, *Which of you shall convince me of sin?*

Whether was formerly used as an interrogative, and as such was equivalent to the phrase, **which one of two**; as,

"*Whether* is greater, the gift, or the altar that sanctifieth the gift?" —*Matt.* xxiii. 19.

EXERCISES.

I. Write out the following sentences, and draw one line under the personal pronouns of the singular number, and two lines under those of the plural number:

You are all doing well.—He has an excellent character.—We are going to the market.—She is an amiable girl.—It is a beautiful piece of book-making.—They listened with great attention to the reading of Hawthorne's *Marble Faun.*—My brother goes to confession regularly. —Does he read well?—They are good boys.—Blessed is he who has found his work, and who does it.

II. In writing out the following sentences, replace the dash by a personal pronoun:

1. Shun the company of *him* who would lead you to evil.—Those —— rebuke —— for —— laziness are —— friends.—He will fulfil —— promise.—He thinks of what —— does. —— saw what —— bought with —— money.

2. He sent —— furniture on before ——. I left —— books behind me.—These are —— shoes.—Speak kindly to ——. Take —— to the church.

III. Insert a relative pronoun:

1. This is the horse *that* we saw yesterday.—Elizabeth, —— was Queen of England, died in 1603.—He —— speaks the truth does well. —He —— would have the kernel must break the shell.

2. He —— would honor him must not fear dying.—He —— hath ears to hear let him hear.—The book —— he sold was new.—The boy —— fails will lose his place.—All the money —— he had was put in bank.—This is the house —— Jack built.

IV. Insert an interrogative pronoun that will complete the sense:

1. —— discovered America? —— founded the Society of the Brothers of the Christian Schools? —— was the first Christian Martyr? —— of these books did you promise? —— preached last Sunday? —— is the greatest living orator? —— do you know about Mr. Gladstone?

2. —— cow is sick? —— child is lost? —— is the name of the first president? —— is your father's name?

V. Insert the simple personal, the relative, or the compound personal pronoun as the sense requires:

I will go to the party. —— will be elected.—Shall —— go with ——. Where shall —— leave —— ? This is —— the principal approves.— Thomas Jefferson, —— wrote the Declaration of Independence, was elected third president of the United States.—Out of the depths have —— cried unto ——. He —— did it.—She —— was there.—But —— go on forever.—I —— spoke to ——. What fairy music —— have heard.—The volume —— I lent has not been returned.

VI. Change the following sentences into sentences containing a relative or a personal pronoun and a preposition:

This is the book *whereof* I spoke = This is the book *of which* I spoke.

Whereof was the house built?—You do take the means *whereby* I live.—*Whereto* have we already gone?—In the day thou eatest *thereof*, thou shalt surely die.—Be at peace; *thereby* good shall come to you.— There is an island in the bay, and *thereto* we turned our boat.—He knows *whereof* he writes.

VII. Parse the pronouns in the following sentences:

Example.—As the man appeared honest, I employed him.—The boy who studies will learn.—Whose knife is this? John's.—I know what is wanted.

I is a pronoun (*why?*); it is a simple pers. pron. (*why?*); of the first pers. sing. n. (*why?*); of the masc. or the fem. gender (*why?*); in the nom. case, because it is the subj. of the verb *employed*.

Him is a simple pers. pron. (*why?*); of the third pers. sing. n. (*why?*); of the masc. gender (*why?*); in the obj. case, because it is the object of the action expressed by the v. *employed*.

Who is a simple relative pron. (*why?*); it is of the third pers. sing. number (*why?*); of the masc. gender (*why?*); and in the nom. case, because it is the subj. of the v. *studies*.

Whose is an interrogative pron. (*why?*); it is of the third pers. sing.

n. (*why?*); of the neuter gender (*why?*); and in the possessive case, because it denotes the relation of possession.

What is a relative pronoun, third person, singular number, neuter gender, nominative case to the verb *is wanted*. The object of *know* is the whole clause *what is wanted*.

VIII. Name and parse the nouns, articles, adjectives, and pronouns in the following sentences:

1. The summer breezes blow soft and cool.—2. The sweetest flowers fringed the little stream.—3. Not every one treads on marble floors.—4. Nobody knows who invented the alphabet.—5. We cannot wrong others without injuring ourselves.—6. Which of you will go with me?—7. The gardener whose flowers we admired, plucked a few for us.—8. What I do now, you know not.

9. Mark but my fall, and that that ruined me.—

SHAKESPEARE,—*Henry VIII.*

CHAPTER VII.

ANALYSIS OF SENTENCES.

1. Analysis, in grammar, is the separation of a sentence into its parts.

I.—CLASSIFICATION OF SENTENCES AS TO MEANING.

2. With regard to their **meaning,** sentences are divided into four classes: declarative, imperative, interrogative, and exclamatory.

3. A **declarative sentence** is a sentence that affirms or denies; as, *He writes his exercise.—He does not write his exercise.*

4. An **imperative sentence** is a sentence that expresses a command; as, *Write your exercise.*

5. An **interrogative sentence** is a sentence that asks a question; as, *Does he write his exercise?*

6. An **exclamatory sentence** is a sentence that expresses emotion; as, *Alas! what have you done!*

II.—PRINCIPAL PARTS OF SENTENCES.

7. Every sentence contains two **essential parts**, the subject and the predicate.

8. A **proposition** is a thought or judgment expressed in words.

9. A sentence that expresses but one proposition is called **a simple sentence**; as, *Boys play.—The wind blows.—Let the wind blow.*

10. The **subject** of a sentence is that of which something is said; as, *God is love.—The fire burns.*

11. When the subject is only a single word it is called a **simple subject**.

12. The subject with all its modifying words is called the **logical subject**; as,

"Now is *the winter of our discontent*
  Made glorious summer."—SHAKESPEARE,—*Richard III.*

Here *winter* is the grammatical subject; *the winter of our discontent* is the logical subject.

13. The **grammatical subject** of a sentence may be:

  (1) **A noun**; as, *Brevity* is the soul of wit.
  (2) **A pronoun**; as, *I* am far from home.
  (3) **A verb in the infinitive mood**; as, *To die* is a gain.
  (4) **A phrase**; as, *To forgive one's enemies* is a Christian duty.
  (5) **A clause**; as, *What is worth doing* is worth doing well.

14. In **imperative sentences** the subject *thou* or *you* is frequently understood ; as,

Honor thy father and thy mother.—Give him a book; that is, *honor thou, give thou.*

15. **Thou** is still employed in poetry and in solemn forms of expression ; as,

"Lead *Thou* me on."—NEWMAN.

16. The **predicate** of a sentence is that which is said of the subject ; as, *Henry reads.—The day is bright.*

17. When the predicate is a single word it is called a **simple predicate**.

18. The **grammatical predicate** is simply the verb.

19. The **logical predicate** includes the verb, with the object or attribute, and all adjuncts of the verb, object, or attribute.

20. Two or more subjects united by a conjunction, and having the same predicate, form a **compound subject**; as, *Mary and Margaret knit the stockings.*

21. Two or more predicates united by a conjunction, and having the same subject, form a **compound predicate**; as, *The seasons come and go.*

22. Besides a subject and a predicate, a sentence usually contains an **object** or an **attribute**.

23. The **object** of a sentence may be :

(1) A noun ; as, "Keep Thou my *feet*."
(2) A pronoun ; as, "God pity *them* both, and pity *us* all."
(3) A verb in the infinitive mood ; as, Bernard is learning *to write*.
(4) A phrase ; as, Dare *to be true*.

(5) **A clause**; as,

> Breathes there the man, with soul so dead,
> Who never to himself hath said,
> "*This is my own, my native land*"?—Scott.

24. A grammatical object may be governed by a transitive verb, a participle, or a preposition.

25. The object of a **transitive verb** expresses the name, phrase, or clause in which the action of the verb is terminated.

26. The object of a **participle** expresses the name, phrase, or clause in which the action of the participle terminates.

27. The object of a **preposition** expresses the name, phrase, or clause in which the relation of the preposition terminates.

28. The **attribute** of a sentence is the word completing the predicate and relating to the subject; as, *The flowers are beautiful.*

29. Attributes belong to intransitive verbs and to the passive voice of transitive verbs.

30. The **attribute** of a sentence may be:

(1) **An adjective**; as,

> And when the morn came *dim* and *sad,*
> And *chill* with early showers.—Hood.

(2) **A noun**; as, Time is the *warp* of life.
(3) **A pronoun**; as, It is *I.*
(4) **A participle**; as,

> Rest is not *quitting*
> The busy career;
> Rest is the fitting
> Of self to its sphere.—J. S. Dwight.

(5) A verb in the infinite mood; as, To will is *to do*.

(6) A phrase; as,

"The fear of the Lord is *the beginning of wisdom*."

(7) A clause; as, One of the most useful effects of action is *that it renders repose agreeable*.

III.—ADJUNCTS.

31. Adjuncts, or modifiers, are words which modify or limit the sense of the principal words in a sentence; as,

> Under her *torn* hat glowed the wealth
> Of *simple beauty* and *rustic health*.—WHITTIER.

32. Adjuncts may be:

(1) **Words**; as, Under her *torn* hat.
(2) **Phrases**; as, Glowed the wealth *of simple beauty*.
(3) **Clauses**; as, *When I look upon the tombs of the great*, every emotion of envy dies in me.—IRVING.

33. Adjuncts, in regard to their **function,** may be divided into three classes; namely, adjective, adverbial, and explanatory.

34. An **adjective adjunct** is an adjunct that is used to modify or limit a noun or pronoun; as, *All those wicked* men deserve severe punishment.

35. An adjective adjunct may be:

(1) An **article** or an **adjective**; as, *The diligent* scholar improves.
(2) A **noun** or a **pronoun** in the possessive case; as, *Henry's* brother has lost *his* hat.

36. An **adverbial adjunct** is an adjunct used as an adverb; as, He ran *rapidly*.

37. An **explanatory adjunct** is an adjunct used to explain a preceding noun or pronoun; as, *My friend Joseph is well.*

38. Adjuncts are called **primary** when they modify the subject or the predicate in a sentence; they are called **secondary** when they modify other adjuncts.

IV.—PHRASES.

39. A **phrase** is any group of words not containing a finite verb and its subject, and which, taken as a whole, performs the office of a single word; as, *In the morning.—Resting on their oars.—Being in time.*

40. A phrase may be substantive, adjective, adverbial, explanatory, or independent.

- (1) **Substantive**; as, *To serve God* is our duty.—James promises *to write.—Writing a book* is no easy task.
- (2) **Adjective**; as, *Faithful to his promise,* he came at the appointed time.—A thing *of beauty* is a joy forever.—The desire *to do good* is praiseworthy.—The book *on the table* is mine.
- (3) **Adverbial**; as, The soldier was brave *on the battlefield.—* The boys walked *along the road.*
- (4) **Explanatory**; as, Frank, *the brother of Charles,* is here.
- (5) **Independent**; as, *To come to the point,* did you strike your friend?

41. A **substantive phrase** is a phrase that takes the place of a noun; as, *Always to do the right is the road to peace of soul.*

42. A substantive phrase may be:

- (1) **Infinitive** in form; as, *To strike the weak* is cowardly.
- (2) **Participial**; as, *Reading bad books* is injurious to the soul. These two forms are interchangeable.

43. A substantive phrase may be:

(1) The subject of a sentence; as, *To forgive one's enemies* is a Christian duty.
(2) The object of a transitive verb or preposition; as, He considered *the reading of Shakespeare* very profitable.
(3) The attribute of an intransitive or neuter verb; as, He was ashamed *to be seen there*.

44. An **adjective phrase** is a phrase that performs the functions of an adjective in qualifying a noun or a pronoun:

(1) A noun; as,

> Philosophy, *baptized*
> *In the pure fountain of eternal love,*
> Has eyes indeed.—COWPER,—*The Task.*

(2) A pronoun; as, Put not your trust in him *with two faces*.

45. An **adverbial phrase** is a phrase that performs the functions of an adverb in modifying a verb, an adjective, or another adverb:

(1) A verb; as, "The judge rode slowly *down the lane*."
(2) An adjective; as, The sailor was nimble *in the rigging*.
(3) An adverb; as, This is good enough *for me*.

46. An **explanatory phrase** is a phrase that explains some other word or phrase in a sentence; as, *Lew Wallace, the author of "Ben Hur,"* was minister to Constantinople.

47. An **independent phrase** is a phrase that has no grammatical connection with any other part of the sentence; as, *To be candid,* I was in fault. *Computing in round numbers,* there were five hundred persons present.

48. An independent phrase may contain:

(1) The name of a person addressed; as, Morning is the best time to study, *my dear friend.*
(2) A pleonasm;[1] as, *A brave boy,* he could not injure others.
(3) A verb in the infinitive; as, His conduct was, *to say the least,* highly reprehensible.
(4) A participle; as, *Speaking candidly,* I do not understand the question.

49. Phrases are divided into simple, complex, and compound.

50. A simple phrase is a phrase not limited by any word or by any other phrase; as, *Beneath the stars.*

51. A complex phrase is one that contains another phrase as an adjunct to its principal part; as, *Beneath the stars of heaven.*

52. A compound phrase is one composed of two or more phrases connected by a conjunction; as, *Going down and looking in.*

V.—PRINCIPAL WORDS AND THEIR MODIFIERS.

53. The **principal words** in any sentence are the noun or pronoun, the verb and its participle, the adjective, and the adverb.

54. A **noun** in a sentence may be modified:

(1) By an **article**; as, *The* library is *a* large one.
(2) By an **adjective**; as, *All* men desire to be happy.
(3) By a **noun** or a **pronoun** in the **possessive case**; as, A *fireman's* life has *its* perils.
(4) By an **explanatory noun** or **pronoun**; as, The novelist

---

[1] A pleonasm is an emphatic repetition of the same idea.

Dickens gave readings in New York.—Alexander *himself* was there.

(5) By a **participle**; as, "Here stood a shattered archway *plumed* with ferns."—TENNYSON.

(6) By an **adjective phrase**; as, William, *weary of fishing,* turned his boat towards the shore.

(7) By an **adjective clause**; as, He endowed the college *in which he was educated.*

(8) By an **explanatory clause**; as, The belief *that there is a purgatory* was held by Plato.

55. A verb may be modified :

(1) By an **adverb**; as, They drove *rapidly.*
(2) By an **adverbial phrase**; as, Fishes glide rapidly *through the water.*—Henry rode quickly *through the town.*
(3) By an **adverbial clause**; as, I came *that I might assist you.*

56. A participle may be modified :

(1) By an **object**; as, By *deserving respect* you will win it.
(2) By an **adverb**; as, The old sailor was discovered *badly beaten.*
(3) By an **adverbial phrase**; as, The youth *inured to hardship* can withstand great fatigue.

57. An adjective may be modified :

(1) By an **adverb**; as, The man is *very irritable.*
(2) By an **adverbial phrase**; as, Be *quick to hear,* but *slow to speak.*
(3) By an **adverbial clause**; as, The distance was greater *than I had imagined.*

58. An adverb may be modified :

(1) By another **adverb**; as, He labors *most faithfully.*
(2) By a **phrase or clause**; as, He acted *conformably to the rules laid down.*

L.--EXERCISES FOR ANALYSIS.

1. Simple Sentences.

Example 1.—*Boys play.*

This is a simple declarative sentence. It is *simple*, because it contains but one proposition; *declarative*, because it expresses an affirmation. *Boys* is the subject, because it is that of which the sentence treats. *Study* is the predicate, because it is that which is said of the subject.

Analyze the following sentences as in the preceding example:

1. Men talk.
2. Students learn.
3. Children cry.
4. Time flies.
5. Birds sing.
6. Horses gallop.
7. Dogs bark.
8. Lions roar.

Example 2.—*Fire melts gold.*
This is a simple declarative sentence.
The subject is *fire;* the predicate, *melts;* gold is the object.

Analyze the following sentences:

1. Integrity inspires confidence.
2. Generosity makes friends.
3. God loves us.
4. Brutus stabbed Cæsar.
5. William defeated Harold.
6. John bought peaches.

Example 3.—*Feathers are light.*
This is a simple declarative sentence.
The subject is *feathers;* the predicate is *are;* and the attribute is *light.*

Analyze the following sentences:

1. Lead is heavy.
2. Gold is yellow.
3. Stars are suns.
4. The moon is a planet.
5. Sailors are brave.
6. Steam is a moving power.
7. Knowledge is power.
8. Union is strength.
9. Diamonds are combustible.
10. Ice is crystallized water.
11. Climate affects plants.
12. Heat is a mode of motion.

ANALYSIS OF SENTENCES. 61

Example 4.—The old wooden clock stopped.
This is a simple declarative sentence.
The subject is *clock;* the predicate is *stopped.*
The subject is modified by the adjective adjuncts *the, old,* and *wooden.*

Analyze the following sentences:

1. The young speaker was applauded.
2. The large steamer sank.
3. The weary little child slept.
4. The wooden house fell.
5. An honest man prospers.
6. The dark clouds lower.

Example 5.—The full moon sometimes shines brightly.
This is a simple declarative sentence.
The subject is *moon;* the predicate is *shines.*
The subject is modified by the adjective adjuncts *the* and *full;* the predicate is modified by the adverbial adjuncts *sometimes* and *brightly.*

Analyze the following sentences:

1. The south wind blew softly.—2. Industrious people rise early.—3. The strong north wind changed suddenly.—4. All those various questions can be settled peaceably.—5. The dark, threatening clouds were soon dissolved.—6. Your venerable father will be cordially welcomed.—7. Mental inaction is mental rusting.—8. The moon is a burnt cinder.

II.—SECONDARY MODIFIERS.

Example 1.—A most horrible catastrophe happened quite recently.
This is a simple declarative sentence.
The subject is *catastrophe;* the predicate is *happened.*
The subject is modified by the adjective adjuncts *a* and *horrible; horrible* is modified by the adverbial adjunct *most.* The predicate-verb *happened* is modified by the adverbial adjunct *recently,* and *recently* is modified by the adverbial adjunct *quite.*

Analyze the following sentences:

1. Our last entertainment was highly enjoyed.—2. People now travel very rapidly.—3. Irving writes with ease, elegance, and grace.—4. That very inconsiderate youth acted too hastily.—5. Fair science frowned not on his humble birth.—6. Trifles often lead to serious results.—7. You are entirely too anxious.

Example 2.—*Young Edward always studies his difficult lessons thoroughly.*
This is a simple declarative sentence.
The subject is *Edward;* the predicate, *studies;* the object, *lessons.*
The subject is modified by the adjective adjunct *young;* the predicate is modified by the adverbial adjuncts *always* and *thoroughly;* the object is modified by the adjective adjuncts *his* and *difficult.*

Analyze the following sentences:

1. New York City has a very fine harbor.—2. Some good artists occasionally paint pictures of inferior merit.—3. Washington Irving is not a trustworthy historian.—4. Many wild beasts inhabit the African continent.—4. George caught a very large salmon.—5. Obliging conduct produces deserved esteem.

Example 3.—*Cartier was a bold navigator.*
This is a simple declarative sentence. The subject is *Cartier;* the predicate, *was;* the attribute, *navigator.*
The subject is unmodified; the attribute is modified by the adjective adjuncts *a* and *bold.*

Analyze the following sentences:

1. Honesty is the best policy.—2. Scott is an instructive writer.—3. Good execution is always aimed at by the true artist.—4. Henry is a faithful boy.—5. Cardinal Manning is the poor man's friend.—6. Disappointment has too frequently been their fate.

Example.—*Knowledge and virtue elevate and purify the mind.*
This is a simple declarative sentence. The subject is compound, consisting of *knowledge* and *virtue,* connected by the conjunction *and.*

ANALYSIS OF SENTENCES. 63

The predicate is also compound, consisting of *elevate* and *purify*, connected by *and*. The object is *mind*.

The subject is unmodified; the predicate is unmodified; the object is modified by the article *the*.

Analyze the following sentences:

1. Joy and sorrow are woven into the life of every man.—2. Kingdoms and empires rise, flourish, and decay.—3. Wealth, honor, and happiness forsake the indolent.—4. Madison, Hamilton, and Jay discussed the Constitution.—5. Vanity and presumption have ruined many a promising youth.—6. Pride and prejudice warp the noblest natures.—7. Tennyson and Browning are among the greatest poets of this century.

I. Write a sentence on each of the following words:

Madison	joy	empires
Hamilton	sorrow	honor
Jay	kingdoms	happiness

II. Write sentences containing any two of these words as subject.

III. Write sentences containing any two as object.

III.—SUBSTANTIVE PHRASES.

Example 1.—To teach idle pupils is disagreeable work.
This is a simple declarative sentence.

The subject is the substantive phrase *to teach idle pupils;* *is disagreeable work* is the predicate.

The subject *to teach* is modified by the object *pupils*, and *pupils* is modified by the adjective adjunct *idle*. The predicate *is*, is modified by the attribute *work*, and *work* is modified by the adjective adjunct *disagreeable*.

Example 2.—Joseph deserves to be rewarded.
This is a simple declarative sentence.

The subject is *Joseph;* the predicate-verb, *deserves;* the object, *to be rewarded*.

The subject is unmodified; the predicate is unmodified; the object is unmodified.

Analyze the following sentences:

1. To relieve the poor is our duty.—2. To die for one's country is a great honor.—3. It is our duty to promote peace and harmony among men.—4. To be able to write well is a valuable accomplishment.—5. To open a letter belonging to another is a penal offence.

IV.—ADJECTIVE PHRASES.

Example.—*A mind conscious of no guilt reposes securely.*
This is a simple declarative sentence.
The subject is *mind;* the predicate, *reposes.*

The subject is modified by the adjective phrase *conscious of no guilt;* the principal word, *conscious,* is modified by the adverbial phrase *of no guilt,* and *guilt* is modified by the adjective adjunct *no.*

The predicate is modified by the adverbial adjunct *securely.*

Analyze the following sentences:

1. The esteem of wise men is the greatest of temporal encouragements.—2. The bounty displayed on the earth equals the grandeur manifested in the heavens.—3. The way to acquire knowledge is to labor for it.—4. His willingness to be just in the matter was apparent to all.

V.—ADVERBIAL PHRASES.

Example.—*We took our small trunk with us.*
This is a simple declarative sentence.
The subject is *we;* the predicate, *took;* the object, *trunk.*

The subject is unmodified; the predicate is modified by the adverbial phrase *with us;* the object is modified by the adjective adjuncts *our* and *small.*

Analyze the following sentences:

1. The two boys carried the basket of apples between them.—2. Abstain from injuring others.—3. In the spring the flowers will bloom.

4. Browning deals with the morbid in souls. He ranks among our greatest poets. He writes in a harsh and difficult style.

VI.—EXPLANATORY AND INDEPENDENT PHRASES.

Example.—*To be candid, I was in fault.*
This is a simple declarative sentence.
The subject is *I;* the predicate, *was.*
The subject is unmodified; the predicate-verb is modified by the adverbial phrase *in fault.* *To be candid* is an independent phrase.

Analyze the following sentences:

1. His conduct, generally speaking, was honorable.—2. To speak plainly, your evil habits are your worst enemies.—3. I was not aware of his being a lawyer.

VII.—COMPLEX PHRASES.

Example.—*They waited in great anxiety for the morning.*
This is a simple declarative sentence.
The subject is *they;* the predicate, *waited.*
The subject is unmodified; the predicate is modified by the complex adverbial phrase *in great anxiety for the morning.* The principal word of the first part, *anxiety,* is modified by the adjective adjunct *great.* The principal word of the second part, *morning,* is modified by the adjective adjunct *the.*

Analyze the following sentences:

1. We require clothing in the summer to protect the body from the heat of the sun.—2. This sentence is not too difficult for me to analyze.—3. The merchant offered the position to a man of integrity.—4. In reading his friend's letter without permission he was guilty of a dishonorable act.

VIII.—COMPOUND PHRASES.

Example.—*The maple-tree grows in this valley, and on yonder hills.*
This is a simple declarative sentence.

The subject is *maple-tree;* the predicate, *grows.*

The subject is modified by the adjunct *the.* The predicate *grows* is modified by the compound adverbial phrase *in this valley and on yonder hills,* taken as a whole. The principal word of the first phrase is *valley,* which is modified by the adjective adjunct *this;* the principal word of the second phrase is *hills,* which is modified by the adjective adjunct *yonder.*

Analyze the following sentences:

1. They were seen rising up and departing hastily.—2. Our friend is always the same, in prosperity and under every misfortune.—3. Some Indian tribes were wont to fight with stones, arrows, and spears.

IX.—IMPERATIVE, INTERROGATIVE, AND EXCLAMATORY SENTENCES.

Example 1.—*Employ your time well.*
This is a simple imperative sentence.

The subject is *you* (understood); the predicate, *employ;* the object, *time.* Subject, unmodified; predicate, modified by the adverbial adjunct *well;* object, modified by the adjective adjunct *your.*

Example 2.—*Has he a silver goblet?*
A simple interrogative sentence.

Subject, *he;* predicate, *has;* object, *goblet.*

Subject unmodified; predicate unmodified; object, modified by the adjective adjuncts *a* and *silver.*

Example 3.—*How mournful the story is!*
A simple exclamatory sentence.

Subject, *story;* predicate, *is.*

The subject is modified by the adjective adjuncts *the* and *mournful; mournful* is modified by the adverbial adjunct *how.*

Analyze the following sentences:

1. Have you bought the Venetian blinds?—2. Solomon, the son of David, built the temple of Jerusalem.—3. Envy not the good luck of

prosperous transgressors.—4. How brightly the sun shines!—5. How the base soul rejoices in dishonorable deeds!

Analyze the following miscellaneous sentences:

1. Lexicology is the science of words.—2. Spelling is the art of expressing words by their proper letters.—3. Astronomers cannot count all the stars.—4. What a beautiful sight the rising sun is!—5. Give the poor man an alms.—6. Men of few words are frequently men of many deeds.—7. A small leak will sink a great ship.—8. The telescope was invented towards the end of the sixteenth century.—9. Consecrate the first thoughts of the day to God.—10. The history of the humblest human life is a tale of marvels.—11. A day spent in idleness is a day lost.—12. The service of God should be the great object of our life.—13. The arts prolong, comfort, and cheer human life.—14. Longfellow is the favorite American poet.—15. Peace of mind being lost, we lose the greatest happiness of life.—16. The general at once crossed the river, engaged the enemy, and gained a complete victory.—17. Thou shalt not take the name of the Lord thy God in vain.—18. Cultivate a taste for Christian art.—

19. "Rome has inherited both sacred and profane learning."—20. "Man has a moral and a religious nature."—CARDINAL NEWMAN.—21. "She walks the water like a thing of life."—BYRON.

CHAPTER VIII.

SENTENCE-BUILDING: ITS NATURE.

1. Besides the analysis of sentences, there is also the process of constructing and combining sentences. This process has been called **sentence-building**.

2. Sentence-building is very simple and of general application.

Every conversation carried on is an exercise in sentence-building. Whenever the pupil has been supplying words in a sentence, or transposing the parts of a sentence, or changing the sense of a sentence, or constructing a sentence, he has been sentence-building. Every recitation in which the pupil is made to express himself correctly; every exercise in which he repeats or writes down the substance of his lesson in reading, or in history, or in geography, is a lesson in sentence-building.

3. The object of sentence-building is to teach the pupil how to use the **right word** in the **right place,** according to **correct grammatical forms** of speech.

4. The same thought may be expressed in many forms, each grammatically correct; but there is always **one** form which expresses the thought more **clearly** and more **forcibly** than the others.

5. The best forms of expression cannot be reached at once. They are the result of repeated trials.

It is only after many efforts, much thought, and great painstaking, that the large majority of our best English writers have expressed themselves in the beautiful manner that makes of their compositions our models for all time.

6. In sentence-building, the pupil should not aim too high. Let him seek to be **natural,** and always to express the idea as it presents itself to his mind.

7. After the idea has been set down, it requires to be modified, and **adapted** to the sentences going before and following.

8. In all sentence-building the pupil should strive to be **grammatically correct.**

The pupil should know clearly what he wants to express. When the thought is clear, the expression can be made both clear and forcible.

EXERCISES.

I. Replace by a preposition and a noun the adjective that qualifies the subject:

1. A *prudent* man will not murmur when he is reproved.—2. Will-power over *bodily* organs may be increased by judicious *physical* exercise.—3. An *obedient* man shall speak of victory.—4. The *honest* man will always be trusted.—5. The *polite* man will gain many friends.

II. Replace the word italicized by a noun from the same root, and make the other necessary changes, in each of the following sentences:

Example.—The *meek* are a source of edification to all = *Those who practise meekness* are a source of edification to all = *They that are meekly disposed* are a source of edification to all.

1. The *poor* are worthy of our compassion and assistance.—2. The *obedient* are certain to find favor with God.—3. The *prudent* calculate the consequences of their actions.—4. The *humble* deserve the gift of chastity.—5. The *vain-glorious* seek happiness in human applause.

III. Change the words in italics into the possessive case, and make the other necessary changes accordingly:

1. Publish the virtues of a generous *friend.*—2. Despise the wiles of the *flatterer.*—3. The style *of Cardinal Newman* is greatly admired.—4. God blesses the projects of a virtuous *man.*—5. The poison of the asp is in the tongue of the *slanderer.*

IV. Throw the following sentences into as many forms as there are divisions:

Example.—*Let our lives be active | according as our hearts are calm.*

We may construct this sentence in two ways:

1. In proportion to the calmness of our hearts let our lives be active.
2. The calmer our hearts, the more active be our lives.

This last is the form in which Cardinal Newman expressed the idea.

1. Washington Irving | is more elegant as an author [1] | than he | is accurate as an historian. [2]
2. Like a thing of life [1] | she walks the water. [2]
3. I know [1] | from our old books [2] | that Joseph came of old to Glastonbury. [3]
4. This place will I not leave [1] | until I needs must go [2] | my death to meet. [3] WILLIAM MORRIS,—*Atalanta's Race.*
5. To open, unauthorized, a letter addressed to another, [1] | is considered a felony before the law [2] | and a dishonor before society. [3]
6. My friends, | the excesses of our youth [1] | are | drafts [2] | upon our old age. [3] |

In the foregoing examples other words may be introduced in order to convey the full sense in the new arrangement.

V. Replace the words in italics by a common adjective, and make the other necessary changes accordingly:

1. The soldier *that is courageous* does honor to his colors.—2. The heart *that is humble* obtains many blessings from God.—3. The pupil *that is attentive* succeeds.—4. The opinion of the fault-finder is of small avail.—5. The young man *that is modest* is esteemed.

VI. Change the following sentences to others expressing opposite ideas:

1. The *proud* will be humbled.—2. The *wicked* will be punished.—3. The approval of *conscience* brings peace of soul.—4. *Old age* possesses experience.—5. *Youth* is a spendthrift of time.

VII. Replace the words in italics by a common adjective form having the same root, and make all other necessary changes:

1. *Purity* shall receive a special reward in Heaven.—2. *Courage* does not shrink in the presence of danger.—3. *Prudence* does not act without due deliberation.—4. *Envy* is the passion of small souls.—5. *Fickleness* never accomplishes anything great.

VIII. Construct sentences each of which shall contain one of the following words and its opposite:

Proud, deliberate, begun, yield, bitter.

IX. Connect an additional proposition with each of the sentences here given by means of the word WHEN:

1. We should offer our hearts to God ——. 2. We write a good sentence ——. 3. We lead a Christian life ——. 4. We are certain of having our prayers heard ——. 5. Why think to live long ——?

X. Transpose the terms of the proposition, by placing the subject before the verb, and the attribute after the verb.

1. The two eyes of history are geography and chronology.—2. The most beautiful ornament of the soul is innocence.—3. The passion of noble hearts is love of country.—4. The horror of a Christian soul is slander.

XI. Add a second proposition, which shall be a consequence of the first, in the following sentences:

1. Science is a precious treasure; *therefore*..... 2. Human respect is contemptible; *therefore*..... 3. The poor are our brethren; *therefore*..... 4. Appearances are often deceitful; *therefore*..... 5. Commerce and industry are the fortune of a country;..... 6. We should shun bad companions; *because*.....

XII. Vary the construction of the following sentences without changing the meaning:

1. The wisest is he who does not believe himself to be wise.— 2. We expose ourselves to lose all in striving to gain all.—3. Necessity is the mother of industry.—4. Virtue is a certain mark of a noble heart.— 5. The two-faced man is sooner or later unmasked.—6. "I made shift to make two or three new waistcoats, which I hoped would serve me a good while."—DEFOE,—*Robinson Crusoe.*

XIII. Add a second clause, which shall contain the opposite of the word in italics:

1. *Virtue* is a garment of honor:—2. The *wise* man knows that he knows but little:—3. *Deep* rivers flow in silence:—4. Among the *base*, merit begets envy:—5. *Anger* stirs up fury.

XIV. An excellent practice in sentence-building is to enlarge a simple proposition into several consecutive sentences, each more developed than the preceding one.

Example.—Take the simple sentence, *The farmer sat watching the fire.*

1. Let us first describe the subject *farmer:*
In his arm-chair, warm and comfortable, sat the farmer, watching the fire.

2. Let us then describe how he *sat:*
Indoors, warm and comfortable, by the fire-place, idly sat the farmer, watching the flames and the smoke-wreaths struggling upward from the fire.

3. Finally, let us look at the farmer as the poet describes him sitting by the fire:

> "Indoors, warm by the wide-mouthed fire-place, idly the farmer
> Sat in his elbow-chair, and watched how the flames and the smoke-wreaths
> Struggled together like foes in a burning city."—LONGFELLOW,—*Evangeline.*

In the same manner, out of each of the following sentences, construct three sentences, giving attributes, first to the subject; second, to the predicate; third, to the attribute or object.

1. The farmer's shadow mocked him.

(1) ....
(2) ....
(3) ....
(4) Longfellow has developed the idea as follows:

SENTENCE-BUILDING: ITS NATURE. 73

" Behind him,
Nodding and mocking along the wall, with gesture fantastic,
Darted his own huge shadow, and vanished away into darkness."—*Ibid.*

2. The spiritual world is present.

   (1) ....
   (2) ....
   (3) ....
   (4) Cardinal Newman has developed this idea in the following eloquent and beautiful manner:

"The world of spirits, then, though unseen, is present; present, not future, not distant. It is not above the sky, it is not beyond the grave; it is now and here; the kingdom of God is among us."—*Parochial and Plain Sermons.*

3. He rode into the castle court.

   (1) ....
   (2) ....
   (3) ....
   (4) Tennyson has thus developed this sentence:

   " Then rode Geraint into the castle court,
   His charger trampling many a prickly star
   Of sprouted thistle on the broken stones."—*Geraint and Enid.*

4. We all know that everything here below is fleeting.

   (1) ....
   (2) ....
   (3) ....
   (4) Browning has developed this thought as follows:

   "Time fleets, youth fades, life is an empty dream.
   It is the echo of time; and he whose heart
   Beat first beneath a human heart, whose speech
   Was copied from a human tongue, can never
   Recall when he was living yet knew not this."—*Paracelsus.*

Note how the generalities of the first proposition are reduced to particulars in Browning's development: *everything here below = time, youth, life; we all know = he whose heart first beat beneath a human heart . . . . can never recall when he was living yet knew not this.*

5. A secluded life finds many a lesson in Nature.

(1) ....
(2) ....
(3) ....
(4) In the following manner does Shakespeare express the same idea:

"And this our life, exempt from public haunt,
Finds tongues in trees, books in the running brooks,
Sermons in stones, and good in everything."—*As You Like It.*

XV. Write six short sentences describing the persons and things in the room in which you now are.

Add attributes or adjuncts to the principal parts in each of the sentences that you have just written.

XVI. Translate into your own words the following passage:

"What doth the poor man's son inherit?
Stout muscles and a sinewy heart,
A hardy frame, a hardier spirit.
King of two hands, he does his part
In every useful toil and art;
A heritage, it seems to me,
A king might wish to hold in fee."

—James Russell Lowell.

CHAPTER IX.

VERBS.

1. **A verb** is a word that expresses being, action, or the being acted upon; as, Truth *is;* Mary *studies her lesson;* The horse **runs**; James **was punished.**

2. Verbs may be classified as regards their **form** and as regards their **meaning**.

3. The grammatical **form** of the verb is the change the verb undergoes in expressing time and state of being, action, or passiveness.

4. The grammatical **meaning** of the verb is the verb as taken in a transitive, intransitive, or unipersonal sense.

I. CLASSIFICATION OF VERBS AS TO FORM.

5. **Verb-forms** are either finite or infinitive.

6. The **infinitive forms** are those forms of the verb which are independent of person and number; as, *to read, writing*.

7. The infinitive forms are **twofold**; namely, the root-infinitive and the participial infinitive.

8. The **root-infinitive** is the simplest verbal form that may be united with the preposition *to;* as, *to be, to do, to speak*. *Be, do*, and *speak* are called the **roots** of the verb.

9. The **participial infinitive** is the root of the verb with the ending -ing; as, *sleeping, rowing*. The participial infinitive is known as the **imperfect participle**.

10. By reason of the **absence of limitations** of person and number in the root-infinitive and the participial infinitive, these forms assume the functions of other parts of speech; as, *For me to die is gain; The rising of the sun is a beautiful sight.*

In these sentences, the root-infinitive *to die* and the participial infinitive *rising* are subjects of the verb *is*, and perform the functions of nouns.

The infinitives may also be the **object** of a verb or of a preposition.

76 ETYMOLOGY.

11. **Verbs** are divided as regards their **finite forms**—that is, as regards the forms of their principal parts—into three classes; namely, regular, irregular, and defective.

12. **A regular verb** is a verb that forms its simple imperfect tense and perfect participle by the addition of **-d** or **-ed** to the root; as, *reap, reaped; wish, wished*.

13. **An irregular verb** is a verb that does not form its imperfect tense and perfect participle by adding -d or -ed to the root; as, *know, knew, known*.

14. **A defective verb** is a verb that forms no participle, and is not used in all the moods and tenses; as, *can, would*.

Modern grammarians call the regular verbs **weak**, and several of the irregular verbs, **strong**.

To the **weak verbs** also belong those verbs whose past tense ends in **t**. This t is, in nearly every instance, a contraction of the more regular form in -d or -ed. (Orthog. chap. i. 17.)

The **strong verbs** are those that form their imperfect tense by a change of **vowel** only; as, *get, got; speak, spoke*.—The perfect participle of strong verbs formerly ended in n or en; as, *spoken*.

II. CLASSIFICATION OF VERBS AS TO MEANING.

15. Verbs are divided, as regards their **grammatical meaning**, into three classes : transitive, intransitive, and unipersonal.

16. **A transitive verb** is a verb that expresses action communicated from a subject to an object; as, *The boy reads the book*.

17. **An intransitive verb** is a verb that expresses being, or state, or action not communicated to an object; as, *John awakes; George walks*.

18. **A unipersonal verb** is a verb used only in the third person singular and with the pronoun **it**; as, *it rains; it*

seems *good;* ***methinks*** = *it thinks me,* or *it appears to me.*

The form **methinks** is erroneously considered an affectation for *I think.* On the contrary, it is a remnant of a whole class of unipersonal verbs employed in older stages of the language, and is not to be construed into the expression *I think.* Some grammarians call the **unipersonal** verb **impersonal.**

III.—MODIFICATION OF VERBS.

19. Verbs have **five** kinds of modification or inflection: voice, mood, tense, person, and number.

VOICE.

20. **Voice** is a modification of **transitive verbs** which distinguishes their subject as acting upon an object, or as being acted upon.

21. There are **two** voices, the active and the passive.

22. The **active voice** is that form of the verb in which the subject acts upon an object; as, *Wolfe* ***defeated*** *Montcalm.*

23. The **passive voice** is that form of the verb in which the subject is acted upon; as, *Montcalm* ***was defeated*** *by Wolfe.*

In the **passive voice** the object of the action becomes the subject of the verb. When the same verb is employed in both voices, that which was the object of the verb in the **active voice** becomes its subject in the **passive voice.**

24. The passive voice is formed by the addition of the perfect participle of the principal **verb** to the auxiliary **be** through all its inflections; as, *The spell* ***is broken.***

A few intransitive verbs assume the passive form even while used in an active sense; as,

"Octavius *is* already *come* to Rome."—SHAKESPEARE.

25. English writers use other forms of the passive; as, *The house is **being built**.*

This is equivalent to the form, *The house is a-building* = on-building = in-building = in the act of building.

MOOD.

26. **Mood** is that modification which shows the particular manner in which the verb is employed.

27. There are **five moods**; namely, the infinitive, the indicative, the potential, the subjunctive, and the imperative.

28. The **infinitive mood** is a form of the verb used to express action or being without limitation of person and number; as, *I came **to see** him.*

The infinitive mood is used without any subject, and may itself be subject or object.

In modern English, the infinitive is expressed by *to* before the verb. In old English, it was expressed by the suffix **an**; as, *drinc-an,* to drink.

29. The **indicative mood** is a form of the verb used to express a direct assertion, or to ask a direct question; as, *John is there; Is John there?*

30. The **potential mood** is a form of the verb used to express possibility, liberty, obligation, or necessity:

(1) **Possibility;** as, "A breath *can make* them as a breath has made."

(2) **Liberty**; as,

> "Men *may come* and men *may go*,
> But I go on forever."—TENNYSON,—*The Brook*.

(3) **Obligation**; as, The merchant *should pay* his debts.

(4) **Necessity**; as,

> "But men *must work*, and women *must weep*,
> Though storms be sudden and waters deep."
> —KINGSLEY,—*The Three Fishers*.

Some modern grammarians identify the **potential** with the **subjunctive** mood.

31. The **subjunctive mood** expresses what is doubtful, supposed or conditional, and contingent or dependent:

(1) **Doubtful**; as, Advise if this *be* worth attempting.

(2) **Supposed** or **conditional**; as, I would go *if I were you*.

(3) **Contingent** or **dependent**; as, *If thou keep promise*, I shall end this strife.

32. The **imperative mood** expresses command, entreaty, desire, request, or exhortation:

(1) **Command**; as,

> "*Blow, blow*, thou winter wind!
> Thou art not so unkind
> As man's ingratitude."—SHAKESPEARE,—*King Lear*.

(2) **Entreaty**; as, *Give* us this day our daily bread.

(3) **Desire**; as, *Be* mine the honor.

(4) **Request**; as, *Let* me call on you to-morrow.

(5) **Exhortation**; as, *Arise, go forth*, and *conquer* as of old

33. The imperative mood has only one person; namely, the **second person**, in the singular and plural numbers.

34. The imperative mood invariably contains the **root** of the verb; as, ***Sing** thou;* ***Play** ye*.

In the forms *let us go, let him speak*, let is the imperative of command or entreaty, and go and speak are verbs in the infinitive mood.

Tense.

35. Tense is a modification of the verb which distinguishes the **time** of action or of state of being.

36. There are **six tenses**: the present, the imperfect, the perfect, the pluperfect, the future, and the future perfect.

37. The **present tense** is the form of the verb that expresses present time; as, *He is.—The girl speaks.*

38. The **imperfect tense** is the form of the verb that expresses action or state of being in a past time; as, *I wrote a letter. I was speaking.*

39. The **perfect tense** is the form of the verb that expresses action or state of being as completed within the present time; as, *I have written a letter to-day.*

40. The **pluperfect tense** is the form of the verb that expresses action or state of being as completed at or before some specified past time; as, *I had written this page when he arrived.*

41. The **future tense** is the form of the verb that expresses action or state of being in some time to come; as, *I shall go to-night.*

42. The **future perfect tense** is the form of the verb that expresses action or state of being as about to be completed at or before a specified future time; as, *I shall have written my letter by noon.*

43. In English there is **change of form** only in the present and the imperfect tense. All other tenses are expressed by means of auxiliary verbs.

VERBS.

NUMBER AND PERSON.

44. The verb follows the **number** and **person** of the noun or pronoun with which it is connected.

45. The verb admits of **two numbers** through all its tenses; namely, the **singular** and the **plural**.

46. The verb admits of **three persons** in both numbers; namely, the **first, second,** and **third**. Thus:

	Singular.	Plural.
First person.	I wait,	We wait,
Second person.	Thou wait-est,	Ye or you wait,
Third person.	He wait-s or wait-eth;	They wait.

47. The verbal root suffers **modification** in the second and third persons singular.

48. In the **second person** singular the modification is -t, -st, or -est; as *shalt, wouldst, heedest*.

49. In modern English the termination of the second person singular is -st or -est; but in old English it was -t. We have remnants of the older form in the words *wilt, shalt, art*.

50. Except in poetry or solemn prose, -s is the usual suffix to the third person singular; as, *He lives in vain who lives for self*.

> "He *prayeth* best, who *loveth* best
> All things both great and small."
> —COLERIDGE,—*The Ancient Mariner.*

51. Four **principal parts** enter into the conjugation of every complete verb; namely, the present, the imperfect, the imperfect participle, and the perfect participle:

(1) The **present** is the verbal root that enters into the present tense of the infinitive mood; as *be* in the verb *to be*.

(2) The **imperfect** is the imperfect tense of the indicative mood, simple form; as, *was, loved*.

(3) The **imperfect participle** is the verbal root, with -ing added; as, *being, loving*. This is also called the **present participle**.

In old English this participle was formed by the suffix -inde, -ende, or -and.

(4) The **perfect participle** is the verbal root with the suffix -en or -ed; as, *been, loved, handed*.

52. These are called the principal parts, because from them and by means of them all the other parts of the verb are formed.

53. A verb that is lacking in any of the principal parts is called a **defective verb**.

IV.—CONJUGATION OF VERBS.

54. The **conjugation** of a verb is the regular arrangement of the verb in all its moods, tenses, persons, and numbers.

AUXILIARY VERBS.

55. An **auxiliary verb** is a verb that aids in the conjugation of other verbs.

56. The **auxiliaries** are **be, do, have, shall, will, may, can,** and **must**.

57. The auxiliary verbs **do, be, will,** and **have** are often used as principal verbs; as, *George **does** well; I **am** here; God **wills** some things, and other things He permits; Thomas **has** money*.

The other auxiliaries are defective. Will has a negative form nill. Must has a provincial equivalent in the word mun. I *mun* go = I *must* go. The word *mun* originally meant *to think, to consider*.

58. *The principal parts of the auxiliaries are :—*

Present.	Imperfect.	Imperfect Participle.	Perfect Participle.
do	did	doing	done
be	was	being	been
have	had	having	had
shall	should	——	——
will	would	——	——
may	might	——	——
can	could	——	——
must	must	——	——

FORMS OF CONJUGATION.

59. Verbs admit of **four forms** of conjugation; namely, the affirmative, the negative, the interrogative, and the negative-interrogative.

60. The **affirmative form** is the form in which a statement, whether direct or indirect, is made.

61. The **direct-affirmative form** may be simple, emphatic, progressive, or intentional.

62. All transitive and intransitive verbs admit of these four forms of affirmation in the present and imperfect tenses of the indicative mood. Thus :—

	Simple.	Emphatic.	Progressive.	Intentional.
Pres.	I write,	I do write,	I am writing,	I am going to write,
Imperf.	I wrote.	I did write.	I was writing.	I was going to write.

(1) The **simple form** expresses action without the aid of auxiliaries.

(2) The **emphatic form** expresses action with the aid of the auxiliaries *do* and *did*.

(3) The **progressive form** expresses a continuance of action through all the moods and tenses.

(4) The **intentional form** expresses action about to be done,

and is formed by the addition of the word *going*, with the infinitive of the verb, to the verb *be* in all its moods and tenses.

63. The **negative form** of a verb is the form employed in expressing negation or denial; as, *William **does not play***.

64. A verb is conjugated **negatively** in its **finite** forms by placing the adverb **not** after the verb or after its first auxiliary; as, *he **speaks not**; he **does not speak**; he **has not spoken***.

65. A verb is conjugated negatively in its **infinitive** forms by placing the adverb **not** before:

(1) The **infinitive**; as, *Not* to speak, *not* to have spoken.
(2) The **participle**; as, *Not* speaking, *not* having spoken.

66. The **interrogative form** of a verb is the form employed in asking a question; as, *Can he read? Shall I go?*

67. A verb is conjugated **interrogatively** by placing the subject immediately after the verb or after the first auxiliary; as, *Has man the right to judge his neighbors?*

68. The interrogative form is used only in the tenses of the **indicative** and the **potential** mood.

69. The subject is also placed after the verb:

(1) In the **indicative** mood; as,

"Up *rose* old *Barbara Fritchie* then
Bowed with her four score years and ten."—WHITTIER.

(2) In the **subjunctive** mood, when the conditional circumstance is expressed without the conjunction; as, *Were I present*, I would have helped you=*If I were present*, I would have helped you.

70. The **negative-interrogative form** of the verb is that form in which a question is asked negatively; as, *Shall I not stay?*

71. A verb is conjugated negatively and interrogatively by placing the subject and the adverb **not** after the auxiliary; as, *May I not write? Does he not speak?*

In familiar speech questions and negations are expressed by means of the present and the imperfect indicative of the auxiliary **do**; as, *Does he sing? Did he not sing? He does not sing.*

The **negative-imperative** also employs the auxiliary **do**; thus the form *Do not speak* is of more general usage than the form *Speak not.*

V.—CONJUGATION OF THE VERB HAVE.[1]

Principal Parts.

Present.	*Imperfect.*	*Imperfect Participle.*	*Perfect Participle.*
Have.	Had.	Having.	Had.

INFINITIVE MOOD.

Present Tense.
To have.

Perfect Tense.
To have had.

INDICATIVE MOOD.

Present Tense.

Singular.
1. I have,
2. Thou hast,
3. He has;

Plural.
1. We have,
2. You have,
3. They have.

Imperfect Tense.

Singular.
1. I had,
2. Thou hadst,
3. He had;

Plural.
1. We had,
2. You had.
3. They had.

---

[1] *Have* is a transitive verb used only in the ACTIVE VOICE.

Perfect Tense.

SIGNS: *Have, hast, has.*

Singular.
1. I have had,
2. Thou hast had,
3. He has had;

Plural.
1. We have had,
2. You have had.
3. They have had.

Pluperfect Tense.

SIGNS: *Had, hadst.*

Singular.
1. I had had,
2. Thou hadst had,
3. He had had;

Plural.
1. We had had.
2. You had had.
3. They had had.

Future Tense.

SIGNS: *Shall, will.*[1]

Singular.
1. I shall have,
2. Thou wilt have,
3. He will have;

Plural.
1. We shall have,
2. You will have,
3. They will have.

Future Perfect Tense.

SIGNS: *Shall have, will have.*

Singular.
1. I shall have had,
2. Thou wilt have had,
3. He will have had;

Plural.
1. We shall have had,
2. You will have had,
3. They will have had.

---

[1] *Shall* in the first person *foretells;* used in the second and third persons, it *promises, commands,* or *threatens;* as, "*I shall go to-morrow.*"—"*You shall go without fail, or suffer the consequences.*"

Will, used in the first person, *promises* or intimates a *determination;* in the second and third persons, it only *foretells;* as, "*I will go without fail.*"—"*They will go, if possible.*" (See *Introductory Etymology,* pp. 71, 72.)

VERBS.

POTENTIAL MOOD.

Present Tense.

SIGNS: *May, can,* or *must.*

Singular.
1. I may have,
2. Thou mayst have,
3. He may have;

Plural.
1. We may have,
2. You may have,
3. They may have.

Imperfect Tense.

SIGNS: *Might, could, would,* or *should.*

Singular.
1. I might have,
2. Thou mightst have,
3. He might have;

Plural.
1. We might have,
2. You might have,
3. They might have.

Perfect Tense.

SIGNS: *May have, can have,* or *must have.*

Singular.
1. I may have had,
2. Thou mayst have had,
3. He may have had;

Plural.
1. We may have had,
2. You may have had,
3. They may have had.

Pluperfect Tense.

SIGNS: *Might have, could have, would have,* or *should have.*

Singular.
1. I might have had,
2. Thou mightst have had,
3. He might have had;

Plural.
1. We might have had,
2. You might have had,
3. They might have had.

SUBJUNCTIVE MOOD.

Present Tense.

Singular.
1. If I have,
2. If thou have,
3. If he have;

Plural.
1. If we have,
2. If you have,
3. If they have.

Imperfect Tense.

Singular.	*Plural.*
1. If I had,	1. If we had,
2. If thou hadst, *or* had,	2. If you had,
3. If he had;	3. If they had.

IMPERATIVE MOOD.
Present Tense.

Singular.	*Plural.*
2. Have thou, *or* do thou have.	2. Have you, *or* do you have.

Participles.

Imperfect.	*Perfect.*	*Preperfect.*
Having.	Had.	Having had.

VI.—CONJUGATION OF THE VERB BE.[1]

Principal Parts.

Present.	*Imperfect*	*Imperfect Participle.*	*Perfect Participle.*
Be.	Was.	Being.	Been.

INFINITIVE MOOD.

Present Tense.	Perfect Tense.
To be.	To have been.

INDICATIVE MOOD.
Present Tense.

Singular.	*Plural.*
1. I am,	1. We are,
2. Thou art,	2. You are,
3. He is;	3. They are.

Imperfect Tense.

Singular.	*Plural.*
1. I was,	1. We were,
2. Thou wast,	2. You were,
3. He was;	3. They were.

---

[1] For the origin of the forms *am, was, be*, see *Development of Old English Thought*, p. 6.

VERBS.

Perfect Tense.

Singular.
1. I have been,
2. Thou hast been,
3. He has been;

Plural.
1. We have been,
2. You have been,
3. They have been.

Pluperfect Tense.

Singular.
1. I had been,
2. Thou hadst been,
3. He had been;

Plural.
1. We had been,
2. You had been,
3. They had been.

Future Tense.

Singular.
1. I shall be,
2. Thou wilt be,
3. He will be;

Plural.
1. We shall be,
2. You will be,
3. They will be.

Future Perfect Tense.

Singular.
1. I shall have been,
2. Thou wilt have been,
3. He will have been;

Plural.
1. We shall have been,
2. You will have been,
3. They will have been.

POTENTIAL MOOD.

Present Tense.

Singular.
1. I may be,
2. Thou mayst be,
3. He may be;

Plural.
1. We may be,
2. You may be,
3. They may be.

Imperfect Tense.

Singular.
1. I might be,
2. Thou mightst be,
3. He might be;

Plural.
1. We might be,
2. You might be,
3. They might be.

Perfect Tense.

Singular.   *Plural.*
1. I may have been,   1. We may have been,
2. Thou mayst have been,   2. You may have been,
3. He may have been;   3. They may have been.

Pluperfect Tense.

Singular.   *Plural.*
1. I might have been,   1. We might have been,
2. Thou mightst have been,   2. You might have been,
3. He might have been;   3. They might have been.

SUBJUNCTIVE MOOD.
Present Tense.

Singular.   *Plural.*
1. If I be,   1. If we be,
2. If thou be,   2. If you be,
3. If he be;   3. If they be.

Imperfect Tense.

Singular.   *Plural.*
1. If I were,   1. If we were,
2. If thou were, *or* wert,   2. If you were,
3. If he were;   3. If they were.

IMPERATIVE MOOD.
Present Tense.

Singular.   *Plural.*
2. Be thou, *or* do thou be.   2. Be you, *or* do you be.

Participles.

Imperfect.	*Perfect.*	*Preperfect.*
Being.	Been.	Having been.

VII.—CONJUGATION OF THE TRANSITIVE VERB LOVE.

ACTIVE VOICE.

Principal Parts.

Present.	*Imperfect.*	*Imperfect Participle.*	*Perfect Participle.*
Love.	Loved.	Loving.	Loved.

VERBS.

Infinitive Mood.

Present Tense.
To love.

Perfect Tense.
To have loved.

Indicative Mood.

Present Tense.

Singular.
1. I love,
2. Thou lovest,
3. He loves;

Plural.
1. We love,
2. You love,
3. They love.

Imperfect Tense.

Singular.
1. I loved,
2. Thou lovedst,
3. He loved;

Plural.
1. We loved,
2. You loved,
3. They loved.

Perfect Tense.

Signs: *Have, hast, has.*

Singular.
1. I have loved,
2. Thou hast loved,
3. He has loved;

Plural.
1. We have loved,
2. You have loved,
3. They have loved.

Pluperfect Tense.

Sign: *Had.*

Singular.
1. I had loved,
2. Thou hadst loved,
3. He had loved;

Plural.
1. We had loved,
2. You had loved,
3. They had loved.

Future Tense.

Signs: *Shall, will.*

Singular.
1. I shall love,
2. Thou wilt love,
3. He will love;

Plural.
1. We shall love,
2. You will love,
3. They will love.

ETYMOLOGY.

Future Perfect Tense.

SIGNS : *Shall* or *will have.*

Singular.
1. I shall have loved,
2. Thou wilt have loved,
3. He will have loved;

Plural.
1. We shall have loved,
2. You will have loved,
3. They will have loved.

POTENTIAL MOOD.

Present Tense.

SIGNS : *May, can,* or *must.*

Singular.
1. I may love,
2. Thou mayst love,
3. He may love;

Plural.
1. We may love,
2. You may love,
3. They may love.

Imperfect Tense.

SIGNS : *Might, could, would,* or *should.*

Singular.
1. I might love,
2. Thou mightst love,
3. He might love;

Plural.
1. We might love,
2. You might love,
3. They might love.

Perfect Tense.

SIGNS : *May have, can have,* or *must have.*

Singular.
1. I may have loved,
2. Thou mayst have loved,
3. He may have loved;

Plural.
1. We may have loved.
2. You may have loved,
3. They may have loved.

Pluperfect Tense.

SIGNS : *Might have, could have, would have,* or *should have.*

Singular.
1. I might have loved,
2. Thou mightst have loved,
3. He might have loved;

Plural.
1. We might have loved,
2. You might have loved,
3. They might have loved.

VERBS.

SUBJUNCTIVE MOOD.
Present Tense.

Singular.
1. If I love,
2. If thou love,
3. If he love;

Plural.
1. If we love,
2. If you love,
3. If they love.

Imperfect Tense.

Singular.
1. If I loved,
2. If thou loved,
3. If he loved;

Plural.
1. If we loved,
2. If you loved,
3. If they loved.

IMPERATIVE MOOD.
Present Tense.

Singular.
2. Love thou, *or* do thou love.

Plural.
3. Love you, *or* do you love.

Participles.

Imperfect.
Loving.

Perfect.
Loved.

Preperfect.
Having loved.

VIII.—CONJUGATION OF THE TRANSITIVE VERB LOVE.

PASSIVE VOICE.

Principal Parts.

Present. *Imperfect.* *Imperfect Participle.* *Perfect Participle.*
Love.   Loved.   Loving.   Loved.

INFINITIVE MOOD.

Present Tense.
To be loved.

Perfect Tense.
To have been loved.

INDICATIVE MOOD.
Present Tense.

Singular.
1. I am loved,
2. Thou art loved,
3. He is loved;

Plural.
1. We are loved,
2. You are loved,
3. They are loved.

Imperfect Tense.

Singular.
1. I was loved,
2. Thou wast loved,
3. He was loved;

Plural.
1. We were loved,
2. You were loved,
3. They were loved.

Perfect Tense.

Singular.
1. I have been loved,
2. Thou hast been loved,
3. He has been loved;

Plural.
1. We have been loved,
2. You have been loved,
3. They have been loved.

Pluperfect Tense.

Singular.
1. I had been loved,
2. Thou hadst been loved,
3. He had been loved;

Plural.
1. We had been loved,
2. You had been loved,
3. They had been loved.

Future Tense.

Singular.
1. I shall be loved,
2. Thou wilt be loved,
3. He will be loved;

Plural.
1. We shall be loved,
2. You will be loved,
3. They will be loved.

Future Perfect Tense.

Singular.
1. I shall have been loved,
2. Thou wilt have been loved,
3. He will have been loved;

Plural.
1. We shall have been loved,
2. You will have been loved,
3. They will have been loved.

POTENTIAL MOOD.

Present Tense.

Singular.
1. I may be loved,
2. Thou mayst be loved,
3. He may be loved;

Plural.
1. We may be loved,
2. You may be loved,
3. They may be loved.

Imperfect Tense.

Singular.
1. I might be loved,
2. Thou mightst be loved,
3. He might be loved;

Plural.
1. We might be loved,
2. You might be loved,
3. They might be loved.

Perfect Tense.

Singular.
1. I may have been loved,
2. Thou mayst have been loved,
3. He may have been loved;

Plural.
1. We may have been loved,
2. You may have been loved,
3. They may have been loved.

Pluperfect Tense.

Singular.
1. I might have been loved,
2. Thou mightst have been loved,
3. He might have been loved;

Plural.
1. We might have been loved,
2. You might have been loved,
3. They might have been loved.

SUBJUNCTIVE MOOD.
Present Tense.

Singular.
1. If I be loved,
2. If thou be loved,
3. If he be loved;

Plural.
1. If we be loved,
2. If you be loved,
3. If they be loved.

Imperfect Tense.

Singular.
1. If I were loved,
2. If thou wert, *or* were loved,
3. If he were loved;

Plural.
1. If we were loved,
2. If you were loved,
3. If they were loved.

IMPERATIVE MOOD.
Present Tense.

Singular. 2. Be thou loved, *or* do thou be loved.
Plural. 2. Be you loved, *or* do you be loved.

Participles.

Imperfect. *Perfect.* *Preperfect.*
Being loved. Loved. Having been loved

IX.—PROGRESSIVE FORM OF THE VERB STUDY.

Principal Parts of the Simple Verb.

Present. *Imperfect.* *Imperfect Participle.* *Perfect Participle.*
Study. Studied. Studying. Studied.

INFINITIVE MOOD.

Present Tense. Perfect Tense.
To be studying. To have been studying.

INDICATIVE MOOD.

Present Tense.

Singular. *Plural.*
1. I am studying, 1. We are studying,
2. Thou art studying, 2. You are studying,
3. He is studying; 3. They are studying.

Imperfect Tense.

Singular. *Plural.*
1. I was studying, 1. We were studying,
2. Thou wast studying, 2. You were studying,
3. He was studying; 3. They were studying.

Perfect Tense.

Singular. *Plural.*
1. I have been studying, 1. We have been studying,
2. Thou hast been studying, 2. You have been studying,
3. He has been studying; 3. They have been studying.

Pluperfect Tense.

Singular. *Plural.*
1. I had been studying, 1. We had been studying,
2. Thou hadst been studying, 2. You had been studying,
3. He had been studying; 3. They had been studying.

Future Tense.

Singular.
1. I shall be studying,
2. Thou wilt be studying,
3. He will be studying;

Plural.
1. We shall be studying,
2. You will be studying,
3. They will be studying.

Future Perfect Tense.

Singular.
1. I shall have been studying,
2. Thou wilt have been studying,
3. He will have been studying;

Plural.
1. We shall have been studying,
2. You will have been studying,
3. They will have been studying.

POTENTIAL MOOD.
Present Tense.

Singular.
1. I may be studying,
2. Thou mayst be studying,
3. He may be studying;

Plural.
1. We may be studying,
2. You may be studying.
3. They may be studying.

Imperfect Tense.

Singular.
1. I might be studying,
2. Thou mightst be studying,
3. He might be studying;

Plural.
1. We might be studying,
2. You might be studying,
3. They might be studying.

Perfect Tense.

Singular.
1. I may have been studying,
2. Thou mayst have been studying,
3. He may have been studying;

Plural.
1. We may have been studying,
2. You may have been studying,
3. They may have been studying.

Pluperfect Tense.

Singular.
1. I might have been studying,
2. Thou mightst have been studying,
3. He might have been studying;

Plural.
1. We might have been studying,
2. You might have been studying,
3. They might have been studying.

Subjunctive Mood.

Present Tense.

Singular.
1. If I be studying,
2. If thou be studying,
3. If he be studying;

Plural.
1. If we be studying,
2. If you be studying,
3. If they be studying.

Imperfect Tense.

Singular.
1. If I were studying,
2. If thou were *or* wert studying,
3. If he were studying;

Plural.
1. If we were studying,
2. If you were studying,
3. If they were studying.

Imperative Mood.

Present Tense.

Singular. 2. Be thou studying, *or* do thou be studying.
Plural. 2. Be you studying, *or* do you be studying.

Participles.

Imperfect.
Being studying.

Perfect.
—

Preperfect.
Having been studying

REMARKS ON THE CONJUGATIONS.

72. In the **indicative mood**, the verb is conjugated in all six tenses.

73. In the **potential mood**, the verb is conjugated in four tenses; namely, the present, the imperfect, the perfect, and the pluperfect.

74. The **subjunctive mood** is generally represented as having two tenses; namely, the present and the imperfect. But this mood in reality admits equally well of the perfect and the pluperfect tense. Thus the verb **love** can be conjugated as follows:

Subjunctive Mood.

Perfect Tense.

Singular.	Plural.
1. If I have loved,	1. If we have loved,
2. If thou have loved,	2. If you have loved,
3. If he have loved,	3. If they have loved.

Pluperfect Tense.

Singular.	Plural.
1. If I had loved,	1. If we had loved,
2. If thou had *or* hadst loved,	2. If you had loved,
3. If he had loved;	3. If they had loved.

75. The subjunctive mood is usually introduced by the conjunctions **if, though, that, unless, lest, except.**

Sometimes the subjunctive mood retains precisely the same forms as the indicative mood, and sometimes it differs from the indicative as here conjugated.

76. In the **imperative mood**, the verb is conjugated in one tense; namely, the present.

The imperative mood is sometimes conjugated in the future tense, in the second and third persons, as follows:[1]

Singular.	Plural.
2. Thou shalt write,	2. You shall write,
3. He shall write;	3. They shall write.

So, in the wording of the Ten Commandments, the idea expressed is one of command, not of futurity; as, *Thou shalt not steal, Thou shalt not bear* false witness.

77. In the **infinitive mood**, the verb has two forms; namely, the present and the perfect.

---

[1] Adams, *The English Language*, p. 109.

These forms do not really carry with them the idea of time. The present infinitive conveys the idea of indefinite action; as, *I wanted to speak.* The perfect infinitive conveys the idea of completed action; as, He is said *to have spoken.*

EXERCISES ON VERBS.

Oral Exercises.

I. What is a VERB? (1)—*Name the verbs in the examples given in the definition.*—*Conjugate the verb* HAVE, *in regular order, as far as the potential mood.*—*Give the first person singular in all the tenses of the indicative mood.*

II. How is the subject of a verb found? (68)—*Conjugate the verb* HAVE, *commencing at the potential mood, and continuing to the end.*—*With regard to their meaning, how are verbs divided?* (4, 15)—*What is a transitive verb?* (16)—*An intransitive verb?* (17)—*Conjugate the verb* BE *in regular order in the potential mood; in the subjunctive mood; in the indicative mood.*

III. Form another verb from each of the following words by prefixing over-, re-, sur-, *or* un-.

1. gain	2. write	3. charge
work	mount	do
look	light	cover

What are the person and number of a verb? (44, 45)—*What is voice?* (20)—*How many voices are there?*—*Name them.* (21)—*What is the active voice?* (22)—*Conjugate the verb* LOVE, *active voice, in regular order, in the potential mood; in the subjunctive mood.*

Conjugate the verb CALL, *active voice, in the indicative mood; in the potential mood.*—*What is a regular verb?*

(2)—What is the passive voice? *(23)—What are weak verbs?—What are strong verbs?* (14)

For what is the present tense used? *(37)—The imperfect?* *(38)—The perfect?* *(39)—Give the principal parts, the infinitive, the imperative, and the participles of* LOVE.

When is the pluperfect tense used? *(40)—The future?* *(41)—The future perfect?* (42)

IV. When is the potential mood used? *(29)—Conjugate the verb* LOVE *in the passive voice.—When is the subjunctive mood used?* *(30)—When is the infinitive mood used?* (27) *—When is the imperative mood used?* *(31)—What are the principal parts of a verb?* *(51)—What is the conjugation of a verb?* (54)

WRITTEN EXERCISES.

I. Underline the verbs in the following stanzas:

>Heaven is not gained by a single bound,
>But we build the ladder by which we rise
>From the lowly earth to the vaulted skies,
>And we mount to its summit round by round.

>I count this thing to be grandly true:
>That a noble deed is a step toward God,—
>Lifting the soul from the common sod
>To a purer air and a broader view.—J. G. HOLLAND.

II. Insert a suitable verb in the following sentences:

1. A good Christian *knows* how to be patient in trials.—2. It —— not enough to commence well, we should also —— well.—3. God commands us to —— and —— our parents.—4. We should —— compassion on the poor who —— our assistance.—5. Constant labor —— the road to success.—6. Time —— so precious, we must nevei —— it. 7. The law of God —— us to covet our neighbor's goods.—8. Speech —— silver; but silence —— gold.

ETYMOLOGY.

III. Where the dash occurs, insert a suitable verb:

1. His wisdom —— him bitter experience.—The rivulet —— with a noiseless current.—A man ——, but a nation ——.
2. All that lives must ——. The wind —— furiously and shook the house.—Evil communications —— good manners.

IV. Indicate orally, or by means of the letter t *or* i, *whether the verb is transitive or intransitive:*

1. Perseverance overcomes all obstacles.—Francis broke the bottle.—The lightning shot forth from the clouds and struck the oak.—Victoria is queen of England.
2. Eight hundred years have passed since the dedication of Westminster Abbey.—A thoughtless person is one who does not reflect upon the consequences of what he does.—"In another moment down went Alice after it, never once considering how in the world she was to get out again."—*Alice in Wonderland.*

V. Conjugate in the indicative present, imperfect, and future; potential present and imperfect; subjunctive present:

Yield, convict, procure, possess, attend, control.

VI. Conjugate in the indicative perfect, pluperfect, future perfect; potential perfect, pluperfect; subjunctive imperfect:

Perish, cry, mention, discover.

VII. Conjugate in the principal parts, infinitive mood, imperative mood, and give participles:

recite	arrest	perish	publish
succeed	heat	bless	bewail
boast	jump	took	turn

VIII. Conjugate in the potential and the subjunctive, active voice:

Unfurl, owe, prepare, answer, exhaust, suffer.

IX. Conjugate the verbs FINISH, REFLECT, ACCEPT, *in the first three tenses of the indicative mood, active voice; and* SERVE, WATCH, SATISFY *in the first three tenses of the potential mood, passive voice.*

X. Conjugate in the infinitive, imperative, indicative future and future perfect, and present and imperfect:

Pardon, instruct, dream, describe, represent, persuade.

XI. Conjugate WISH, PROVIDE, ADORE *in the first person plural, active voice, through all the tenses of the indicative mood.*

XII. Change the verbs in the following passage into the indicative present:

His death was a shock to the literary world, and a deep affliction to a wide circle of intimates and friends; for, with all his foibles and peculiarities, he was fully as much beloved as he was admired. Burke, on hearing the news, burst into tears. Sir Joshua Reynolds threw by his pencil for the day, and grieved more than he had done in times of great family distress.—W. IRVING,—*Life of Goldsmith.*

XIII. Change the verbs in the following sentences to the form of the future tense:

You love your brother.—You never annoy your neighbor.—You speak the truth.—You avoid evil companions.—You pay attention to your teacher.—You always employ your time well.—You render to every man his due.—You love and venerate your parents.

Which expressions in the future form express FUTURITY, **and which** COMMAND? **(76)**

XIV. Change the verbs to the passive voice:

Robinson Crusoe brought his man Friday with him.—Whom did the Queen of France visit?—Mary's mother loves her.—George recited the lesson.—The tailor has made the coat.

XV. Where the dash occurs, insert a suitable auxiliary of the potential mood:

He —— be here this evening. —— you go with him? —— I go also?—You —— do as you are told.—He —— have had the position. —— you assist this poor man?—I —— have spoken sooner.

Draw one line under the subject and two lines under the predicate:

The time when we first begin really to know anything about Britain is between fifty and sixty years before the birth of our Lord Jesus Christ, you know. I suppose this is the way Christian nations reckon time; such a thing happened so many years before, or so many years after the birth of Christ. At that time the greatest people in the world were the Romans.—FREEMAN.

XVI. Supply the predicate:

1. Life *is* what we *make* it.—The sun and moon —— light.—The boys —— playing.—It —— he.—His remark —— inappropriate.—The sheep —— wool.—This lace —— in France.—He —— all the way.—The city —— this year.—He —— yesterday.—They —— their parents.

2. She —— last Tuesday.—The man —— miserably.—Cowards —— many times before their deaths.—It —— wise to be humble.—Newton —— very modest.—The Emperor Augustus —— a patron of the fine arts.—The labors of Alexander Hamilton as a statesman —— invaluable.

XVII. Where the dash occurs, insert one or other of the following verbs in the indicative present:

To like, to be, to visit, to enjoy, to will.

The air —— mild this morning, the birds sing as in spring, and some sunshine —— my little room.—I —— it thus, and —— myself as much in it as in the most beautiful place in the world, all solitary though it ——. This is because I make of it just what I ——, a drawing-room, a church, an academy.—EUGÉNIE DE GUÉRIN,—*Journal.*

XVIII. Where the dash occurs, insert one or other of the following verbs of the imperfect tense of the indicative:

To glory, to brook, to owe, to presume, to hesitate, to thwart, to obey, to spot, to pour, to seem, to employ, to pursue, to inflict.

He was careful that his favorites should —— everything to himself, and —— in the parade of their power and opulence, because they were of his own creation. But if he was a bountiful master, he was a most vindictive enemy. His temper could not —— contradiction. Whoever —— to —— his will, or —— to —— his desires, was —— out for his victim, and was —— with the most unrelenting vengeance. We are told that in his paroxysms his eyes were —— with blood, his countenance —— of flame, his tongue —— a torrent of abuse and imprecation, and his hands were —— to —— vengeance on whatever came within his reach.—LINGARD,—*On Henry II.*

XIX. Where the dash occurs, insert a verb of the indicative imperfect or perfect, as the sense may require:

1. The heat *was* intense.—The officers —— chosen.—Mary —— to secure the approbation of her teacher.—The charms of summer ——. He —— me a pencil.—The multitude —— divided.—The President and Vice-President —— there.

2. Pompey —— a Roman general.—Jane —— yesterday.—Peter —— after the cow.—New York —— nearly two million inhabitants.—The sun —— slowly.—The boys —— to their father.—The pupils —— their lessons well.—Charles —— on the farm.

3. Mary —— lessons in vocal music.—Margaret —— to mass this morning early.—Alice —— a beautiful letter.

XX. Where the dash occurs in the first paragraph, insert a suitable verb of the indicative pluperfect; and in the second, a verb of the future or future perfect:

1. Thomas *had reached* Albany before Agnes started.—John —— his letter when you came to see him.—Rose —— her brother before we reached home.—You —— there before we arrived.—George —— when James met his father.

2. They —— the vessel by to-morrow noon.—I —— there before you get home.—You —— your lessons before I have my exercise written.—George —— his clothes before evening.

XXI. Where the dash occurs, insert a suitable verb of the infinitive or imperative mood, as the sense may require:

1. *Be* industrious if you would succeed in life.—The lady has started to —— Washington. —— in immediately out of the storm.

2. —— thy neighbor as thyself.—Those who serve God faithfully, deserve to —— by him.

XXII. Change the object in each sentence to the plural, and make the other necessary changes to complete the sense:

Persuade the boy to tell the truth.—He forgave the man that was guilty.—Bring the flower that was plucked last evening.—We admire an object that is beautiful.—The officer rewarded the man who was faithful to his duty.—Forgive the enemy who asks your pardon.

XXIII. Insert the following words as the object of the verb in the sentences here given:

1. Thirst, water, trash, peace, purse, truth, soul.—2. Shot, secret, scene, strength, penny, hero, voice.

1. Who steals my ——, steals trash.—He satisfied his ——. Simplicity of life produces —— of mind.—He found —— in it.—Always speak the ——. Truth enlightens the ——. 2. The winds and the waves obey their Creator's ——. "Not a soldier discharged his farewell ——, O'er the grave where our —— we buried."—We can

never find out the —— of life.—A rude wooden cross marks the —— of the battle.—Shall we gain —— by irresolution and inaction?—I will give you a —— to row us over the ferry.

XXIV. Where the dash occurs in the following passage, insert suitable verbs in the passive voice from the list furnished:

Dissolve, excite, make, form, compose.

That the diamond —— —— —— of the same material as coal; that water —— —— chiefly —— of an inflammable substance; that acids —— —— almost all —— of different kinds of air; and that one of those acids, by whose strength almost any of the metals —— ——, —— —— —— of the self-same ingredients with the common air we breathe: these surely are things by which the wonder of any reflecting mind —— ——.

X.—IRREGULAR VERBS.

78. An **irregular verb** is a verb that does not form its imperfect tense and perfect participle by assuming -d or -ed; as, *see, saw, seeing, seen.*

79. Several of the irregular verbs form their principal parts by change of **vowel.** They are called **strong verbs.** Their perfect participle originally ended in -n or -en.

80. Several verbs are only apparently irregular. Such are those whose imperfect tense is formed by -d or -t, without a change of vowel. They are ranked among the **weak verbs,** as are all regular verbs.

81. Derivatives and compounds generally follow the form of the simple verb; as, *foresee, foresaw, foreseeing, foreseen; oversee, oversaw, overseeing, overseen.* The exceptions are *behave* and *welcome,* which are regular.

1. Verbs that Vary in all Three Parts.[1]

Present.	Imperfect.	Perfect Participle.
am or be	was	been
arise	arose	arisen
bear (*to bring forth*)	bore, **bare**	born
bear (*to uphold*)	bore, **bare**	borne
beat	beat, bet	**beaten**, or beat
begin	began	begun
bid	bid, **bade**	**bidden**, bid
bite	bit	**bitten**, bit
blow[2]	blew	blown
break	broke, **brake**	broken
chide	chid	**chidden**, chid
choose	chose	chosen
cleave *to* (*split*)	clove, cleft	cloven, cleft
come	came	come
do	did	done
draw	drew	drawn
drink	drank	drank, **drunk**
drive	drove	driven
eat	ate, eat[3]	**eaten**, or eat
fall	fell	fallen
fly	flew	flown
forbear	forbore	forborne
forget	forgot	**forgotten**, forgot
forsake	forsook	forsaken
freeze	froze	frozen
get	got	**gotten**, got
give	gave	given

[1] Where there are two forms for the same part, the older form is printed in bold type. As the *imperfect participle* has no variation, and is always formed by adding *ing* to the present, it is omitted from the list here given.

[2] *Blow, to bloom*, and *blow*, the word used when speaking of the wind, have both the same parts.

[3] Scott uses *eat* for *ate*, in *Waverley*, ch. xi.—Shakespeare has *eat* for *eaten*, in *King John*, I. i.

VERBS.

Present.	Imperfect.	Perfect Participle.
go	went[1]	gone
grow	grew	grown
hide	hid	hidden, hid
hold	held	held, holden
know	knew	known
lade (*to load*)[2]	laded	laden
lie (*to recline*)	lay	lain, lien[3]
ride	rode	ridden
ring	rang, rung	rung
rise	rose	risen
run	ran, run	run
see	saw	seen
shake	shook	shaken[4]
shrink	shrank	shrunk
sing	sang, sung	sung
sink	sank, sunk	sunk
slay	slew	slain
smite	smote	smitten, smit[5]
speak	spoke, spake	spoken
spit	spit, spat	spit, spitten, spitted
spring	sprang, sprung	sprung
steal	stole	stolen
stride	strode	stridden
strive	strove	striven
swear	swore	sworn
swim	swam, swum	swum

[1] The imperfect *went* comes from the present of another verb, *wend*, which also meant *to go*, but which is now used in a different sense and is conjugated regularly.

[2] Lade, *to dip*, is regular.

[3] *Lien* is now archaic, but it was used by Shakespeare and in the King James version of the Bible.

[4] Milton uses *shook* for *shaken:*

—all earth
Had to her centre *shook.*—*Paradise Lost*, vi., 219.

[5] Shakespeare uses *smote* for *smitten* (*Coriolanus* III., i.), *wrote* for *written* (*Cymbeline* III., v.), *arose* for *arisen* (*Comedy of Errors* V., i.), *rode* for *ridden* (*Henry IV.*, v. iii.).

Present.	Imperfect.	Perfect Participle.
take	took	taken
tear	tore	torn
throw	threw	thrown
tread	trod	**trodden**, trod
wear	wore, ware	worn
write	wrote	**written**, writ
weave	wove	**woven**, wove

2. VERBS WHOSE IMPERFECT TENSE AND PERFECT PARTICIPLE ARE ALIKE.

Present.	Imperfect.	Perfect Participle.
abide	abode	abode
bend	bent	bent
beseech	besought	besought
bet	bet	bet
bind	bound	bound
bleed	bled	bled
breed	bred	bred
bring	brought	brought
burst	burst	burst
buy	bought	bought
cast	cast	cast
catch	caught	caught
cling	clung	clung
cost	cost	cost
creep	crept	crept
cut	cut	cut
dig	dug	dug
feed	fed	fed
feel	felt	felt
fight	fought	fought
find	found	found
flee	fled	fled
fling	flung	flung

Present.	Imperfect	Perfect Participle.
grind	ground	ground
have	had	had
hear	heard	heard
hit	hit	hit
hurt	hurt	hurt
keep	kept	kept
lay	laid	laid
lead	led	led
leave	left	left
lend	lent	lent
let	let	let
lose	lost	lost [1]
make	made	made
mean	meant	meant
meet	met	met
pay	paid	paid
put	put	put
read	read [2]	read [2]
rend	rent	rent
rid	rid	rid
say	said	said
seek	sought	sought
sell	sold	sold
send	sent	sent
set	set	set
shed	shed	shed
shine	shone	shone
shoe	shod	shod
shoot	shot	shot

---

[1] In older forms of English speech the perfect participle was *losen*, in which, according to the law governing the interchange of letters (*Orthography*, ch. i., 22), *s* was changed to *r*, and *losen* became *loren*, which, according to another law (*Ibid.* 15), became *lorn*. Spenser uses *lorn* for *lost*: "After he had fair Una *lorn*."—*Faerie Queen*, I., 42.—A remnant of this older form is still retained in the word *forlorn*.

[2] Pronounced *red*.

Present.	*Imperfect.*	*Perfect Participle.*
shut	shut	shut
sit	sat	sat
sleep	slept	slept
slide	slid	slid
sling	slung	slung
slink	slunk	slunk
slit	slit	slit, slitted
speed	sped	sped
spend	spent	spent
spin	spun	spun
split	split	split
spread	spread	spread
stand	stood	stood
stick	stuck	stuck
sting	stung	stung
strike	struck	struck
string	strung	strung
sweep	swept	swept
swing	swung	swung
teach	taught	taught
tell	told	told
think	thought	thought
thrust	thrust	thrust
weep	wept	wept
win	won	won
wind	wound	wound
wring	wrung	wrung

8. VERBS BOTH REGULAR AND IRREGULAR IN THEIR PRINCIPAL PARTS.

Present.	*Imperfect.*	*Perfect Participle.*
awake	awoke, awaked	awaked
bereave	bereft, bereaved	bereft, bereaved
blend	blended	blended, blent

VERBS.

Present.	Imperfect.	Perfect Participle.
build	built, builded [1]	built, builded
burn	burned, burnt	burned, burnt
cleave (*to cling to*)	cleaved, clave	cleaved
climb	climbed, clomb [2]	climbed
clothe	clothed, clad	clothed, clad
crow	crowed, crew	crowed
dare (*to venture*)	dared, durst	dared
deal	dealt, dealed	dealt, dealed
dream	dreamed, dreamt	dreamed, dreamt
dwell	dwelt, dwelled	dwelt, dwelled
gild	gilded, gilt	gilded, gilt
gird	girded, girt	girded, girt
grave	graved	graven, graved
hang	hung, hanged [3]	hung, [4] hanged
hew	hewed	hewn, hewed
kneel	knelt, kneeled	knelt, kneeled
knit	knit, knitted	knit, knitted
light	lighted, lit	lighted, lit
mow	mowed	mown, mowed
pen (*to inclose*)	pent, penned	pent, penned
quit	quit, quitted	quit, quitted
rive	rived	riven, rived
rot	rotted	rotten, rotted
saw	sawed	sawn, sawed
shape	shaped [5]	shapen, shaped
shave	shaved	shaven, shaved

---

[1] The -*t* in *built* stands for the original letters -*d* + -*de* which became -*de*, then -*te*, and finally -*t*. This last change took place in the fourteenth century. The form *builded* is still sometimes used. Thus Emerson says: "They *builded* better than they knew."

[2] Milton uses *clomb*: "So *clomb* this first grand thief into God's fold."—*Paradise Lost*, iv., 192. Byron also: "We forded the river and *clomb* the high hills."—*Siege of Corinth*.

[3] Regular when it denotes the taking of life.

[4] *Hung* is a contraction of the old English form *hongen*.

[5] The old imperfect *shope* was in use in the sixteenth century.

Present.	Imperfect.	Perfect Participle.
shear	sheared	shorn, sheared
show	showed	shown, showed
sow	sowed	sown, sowed
spell	spelt, spelled	spelt, spelled
spill	spilt, spilled	spilt, spilled
strew	strewed	strewn, strewed
strow	strowed	strown, strowed
swell	swelled	swollen, swelled
thrive	thrived, throve	thriven, thrived
wax	waxed	waxen, waxed
whet	whet, whetted	whet, whetted
work	wrought, worked	wrought, worked

XI.—DEFECTIVE VERBS.

82. A **defective verb** is a verb that, in its present state, forms no participles, and is not used in all the moods and tenses. The following are defective verbs:

83. Worth = *be.*—"*Wo worth the day!*"— *Ezech.* xxx. 2.

This phrase means "*Woe be to the day!*" It is the only phrase in which *worth* in this sense is met with in modern English.

Worth is from the old English *weorthan*=to become.

84. Beware is used only in those tenses in which the form **be** is retained in the conjugation of the verb **be**; namely:

(1) The infinitive present; as, Strive *to beware*.
(2) The indicative future; as, He *will beware*.
(3) The potential present; as, You *must beware*.
(4) The potential past; as You *should beware*.
(5) The subjunctive present; as, If *you beware*.
(6) The imperative; as, *Beware* of bad company.

In the indicative present of the verb *be*, we meet the forms *I am*, *he is*. Now, we cannot say *I beware*, *he bewares*.

85. Ought (*should*) is derived from *owe*, of which it is the imperfect tense.

Shakespeare uses ought in this sense:
"You ought him a thousand pounds;"
that is, "You *owed* him."

Ought is now used in the present and the imperfect tense to express moral obligation. It is invariable except in the second person singular.

Singular.	*Plural.*
1. Ought,	1. Ought,
2. Ought-est,	2. Ought,
3. Ought;	3. Ought.

86. Would (meaning *earnest desire*) is rarely used except in the expressions *would God, would Heaven; would to God, would to Heaven; I would that, would that I could*, and the like. **Would** is originally the imperfect tense of **will**, but, like *ought*, expresses present time in the examples here given.

The colloquial expression **won't** comes from **wol-not**, according to laws already laid down (*Orth.* ch. i. 15, 20).

Wol is another form for **will**, and was in use up to the thirteenth century.

Nill is a contracted form of **ne-will**, *not-will*, according to the same laws (*Ibid.*).

Willy nilly=*will-he, nill-he*, or *will-ye, nill-ye*. (*Taming of the Shrew*, II. i.) Cromwell writes: "They, *will they, nill they*, shall fulfil the good pleasure of God."—CARLYLE,—*Cromwell's Letters and Speeches*, Letter 67.

87. Quoth (*say, said*) is used only in the first and the third person singular of the indicative present and past.

It is invariable, and is always placed before its subject, as, "*Quoth I.*—" *Quoth he.*"—

"Quoth the Raven, nevermore."—EDGAR ALLAN POE.

Quoth was originally the form of the imperfect tense. We have a remnant of the present tense in the syllable *queath* of the word *bequeath*.

88. Wit is now used only in the infinitive present, when it is taken adverbially, and means *namely*.

To wit originally meant *to know*. Its present tense is **wot**; it is the same through all the persons.

The word *wot* is of frequent occurrence in Shakespeare. The imperfect tense is *wist;* this is also the same through all the persons. To illustrate its use: the Rheims-Douay version of the Bible reads: "For he *knew* not what he said." The King James version reads: "For he *wist* not what to say." (*Mark* ix. 6.) An English proverb reads: "Beware of *had I wist;*" that is, "Beware of having to say afterwards with regret, *had I known*." The imperfect participle of *wit* is retained in the words *unwitting, unwittingly*, still in use.

89. Must was originally itself an imperfect tense. It is now used in all persons and in past and present tenses to denote necessity and obligation.

The present tense of must was môt. Spenser used the old verb form:

Fraelissa was as fair, as fair *mote* be.—*Faërie Queen.*

90. Durst is the imperfect tense of *dare*. Like *must*, it is used both in the present and past tenses. So, also, the form **dare** is correctly used in the third person singular; as,

"A bard to sing of deeds he dare not imitate."—SCOTT,—*Waverley*.

When dare signifies *to challenge*, it becomes a regular verb.

91. Need, as a verb, used negatively, loses its ending **s** in the third person singular; as, *It need not be; he need not come.*

92. When the infinitive following has the particle **to** omitted, **need** is also used without the **s** in the third person singular; as, *It need scarcely be said; all that need be said.*—NEWMAN.

93. But when the particle **to** is expressed, the **s** is added; as, *It needs to be said.*

The same rule holds good for the verb **dare.** The phrase must needs is an emphatic form of necessity; as, *He must needs go to Rome.* The word *needs* is an adverb in this instance.

EXERCISES.

I. Conjugate in the second and third persons singular, indicative mood:

Deal, buy, dig, catch, come, bring, cut, do, clothe.

II. Conjugate in the first person, singular and plural, indicative and potential moods:

Feel, eat, find, drink, dwell, drive, fling, fall, fly, forgive.

III. Conjugate in the infinitive, subjunctive, imperative moods, and give the participles:

Freeze, get, give, keep, hold.

IV. Conjugate in the indicative and potential, second person singular and plural, passive voice:

Lend, lead, meet, pay, make, let, lose, make, read.

V. Change to the plural the words in italics:

He rows the boat.—*Thou walkest* too fast.—*I* went to the library. —*He* spoke of *his* fine horses.—*My* book *was* found.—The *base ball team is* here. *It is* new and large.—*Thou art* the *man.*—*I know him* to be honest.

VI. *Change to the singular form:*

The birds were on the trees.—The boats contain the boys.—You rest when you should labor.—The pupils received their rewards.—The books were given to the girls.—We visited the gardens last week.

VII. *Change to the plural form the words in italics:*

Remember, boy, when *thou makest* a mistake *thou canst* correct it, if *thou takest* the means that are pointed out to *thee.*—Guide *thyself* by the rules of justice.—They gave *thee* the book that *thou didst lend* some time since to *thy* friend.—The *crucifix is* beautifully carved.— The *carpet was* greatly admired.

VIII. *Supply an irregular verb in the following sentences:*

1. I *awoke* this morning at two o'clock.—I —— the Lord with all my heart.—He —— a new carriage.—Oliver —— the trumpet.—Alexander —— a large trout.—Anna —— when I arrived.—James —— me tell you that he —— to see you.

2. The ship —— in England.—He is —— to fulfil the contract.—Isaac —— his pains patiently.—Thomas —— me the Bible.—Do as your father —— you.—The dam ——. The table is ——.

IX. *Give the following verbs such inflections as they take:*

Beware, ought, quoth, wot, dare.

X. *Replace the emphatic form of the verb by the simple form in the following sentences:*

They *do love* to work.—I know that he *did intend* to go.—They *did expect* to be there.—We *did propose* the meeting.—Henry *did sell* the house.—He *did make* a great mistake in acting unkindly.—You *did wrong* your friend when you *did speak* ill of him.

XI. Change the verbs in the following sentences into the progressive form and state the change of meaning brought about by the change of form:

Example.—Simple form: *John writes* = Progressive form: *John is writing.*

1. William studied his lessons.—2. Henry will go to the dock.—3 Eliza may write to her aunt.—4. Ida proposed to stay with her sister —5. "The saint, the father, and the husband prays."—BURNS.

XII. Change the verbs in the following sentences into the intentional form:

Example.—Simple form: *John had written.* Intentional form: *John had been going to write.*

1. Fools rush in where angels fear to tread.—2. Adversity was a good school.—3. Carlyle wrote *The French Revolution.*—4. The war occurred.—5. The book was printed.—6. Napoleon betrayed the Pope.

XII.—INFINITIVES.

1. The verb has two forms in the **infinitive mood**: the present and the perfect.

2. The **present infinitive** is the verb in its simplest form with the preposition to prefixed; as, *to ride, to be deceived.*

3. The **perfect infinitive** is the perfect participle of the verb, preceded by the infinitive to **have**; as, *to have ridden, to have been deceived.*

4. The infinitive forms are chiefly used as **verbal nouns.** As such they enter largely into the construction of infinitive phrases.

5. **Infinitive phrases** may be:

>   (1) The subject of a verb; as, *To read good books* is useful.
>   (2) The object of a transitive verb; as, James loves *to read good books.*

(3) An **attribute**; as, To work is *to pray.*
(4) In **apposition with a noun**; as, It is a noble task *to train the tender soul.*
(5) An **adjective**; as, There is a time *to laugh* and a time *to be serious.*
(6) An **adverb**; as, He is always ready *to find fault.*
(7) **Independent**; as, *To make a long story short*, they escaped all perils.

6. The present infinitive is used when the verb in the sentence expresses an act or state of being **before** or at **the time of** the act expressed by the infinitive:

(1) **Before the act**; as, I meant *to write* to you before to-day.
(2) **At the time of the act**; as, He seemed *to enjoy* the play last night.

7. The perfect infinitive is used when the verb expresses an act or state of being **following** the act expressed by the infinitive; as, *He appeared* **to have seen** *better days.*

EXERCISES.

I. Where the dash occurs insert the present infinitive:

He was expected —— present.—Henry and John are —— to-morrow.—They started —— for the train.—I intended —— for Europe.—They are —— in the hotel. —— is all he asks.—You need not ——.

II. Where the dash occurs insert the perfect infinitive:

You ought —— with your father. —— so many friends, was a sufficient proof of the esteem in which he was held.—She was thought —— the letter.—Thomas will be known —— the essay.—He was said —— over the country.

III. Write out the verbs in the infinitive mood, present and perfect tenses, and state the reasons why they are in those respective tenses:

They were said to have been sick.—I intend to write.—Ralph has neglected to read the editorial.—We have forgotten how to spell.—To be believed always comes from speaking the truth.—He believed his friend to have been wrong.

>We have hearts to feel and hands to do,
>And eyes to pierce the darkness through.

>He that lacks time to mourn, lacks time to mend.
>Eternity mourns that.—HENRY TAYLOR.

XIII.—PARTICIPLES.

1. **A participle** is a form of the verb expressing action or state of being without the limitations of number and person.

2. The participle admits of **three forms**: the imperfect, the perfect, and the preperfect.

3. The **imperfect participle** expresses action or state of being as continuing and unfinished; as, *reaping*.

The imperfect participle is also called the **present participle**, and the **participial-infinitive**.

4. The imperfect participle is formed by adding -ing to the root-word of the verb; as, *speak-ing*.

5. The **perfect participle** expresses action or state of being as past; as, *spoken*.

The perfect participle is also called the **past participle**.

6. The perfect participle is formed by adding **-d** or **-ed** to the root of regular, or weak verbs, and **-n** or **-en** to the root of irregular, or strong verbs.

Sometimes, among the irregular or strong verbs, no change occurs in the formation of the perfect participle. Several such are to be found in the list of our irregular or strong verbs.

7. The **preperfect participle** expresses action or state of being as having been completed; as, *having spoken.*

The preperfect participle is also called the **perfect participle.**

8. The preperfect participle is formed by prefixing the word **having** to the perfect participle.

9. The **participial infinitive** assumes the functions of a noun, an adjective, an adverb, and a preposition.

(1) A **noun**; as, The *reading* of good books is beneficial.
(2) An **adjective**; as, They fired a *parting* shot.
(3) An **adverb**; as, The water was *scalding* hot.
(4) A **preposition**; as, He was informed *regarding* the whole proceeding.

10. The following participles are frequently used as prepositions:

barring	notwithstanding	saving
bating	pending	touching
concerning	regarding	
excepting	respecting	

EXERCISES.

I. Copy the following passage, underlining the participles, and naming the kind of participle each is.

PERFECTION.

A friend called on Michael Angelo, who was finishing a statue; some time afterwards he called again; the sculptor was still at work; his friend, looking at the figure, exclaimed, "You have been idle since I saw you last!" "By no means," replied the sculptor, "I have retouched this part, and polished that; I have softened this feature, and brought out this muscle. I have given more expression to this lip, and more energy to this limb." "Well, well," said his friend, "but all these are trifles." "It may be so," replied Michael Angelo, "but recollect that trifles make perfection, and that perfection is no trifle."

II. Where the dash occurs insert a suitable participle:

1. The workman, *spent* with fatigue, fell into a deep sleep.—The art of —— well and fluently is important.—Henry, —— on the pavement, broke his leg.—The retiring president, —— the meeting, withdrew from the platform.

2. Margaret has a —— for good books. —— by the gale, the vessel was dashed against the rocky shore. — — his soldiers over the Alps, Hannibal entered Italy.

3. —— with difficulties and disappointments, La Salle never lost courage.—I have not —— here to-day.—The tyrant Nero, —— many cruel acts, died a miserable death.—Columbus was about —— to Spain.—St. Paul the Apostle, —— in the reign of Nero, was witness of his cruelties.

CHAPTER X.

ADVERBS.

1. **An adverb** is a word used to modify a verb, an adjective, or another adverb; as, *When you speak, speak slowly, distinctly, and correctly.*

2. Adverbs are derived from **adjectives** and **participles** by the addition of **-ly**; as, from the adjective *slow*, comes the adverb *slowly;* and from the participle *knowing* comes the adverb *knowingly.*

The suffix **-ly** is from the Old English *lic* or *lich*=like.

3. Some adverbs and adverbial phrases are formed by combining a **preposition** with a **noun** or an **adjective**:

(1) Of, replacing the old possessive case; as, *Of-course, of-force, of-truth, of-old, of-late, of-a-day, of-a-truth.*

(2) Of, with the old possessive form; as, *of-Sundays, of-mornings.*

(3) A, standing for the old English **an, on, in**; as, *a-year, a-day,*=yearly, daily; *a-bed, a-foot, a-loft.*

(4) An, on, o, standing for **an** or **on**, and meaning of; as, *man-a-war, two-o-clock, Jack-an-apes.*

(5) A, with old possessive forms; as, *a-nights, now-a-days*=old English *now-on-days.*

(6) Be; as, *be-times, be-side.*

(7) To; as, *to-day, to-night, to-morrow.*

Some adverbs have changed from the old objective to the old possessive form; thus,

Sometime has become **sometimes**.
Alway " " **always**.
Sideway " " **sideways**.

4. Adverbs of **direction** are formed from other adverbs or from nouns by the addition of the suffix **-ward** or **wards**; as, *upward* or *upwards, backward, afterward, downward; homeward, leeward, shoreward.*

The suffix **-ward**, in old English **weard**, is allied to **weorthan**, *to be* or *to become*, and hence implies *turning* or *leading to.*

5. Some **adverbial phrases** are formed by prepositions with the comparative and superlative of adjectives:

(1) **Comparative**; as, *for better, for the worse.*
(2) **Superlative**; as, *at last, at most, at best, at least.*

I.—CLASSIFICATION OF ADVERBS.

6. Adverbs are divided into **four** principal classes; namely, adverbs of time, adverbs of place, adverbs of degree, and adverbs of manner.

ADVERBS.

7. Adverbs of time answer the questions *When? How long?* They may express:

(1) **Time absolute:** Ever, never, always, eternally, perpetually, continually, constantly, endlessly, forever, incessantly, everlastingly, evermore, nevermore, aye.

(2) **Time relative:** i. e., *reckoned with, to, or from some other time:* When, whenever, then, meanwhile, meantime, as, while, whilst, till, until, otherwhile, after, afterwards, subsequently, before, late, early, betimes, seasonably.

(3) **Time repeated:** Again, often, oft, oftentimes, sometimes, occasionally, seldom, rarely, frequently, now and then, ever and anon, daily, weekly, hourly, monthly, yearly, annually, anew, once, twice, thrice, four times, and so on.

(4) **Time present:** Now, to-day, nowadays, at present, yet (= *heretofore and now*), as yet.

(5) **Time past:** Yesterday, heretofore, recently, lately, of late, already, formerly, just now, just, anciently, since, hitherto, long since, long ago, erewhile, till now.

(6) **Time future:** Hereafter, henceforth, henceforward, soon, to-morrow, shortly, erelong, by and by, presently, instantly, immediately, straightway, straightways, directly, forthwith, not yet, anon.

8. Adverbs of place answer the questions *Where? Whither? Whence?* They may express:

(1) **Place absolute:** Here, there, yonder, where, everywhere, somewhere, universally, nowhere, wherever, wheresoever, anywhere, herein, therein, wherein, hereabouts, thereabouts, whereabouts, hereabout, thereabout, aground, on high, all over, here and there.

(2) **Place reckoned from some point:** Whence, hence, thence, elsewhere, otherwhere, away, far, afar, far off, out, remotely, abroad, above, forth, below, ahead, aloof, outwards, about, around, beneath, before, behind, over, under, within, without, from within, from without.

(3) **Place reckoned to some point:** Whither, thither, hither, in, up, down, upwards, downwards, inwards, backwards, forwards, hitherward, thitherward, homeward, aside, ashore, afield, aloft, aboard, aground, nigh.

The forms *upward, downward, backward,* and similar words, are also used as **adjectives.**

(4) **Place numerical:** First, secondly, thirdly, next, lastly, finally, at last, in fine. *First* means *in the first place; secondly* means *in the second place,* and so on.

9. **Adverbs of degree** answer the questions *How much? How little?* They may express:

(1) **Extent or degree:** Much, more, most, greatly, far, further, very, too, little, less, least, extra, mostly, entirely, chiefly, principally, mainly, generally, commonly, usually, in general, fully, full, completely, totally, wholly, perfectly, all, together, quite, exceedingly, extravagantly, immeasurably, immensely, excessively, boundlessly, infinitely, inconceivably, clear, stark, nearly, well-nigh, partly, partially, intensely, scarcely, scantily, precisely, enough, exactly, even, everso, just, equally, sufficiently, adequately, proportionately, competently, as, so, however, howsoever, somewhat, at all.

(2) **Exclusion or emphasis:** Merely, only, but, alone, simply, barely, just, particularly, especially, in particular.

(3) **Superposition:** Also, besides, else, still, yet, too, likewise, withal, moreover, furthermore, however, extra, eke, even, nevertheless, anyhow. These adverbs are used when an idea is added to the idea already expressed.

10. **Adverbs of manner** answer the question *How?* They are:

So, thus, well, ill, how, wisely, foolishly, justly, slowly, somehow, anyhow, however, howsoever, otherwise, else, likewise, like, alike, as, extempore, headlong, lengthwise, crosswise, across, aslant, astride, astraddle, adrift, amain, afloat, apace, apart, asunder, amiss, anew, fast, together, separately, aloud, accordingly, agreeably, necessarily, helter-skelter, hurry-skurry, namely, suddenly, silently, feelingly, surprisingly, touchingly, trippingly, lovingly, hurriedly, mournfully, sweetly, proportionally, exactly, heavily, and many others ending in ily and formed from **adjectives** or **present participles.**

II.—MODIFICATION OF ADVERBS.

11. The only **modification** adverbs have is that of comparison.

12. A few adverbs are compared after the manner of adjectives; as, *soon, soon-er, soon-est; early, earli-er, earli-est.*

13. The following adverbs have comparatives and superlatives that are usually employed as **adjectives**:

Positive.	Comparative.	Superlative.
aft	after	aftermost
in	inner	{ innermost { inmost
neath	nether	nethermost
out	{ outer { utter	{ uttermost { utmost
up	upper	{ uppermost { upmost

After, in modern usage, is sometimes employed as an adverb and sometimes as an adjective. Like near, it has lost its comparative meaning. *After* is derived from the old English form *af=of* or *off.*

In retains its adverbial sense in the word *within*, which, with the old English, was known as *inwith.*

Neath does not stand alone in modern English. It is found in such words as, *beneath, underneath.*

These adverbs are all **prepositional** in origin.

14. Most **adverbs of manner** are compared by prefixing the adverbs *more* and *most, less* and *least;* as, *wisely, more wisely, most wisely; culpably, less culpably, least culpably.*

15. The following adverbs are irregular in their comparison:

Positive.	Comparative.	Superlative.
well	better	best
ill	worse	worst
much	more	most
forth	further	furthest
far	farther	farthest
late	later	latest
——	rather	rathest.

The th in *farther* and *farthest* crept into these words by false analogy with *further* and *furthest*. The natural mode of comparing *far* is *far, far-er, far-est.* In the earlier forms of the language *ferrer* was used as the comparative.

Rather is derived from the adjective *rathe=ready.* Milton, in *Lycidas,* speaks of the "rathe primrose." Here *rathe* means *early.*

16. Adverbs may be modified by other adverbs; as, **extremely** *well,* **very** *simply done.*

17. Adverbs may also be modified by adverbial phrases or adverbial clauses.

18. The following is a partial list of the **adverbial phrases** most frequently employed in English:

at length	at times	by and by	in case	now and then
at last	at hand	by no means	from above	ever and anon
at best	as yet	in that	from below	up and down
at all	by chance	inasmuch as	one by one	in and out
at large	by far	in truth	in like manner	here and there
at once	by turns	of purpose	of a truth	of mornings

III.—FUNCTIONS OF ADVERBS.

19. In modifying other words, adverbs perform certain functions which it is customary for grammarians to distinguish. The principal functions are :

(1) **Causative**; as expressed by *whence, thence, wherefore, therefore.*

(2) **Conjunctive**; as expressed by *when, before, besides, since, so.*

(3) **Interrogative**; as expressed by *why, wherefore, whence, how,* when employed in asking questions.

(4) **Affirmative**; as expressed by *yes, yea, indeed, positively, amen.*

(5) **Negative**; as expressed by *no, nay, not, nowise.*

(6) **Potential**; as expressed by *peradventure, perchance, perhaps, may-be, possibly.*

20. The adverb **then** is sometimes used as an adjective by English writers :

"*In my **then** circumstances.*"—THACKERAY,—*The Paris Sketch Book.*
"*After the **then** country fashion.*"—KINGSLEY,—*Westward Ho!*

21. When adverbs are used in pairs and have a mutual relation, they are called **correlative adverbs**. Among the correlative adverbs are :

As–so:—*As* the twig is bent, *so* shall it grow.
When–then:—*When* the heart beats no more, *then* the life ends.
Where–there:—*Where* the carrion is, *there* the buzzard is to be found.
Not only–but:—Oswald communicated *not only* a copy of his commission, *but* a part of his instructions.—BANCROFT.
Not only–but even:—Smuggling and piracy were deemed *not only* not infamous, *but even* honorable.
Not merely–but also:—These are questions, *not* of prudence *merely, but* of morals *also.*

EXERCISES.

I. Mention the adverbs ending in **-ly** *formed from the adjectives given:*

slow	slowly	liberal	——	busy	——
manful	——	general	——	sole	——
pretty	——	hearty	——	whole	——
gay	——	rude	——	feeble	——

II. Write one line under the adjectives and two lines under the adverbs:

Every truth of common sense can bear the test of reason.—We should read authors whose names are generally known and respected.—Study, prosecuted with enthusiasm, is all the more intense and the better sustained.—How can you run so rapidly?

III. Supply an adverb that will complete the sense:

1. He swam *almost* across the river.—He —— mentioned that he had met you.—They labored faithfully ——. Charles was —— this morning.

2. Joseph has —— been promoted. —— did you not go.—He spoke ——. The man was conscious —— the last.—Richard studies his lessons ——. They walked —— down the road.

3. Louis is —— in time.—Be —— the first on whom the news is tried.—Be wise ——; 'tis madness to defer.—Cunning and deception, the meteors of the earth, —— glittering for a time, must pass away.

IV. In copying the following passage, indicate each adverb, its kind and its function; also point out the verbs, nouns, pronouns, adjectives, and adjective pronouns.

"There is a sharp dividing line between youth and manhood. Sometimes we cross it early, and sometimes late, but we do not know that we are passing from one life to another as we step across the boundary. The world seems to us the same for awhile, as we knew it yesterday and shall know it to-morrow. Suddenly, we look back and start with astonishment when we see the past, which we thought so near, already vanishing in the distance, shapeless, confused, and estranged from our present selves. Then we know that we are men, and acknowledge, with something like a sigh, that we have put away childish things."— F. MARION CRAWFORD,—*Sant 'Ilario.*

CHAPTER XI.

PREPOSITIONS.

1. **A preposition** is a word used to express the relation between an object and a preceding name, state, or action.

2. A preposition is generally placed **before** a noun or pronoun, which is called the object of the preposition.

3. The relations expressed may be:

   (1) Between the **object** and a **preceding noun** or **pronoun**; as, There is fruit *in* the dish; the question passed from him *to* me.

   (2) Between the **object** and a **verb**; as, Come *to* me.

   (3) Between the **object** and an **adjective**; as, He is pleased *with* the lesson.

4. The relations expressed by prepositions are:

   (1) **Relation of time**; as, He started *before* sunrise.

   (2) **Relation of place**; as, He went *to* Boston.

   (3) **Relation of instrument**; as, He gained the case *by* the force of his eloquence.

   (4) **Relation of quality**; as, A house *of* stone.

   (5) **Relation of cause**; as, He works *for* money.

   (6) **Relation of purpose**; as, He came *for* a book.

5. Two prepositions are sometimes found together in the same sentence. Sometimes one of them may be parsed as

an adverb and the other as a preposition. "*He went **out of** the house.*"

Here *out* is an adverb modifying *went*, and *of* is a preposition governing *house* and showing the relation between its object and the verb *went-out*.

Sometimes, both words should be considered prepositions; as in the sentences, *The Franks came **from beyond** the Rhine; Draw the bench **from under** the table.*

6. Many words, **prepositional** in their nature, such as *after, about, up, before, beyond, below,* are used as **adverbs.** As such, they have no subsequent term of relation.

Example.—"You may go *before*, but John must stay *behind*." "The eagle flew *up*, then soared *about*, and afterwards descended."

List of Prepositions.

A= *at, on,* or *in;* "The world runs *a* wheels."—Ben Jonson.

Aboard; "*Aboard* ship, dull shocks are sometimes felt."

About; "I must be *about* my Father's business."—St. Luke.—"Roving still *about* the world."—Milton.

Above; "I saw in the way a light from heaven *above* the brightness of the sun."—Acts.

According to; "Proceed *according to* law."

Across; "A bridge is laid *across* the river."—Dryden.

After; "Ye shall not go *after* other gods."—Deuteron.

Against; "Uplift *against* the sky your mighty shapes."

Along; "I hear the waves resounding *along* the shore."

Amid, amidst; "But rather famish them *amid* their plenty."—Shakespeare.—"This work was written *amidst* many interruptions."

Among, amongst; "Blessed art thou *among* women."—"He was always foremost *amongst* them."

Around; "A lambent flame *around* his brows."—Dryden.

As to; "*As to* the parts of the cargo, they were already made fast."

At; "She is *at* church."—"The bell rings *at* noon."

Athwart; "*Athwart* the thickets low."—TENNYSON.
Before; "Who shall go *before* them?"—"*Before* Abraham was, I am."—ST. JOHN.
Behind; "What hope of answer or redress?—
 Behind the veil, *behind* the veil."—TENNYSON.
Below; "One degree *below* kings."—ADDISON.—"*Below* the moon; *below* the knee."—SHAKESPEARE.
Beneath; "Our country sinks *beneath* the yoke."—SHAKESPEARE. "*Beneath* a rude and nameless stone he lies."—POPE.
Beside; "*Beside* him hung his bow."—MILTON.
Besides; "There was a famine in the land *besides* the first famine."—GEN.
Between; New York is *between* Boston and Philadelphia.—"If things should go so *between* them."—BACON.
Betwixt; "*Betwixt* two aged oaks."—MILTON.
Beyond; "*Beyond* any of the great men of my country."—SIDNEY.
But=*except*; "Who can it be *but* perjured Lycon."—DRYDEN.
By; "*By* land, *by* water they renew their charge."—POPE.
Concerning; "I have accepted thee *concerning* this thing."—GENESIS xix.
Down; "His gory visage *down* the stream was sent."—"*Down* the swift Hebrus to the Lesbian shore."—MILTON.
During; He stayed at home *during* the winter.
Ere;   —"Our fruitful Nile
 Flowed *ere* the wonted season."—DRYDEN.
Except; "I have finished all the letters *except* one."—COLLIER.
For; "We take a flashing meteor *for* a star."
From; "Experience *from* the time past to the time present."—BACON.
In; "The golden moments *in* the stream of life rush past us, and we see nothing but sand."—GEORGE ELIOT.
Into; Water enters *into* the fine vessels of plants.
Notwithstanding; I shall go *notwithstanding* the rain.
Of; "It is the duty to communicate *of* those blessings we have received."—FRANKLIN.

Off; The vessel was becalmed *off* Cuba.

On; "Whosoever shall fall *on* this stone shall be broken."—M'T. xxi. 44.

Out of; "Keep thy heart with all diligence; for *out of* it are the issues of life."—Prov. iv. 23.

Over; "I will make thee ruler *over* many things."—Matt. xx t. 23.

Past; "The author was galled *past* endurance by this new stroke."—Macaulay.

Round; "A shoreless ocean tumbled *round* the globe."

Save; "Of the Jews five times received I forty stripes, *save* one."—II. Cor. xi. 24.

Since; "The Lord hath blessed thee *since* my coming."—Gen. xxx. 30.

Till, until; "And he said unto them, trade *till* I come."—Luke xix. 13.

Through; "*Through* these hands this science has passed with great applause."—Sir W. Temple.

Throughout; There was much anxiety felt *throughout* the land.

To; "Stand dumb, and speak not *to* him."—Shakespeare.

Toward, towards; "He set his face *toward* the wilderness."—Num. xxiv. 1.

Under; "Bottles let down into wells *under* water will keep long."—Bacon.

Unto; Verily I say *unto* you.

Up; "In going *up* a hill, the knees will be most weary."—Bacon.

Upon; "Thou shalt take of the blood.... *upon* the altar."—Exod. xxix. 21.

With; "*With* her they flourished, and *with* her they die."—Pope.

Within;
"— *Within* himself
The danger lies, yet lies *within* his power."—Milton.

Without; "There is no living with thee nor *without* thee."—Tatler.

EXERCISES.

I. Supply a suitable preposition :

1. Come *from* Albany.
   Live —— peace.
   Act —— malice.
   Walk —— on the roof.

   2. Open —— facility.
   Engrave —— marble.
   He will die —— hunger.
   Write —— English.

   3. Remain —— home.
   Send her —— school.
   Raise your hearts —— God.
   Punish him —— stealing.

II. Where the dash occurs insert a suitable preposition:

John differs —— him —— appearance.—We sat —— a mossy bank, —— an aged pine, —— whose branches the south wind made pleasant music, while —— us, —— a little distance, the waters —— a tiny brook sang merrily as they danced swiftly —— the slope, —— —— be lost —— the flood —— the mighty river.

III. Supply a suitable participle where the dash occurs, and underline the prepositions:

1. When the sea had —— its fury, it became calm.—The officers were ——, and then the meeting adjourned.—The —— of the bell prevented our hearing the —— of the clock.—The boy, having been ——, was dismissed. —— a noise, I went to the door.

2. He was —— for hearing —— his lesson.—They heard the girl ——. The soldiers were —— the city.—He was —— for his conduct. —We —— at the things that were —— to us.

3. Then shook the hills with thunder —— (*to riv*) /
   Then rushed the steed to battle —— (*to drive*) /
   And louder than the bolts of heaven
   Far flashed the red artillery !—THOMAS CAMPBELL.

CHAPTER XII.

CONJUNCTIONS.

1. A **conjunction** is a word used to join sentences, or the elements of a sentence.

2. The elements of a sentence which the conjunction may connect are:

> (1) **Words**; as, Mary *or* her brother went to town. Here the conjunction *or* connects the words *Mary* and *brother*.
> (2) **Phrases**; as, "His voice was heard above the whistling of the wind *and* the roar of the billows." Here the two phrases "*roar of the billows*" and "*whistling of the wind*" are connected by the conjunction *and*.
> (3) **Clauses**; as, He will write *if* you ask him. Here the conjunction *if* connects the clauses "*you ask him*" and "*he will write.*"

3. Conjunctions may also connect a **consecutive series** of words, phrases, clauses, or sentences.

4. Conjunctions may be **co-ordinate** or **subordinate**.

5. A **co-ordinate conjunction** is that which joins elements—whether words, phrases, or clauses, which are of the same rank, be it one of dependence or independence.

6. The co-ordinate conjunctions may be classed as follows:

> (1) **Copulative**; that is, words linking words, phrases, clauses, or sentences together. Such are the words *and, also, further, moreover*.
> (2) **Adversative**; that is, words expressing opposition between words, phrases, clauses, or sentences. Such are the words *but, yet, still, however, only, notwithstanding*.

(3) **Alternative;** that is, words denoting that the sense conveyed by one out of two or more names, phrases, clauses, or sentences may be chosen or rejected. Such words are: *or, now, else, otherwise.*

(4) **Illative;** that is, words that express a consequence or inference following from what has been said. Such words are: *hence, thence, then; for, because, so; therefore, wherefore, consequently, accordingly.*

7. **A subordinate conjunction** is that which joins a dependent phrase or clause with the phrase or clause on which it depends.

8. The subordinate conjunctions may be classed as follows :

(1) **Conjunctions of cause;** that is, words that express cause or contingency. Such words are: *that, if; unless, except, because, since; although, albeit, though; whereas, provided, inasmuch, as.*

(2) **Conjunctions of time ;** that is, words that express time. Such are: *before, ere, since, after, as soon as; while, whilst, when.*

(3) **Conjunctions of place ;** that is, words that express rest in or motion to or from a place. Such words are: *whence, thence; whither, thither.*

(4) **Conjunctions of comparison;** that is, words that express comparison. Such are: *as, than.*

(5) **Conjunctions of purpose ;** that is, words that express an end, result, or purpose. Such are: *lest, that, so that, in order that.*

(6) **Conjunctions of manner ;** that is, words that express manner. Such words are: *as, as if, how.*

9. When co-ordinate or subordinate conjunctions are used in pairs and have a mutual relation they are called **correlative conjunctions.** Such are :

Both—and.... "Power to judge *both* quick *and* dead."—MIL-
TON.

As—as.... *As* long *as* you please.

So—as.... *So* long *as* you please.

Either—or.... "*Either* he his talking,... *or* he is on a journey."
—I. KINGS xvii. 27.

Neither—nor.... "*Neither* had I transgressed, *nor* thou with
me."—MILTON.

If—then.... *If* he confessed it, *then* forgive him.

Though—yet.... "*Though* he slay me, *yet* will I trust in him."—
JOB xiii. 15.

Nor—nor.... "I whom *nor* avarice *nor* pleasures move."—
WALSH.

Whether—or.... It matters little *whether* I go *or* stay.

10. The correlatives **as-as, so-as, such-as,** are more adjective and adverbial than conjunctive.

(1) **As-as**: "A miss is *as* good *as* a mile." Here the first *as* is an adverb, the second *as* is a conjunctive adverb.

(2) **So-as**: "It is risky to lean on *so* weak a reed *as* he has proven himself." Here *so* is an adverb, and *as* is a conjunctive adverb.

(3) **Such-as**: "*Such* men *as* these should never be intrusted with the work." Here *such* is a pronominal adjective, and *as* is a conjunctive adjective.

In the sentence: "Give me *such as* are good," *such* is a pronominal adjective, taken as a noun and the object of *give; as* is also a pronominal adjective and the subject of *are.*

Some grammarians call *as* in this instance a **demonstrative pronoun.**

11. Conjunctions are not only connectives; they also serve to introduce a sentence; as, *If I were you I would not destroy the house.*

EXERCISES.

I. Where the dash occurs insert a suitable conjunction:

1. Keep good boys' company, —— you will be one of the number. Roll on, thou deep —— dark blue ocean, roll! He is honest —— his judgment is one-sided. If you are going —— I will go.

2. No one will dispute the fact —— Edison is a great inventor. He was selected —— of his personal qualities. The secret of success is nothing more —— doing well what you can do.

II. Where the dashes occur insert correlative conjunctions:

1. Lawn —— white —— driven snow.—2. —— he must leave, —— I also shall go.—3. I am debtor —— to the Greeks and the Barbarians, to the wise —— to the unwise.—4. —— this man sinned —— his parents.—5. *If* you are not afraid, —— why remain silent?—6. I know not —— it be of a public —— a private nature.

III. Name the conjunctions in the following sentences.

1. "In the meadows and the lower ground,
   Was all the sweetness of a common dawn."—WORDSWORTH.

2. That Rousseau had given an equally beautiful picture was no reason why Goethe should not repeat it.

3. Think no man so perfect but that he may err.

4. You will never live to my age unless you keep yourself in breath with exercise.

5. Both Rousseau and Goethe were immoral in their lives and in their writings. Rousseau wielded great influence in French literature; Goethe, in German. Indeed, Goethe's influence has been felt throughout Europe.

6. "Reading maketh a full man, conference a ready man, and writing an exact man. And, therefore, if a man write little, he had need have a great memory; if he confer little, he had need have a present wit; and if he read little, he had need have much cunning, to seem to know that he doth not."—LORD BACON,—*Of Studies.* The word *conference,* as used by Bacon, means *conversation.*

CHAPTER XIII

INTERJECTIONS

1. An **interjection** is a word that expresses emotion; as, *Lo! the conquering nero comes.*

2. The interjection **stands alone**; it has no grammatical relation with any other words; as, *Hush! he is speaking.*

3. There are interjections corresponding to nearly every emotion of the human breast; and the same interjections may express different emotions, according to the **tone of voice.**

4. The principal interjections are those expressing:

   (1) Joy or glad surprise; as, *Oh! ah! Hurrah! Huzza!*
   (2) Pain or suffering; as, *Oh! ah! alas! well-a-day! dear me!*
   (3) Disappointment; as, *Whew!*
   (4) Contempt; as, *Fie! fudge! faugh! pshaw!*
   (5) Calling or directing attention; as, *Hello! ho! hem! lo!*
   (6) Repression; as, *Hist! hush! tut! mum!*
   (7) Imitation; as, *Pop! bang! bow-wow! ding-dong!*
   (8) Greeting or parting; as, *Good morning! good bye! farewell! adieu!*

5. Other parts of speech are used as interjections:

   (1) A noun; as, *Peace!* be still.
   (2) A verb; as, *Hail!* Macbeth. *Behold!* I come.
   (3) An adjective; as, *Welcome!*
   (4) A pronoun; as, *Why!* how could he? *What!* you weep.
   (5) An adverb; as, *Away! Indeed!* is it possible?

6. In the dramas of Shakespeare and other Elizabethan English writers, there are forms of interjections, now

obsolete, which were once oaths or solemn asseverations. Such are :

Marry=Marie=the Blessed Virgin Mary.
Zounds=Our Lord's wounds.
Egad=corruption of an oath including the name of God.

7. Some of our interjections are of foreign origin. Such are :

Grammercy=*Grand merci*, the French for *many thanks*.
Adieu=to God, i.e., *To God I commend you*.
Alas=*ah! lasso*, the Italian for *Ah, miserable me!*
O dear=*O Dio;* the Italian for *O God*.
Amen=*yea, verily, be it so*, in Hebrew.
O dear me=*O Dio mio*, the Italian for *O my God*.

8. Some interjections are composed of English phrases. Such are :

Good bye=God be with ye.
Farewell=*Fare* and *well;* that is, "May you fare or speed well on your journey."
Prithee=I pray thee.
Well-a-way=old English *wâ-lâ-wâ*, equivalent to the modern English words *woe!-lo!-woe!*
Well-a-day=a corruption of *well-a-way*.

The noun **wassail** is derived from the old English salutation *wes hâl* =*wes thu hâl*=*be thou hale*=good health. It was the form of salutation employed in drinking.

EXERCISES.

I. Insert a suitable interjection:

1. *Hark!* the trumpet sounds. ——! they had been friends in youth. ——! for the rarity of Christian charity.

2. ——! to the home of your childhood. ——! you have been caught at last. ——! noble man. ——! that you should act so fool-

ish!*.*—The boy, ——! where was he ? ——! both for the man and his victim.

II. Name and classify the interjections in the following sentences:

 1. Hark! heard you not the thunder's roar ?

 2. Ah, well! for us all some sweet hope lies
  Deeply buried from human eyes.—WHITTIER.

 3. Lickety, lickety, switch, we came to the ford.—BRET HARTE.

 4. O Jones, my dear!—O dear! my Jones,
  What is become of you ?—HOOD.

 5. A fox went out in a hungry plight,
  And he begged of the moon to give him light,
  For he had many miles to trot that night,
  Before he could reach his den, O!—

 6. "Bobolink! Bobolink!
  Now what do you think ?
  Who stole a nest away
  From the plum-tree to-day ?"
  "Not I," said the dog, "bow-wow!
  I wouldn't be so mean, anyhow!"
      —LYDIA MARIA CHILD.

III. Name the different parts of speech in the passage here quoted from Swift:

"There are two faults in conversation, which appear very different, yet arise from the same root, and are equally blameable; I mean an impatience to interrupt others, and the uneasiness of being interrupted ourselves. The two chief ends of conversation are to entertain and improve those we are among, or to receive those benefits ourselves; which whoever will consider, cannot easily run into either of these two errors; because, when any man speaks in company, it is to be supposed he does it for his hearers' sake, and not his own; so that common discretion will teach us not to force their attention, if they are not willing to lend it; nor, on the other side, to interrupt him who is in possession, because that is in the grossest manner to give the preference to our own good sense.—SWIFT.

CHAPTER XIV.

WORDS USED IN VARIOUS SENSES.

1. There are certain words in the language that are used in **various senses**, according to the construction of the sentence into which they enter. The list usually given by grammarians is as follows:

2. **A** or **an** is used as:

   (1) An **article**; as, *A* beautiful face.
   (2) An **adjective**; as, This ribbon costs fifty cents *a* yard.
   (3) A **conjunction**; as, Catch me *an* thou canst, where *an* has the same force and meaning as if. ——Nay, *an* thou'lt mouth, I'll rant as well as thou.—*Hamlet*, V. i. The older writers use *and* for *an* in this sense; as, "*And* you love me, let's do it; I am dog at a catch."—*Twelfth Night*, II. iii.

   Sometimes **and** and **if** are used together; as, "I pray thee, Launce, *and if* thou seest my boy, bid him make haste."—*Two Gentlemen of Verona*, III. i. In these instances the **an** becomes **and** according to the phonetic laws of the language. The d was introduced just as it was introduced into the common pronunciation of the word *drowned*, which was *drownded*.

   In like manner the expression **yon-a** became **yond-er**.

   (4) A **preposition**; as, He lies *a*-bed. Here **a** is the old English preposition **on**, **in**, **an**, and not the article.

3. **About** is used as:

    (1) An **adverb**; as, He walked *about;* there were *about* twenty present.
    (2) A **preposition**; as, He was *about* his father's business.

4. **Above** is used as:

    (1) An **adverb**; as, The sailor went *above.*
    (2) A **preposition**; as, The skylark soars *above* the clouds.
    (3) A **noun**; as, The missile came from *above.*
    (4) An **adjective**; as, The *above* remark.

This last form has not the sanction of some grammarians, but good writers employ it.

5. **Adieu** is used as:

    (1) An **interjection**; as, *Adieu! Adieu!* my native land.
    (2) A **noun**; as, I bade my native land *adieu.*

6. **After** is used as:

    (1) A **preposition**; as, William comes *after* me.
    (2) An **adverb**; as, I saw him *after* you had left.

7. **All** is used as:

    (1) A **pronominal adjective**; as, *All* men; good bye to you *all.*
    (2) An **adverb**; as, We were left *all* alone.

8. **Any** is used as:

    (1) A **pronominal adjective**; as, Are there *any* reasons?
    (2) An **adverb**; as, Is he *any* better?

9. **As** is used as:

    (1) An **adverb**; as, *As* white as snow.
    (2) A **conjunctive adverb**, the correlative of **as, so**; as, *As* far *as* he can go; so weak *as* to need support.
    (3) A **conjunction**; as, "*As* he was ambitious I slew him.

WORDS USED IN VARIOUS SENSES.   145

(4) Part of a conjunctive phrase; as, He looks *as though* he were sick.

(5) Part of a prepositional phrase; as, *As for* me.

(6) Part of a predicate phrase; as, *As follows, as regards.*

In parsing the expressions *as follows, as regards*, some grammarians introduce the pronoun it as the subject; others make as the subject.

(7) A pronoun; as, These are such books *as* I can recommend.

As is derived from the compound word *al-so=ealswa=also*, by the dropping of the l (Orthog. chap. i. 20). Like its root so it was originally pronominal. As such, it was used in the fourteenth century. We have a remnant of its pronominal sense in such vulgarism as this: "Here is the man *as* struck the first blow."

10. **Before** is used as :

(1) An **adverb**; as, He had written *before* I saw him.

(2) A **preposition**; as, Go *before* him.

11. **Both** is used as :

(1) A **pronominal adjective**; as, I like *both*.

(2) A **correlative conjunction**; as, He is *both* old *and* ugly.

12. **But** is used as :

(1) A **preposition**; as, All *but* him had fled.

(2) A **conjunction**; as, I go, *but* I return.

(3) An **adverb**; as, 'Tis *but* a little faded flower; *but* for this.

(4) A **relative**; as, There is no flock *but* has a black sheep= There is no flock *that* has *not* a black sheep. *But* is here equivalent to *that....not*.

So also in the lines :

There is no fireside, howsoe'er defended,
But has one vacant chair.—LONGFELLOW.

But was originally a preposition. It is composed of the two words *be* and *out*. In provincial English it is equivalent to **without**. The modern tendency of the language is to use *but* in a conjunctive sense. We find good writers using the expression *but he*. Cardinal Newman so uses it; and in the Rheims-Douay version of the Scriptures we read: "And that no man might buy or sell, *but he* that hath the character.' —*Apocalypse* xiii. 17.

13. By is used as :

(1) A preposition; as, "Long labors both *by* sea and land he bore."—DRYDEN.

(2) An adverb; as, I saw John go *by*.

(3) An adjective; in the compound words *by-play, by-street*. Here the word *by* means simply *aside* or *incidental*.

(4) A noun; when it is also spelled bye; as, "The Synod of Dort condemneth *upon the bye* even the discipline of the Church of England."—FULLER. Here, *upon the bye* means *in passing*, or *incidentally*. In the same sense we say *by the bye*.

(5) A noun; in the compound words *by-law, by-word*. Here the word *by* has a different origin and meaning. It comes from the Danish word big, which means town. Thus, *by-word* means *town-talk;* as when we say that a person's name is a *by-word*, that is, it is the *talk of the town*. So, *by-law* means *town-law*. The suffix -by in the names *Whitby, Derby* is of the same Danish origin, meaning *town*.

14. Else is used as :

(1) An adjective; as, Nobody *else*.

(2) An adverb; as, How *else* can he travel?

(3) A conjunction; as, He must be generous, *else* he would not have given so freely.

(4) A noun; as, "Would it were *else*."—FORD,—
                                    Witch of Edmonton, II. i.

Else is the possessive *elles* of an old English root el, meaning *other*. Our expression *elsewhere* was formerly *otherwhere*. Hooker so uses it.

15. **Except** is used as :

   (1) A **verb**; as, The tariff-bill *excepts* raw material.
   (2) A **preposition**; as, He saw nothing *except* water.
   (3) A **Conjunction**; as, *Except* the Lord build the house, they labor in vain that build it.

16. **For** is used as :

   (1) A **preposition**; as, He that is not *for* me is against me.
   (2) A **conjunction**; as, Give thanks unto the Lord, *for* He is good; *for* his mercy endureth forever.
   (3) **With a verb**; as, This is a grace *to be prayed for*.
   (4) **With an adverb**; as, *For as much as*.
   (5) **With the preposition to**; as, " There went out some of the people on the seventh day *for to* gather."—Exod. xvi. 27. *King James's Version. For to* here means *in order to.* The form is now considered a vulgarism.

17. **Full** is used as :

   (1) A **noun**; as, He came at the *full* of the moon.
   (2) A **verb**; as, They *full* cloth at the factory.
   (3) An **adjective**; as, A *full* measure.
   (4) An **adverb**; as,
   "*Full* many a flower is born to blush unseen."—Gray.

18. **Ill** is used as :

   (1) A **noun** (in the plural); as, The *ills* of life; "to hastening *ills* a prey."
   (2) An **adjective**; as, He was *ill* on his birthday.
   (3) An **adverb**; as,
   " *Ill* fares the land, to hastening ills a prey."—Goldsmith.

19. **Like** is used as :

   (1) A **noun**; as, *Like* begets *like*.
   (2) An **adjective**; as, They both have *like* chances.

(3) An **adverb**; as,

"The Assyrian came down *like* a wolf on the fold."—BYRON.

(4) A **verb** (transitive); as, He *likes* his dog, but he loves his friends.

(5) A **verb** (unipersonal); as, "I willingly confess that *it likes me* better where I find virtue in a fair lodging."—SIR PHILIP SIDNEY. The form *it likes me* is equivalent to *it pleases me*.

20. **Needs** is used as :

(1) A **noun**; as, His *needs* were many.
(2) A **verb**; as, William *needs* assistance; John *needs* to go.
(3) An **adverb**; as, He must *needs* go; that is, he must go *of necessity*.

The verb **need**, when followed by an infinitive, sometimes loses its personal ending -s; as, It *need* not be. So also, in a former stage of the language, men said **me-think** for **me-thinks**.

21. **Now** is used as :

(1) A **noun**; as, Eternity is a continuous *Now*.
(2) An **adverb**; as, *Now* is the accepted time.
(3) A **conjunction**; as, "*Now* Barabbas was a robber."

22. **Save** is used as :

(1) A **verb**; as, God *save* you all.
(2) A **preposition**; as, Five times received I forty stripes *save* one.
(3) A **conjunction**; as, "And that no man might buy or sell *save he* that hath the mark.—REV. xiii. 17. *King James's Version*. The Rheims-Douay version reads : "*but he* that hath the mark."—APOC. xiii. 17.

23. **So** is used as:

(1) An **adverb**; as, *So* nice we grow.

(2) A conjunction; as, There was nothing for us to do, *so* we returned home.

(3) A pronoun; as,

> We think our fathers fools, so wise we grow;
> Our wiser sons, no doubt, will think us *so*.
> —POPE,—*Essay on Criticism*.

As we have already seen, **so** is the root from which **as** is derived.

24. **The** is used as :

(1) An **article**; as, *The* man.
(2) An **adverb**; as, *The* more, *the* better; " *The* more busy we are, *the* more leisure we have."—HAZLITT.
(3) **The** is also employed with an adverb to form an **adverbial phrase**; as, I like you *the better* for that.

At an early stage of our language **the** had all the inflexions of adjectives, in number, gender, and case.[1] Before comparatives, **the** retains the force of the old instrumental case *thi*; e. g., *the more*=*eo magis*. In like manner, **thus** was originally the instrumental case of **this**.

25. **Till** is used as :

(1) An **adverb**; as, Wait *till* you hear from me.
(2) A **preposition**; as, Stay *till* Wednesday.
(3) A **verb**; as, Farmers *till* the ground.
(4) A **noun**; as, Place the money in the *till*.

Till is of Danish origin. It was sometimes used as a sign of the infinitive. In consequence, our *into* was formerly *intil*. The word first makes its appearance as a preposition in the northern districts of England. We find it in the Durham Gospels, which date from the eleventh century.

26. **Well** is used as :

(1) A **noun**; as, He drew water from the *well*.

---

[1] See *Historical Outlines of English Accidence*, by Dr. R. Morris, pp. 125, 126. This is an admirable book, to which we are indebted for many a hint.

(2) A verb; as, Tears began *to well* from his eyes.
(3) An adjective; as, Is it *well* with thee?
(4) An adverb; as, The exercise was *well* written.

27. While is used as:

(1) A noun; as, It is not worth the *while*.
(2) An adverb; as, *While* he was writing, the visitor entered.
(3) A verb; as, Some people foolishly *while* away precious time.

28. Worth is used as:

(1) A noun; as, Slow rises *worth* by poverty depressed.
(2) An adjective; as, This book is *worth* a dollar.
(3) A verb; as, "Wo *worth* the day."—EZECH. xxx. 2.

Worth originally meant *become*, and also *be*. In fourteenth century English, *worth* was equivalent to *shall be;* as,

"To-morrow *worth* ymade the maiden's bridal."
—*Vision of Piers Plowman,* B. iii. 48.

Ymade is the perfect participle corresponding to our word *made*. In present English the sentence would read:

"To-morrow *shall be made* the maiden's bridal."

29. Yon, Yond, Yonder is used as:

(1) An adjective; as, "Near *yonder* copse."
—GOLDSMITH,—*Deserted Village,* 136.
(2) An adverb; as, The river is *yonder*.
(3) A demonstrative pronoun; as, "*Yonder's* a bad man."
—BEAUMONT AND FLETCHER, II. p. 400.

The Scotch still use **yon** as a pronoun; as, *Yon* says the cows have come home = *that man* says. **Yon** is derived from the same pronominal root with *yea* and *yes*. That root is **ge**.

CHAPTER XV.

ANALYSIS OF COMPLEX SENTENCES.

CLASSIFICATION OF SENTENCES AS TO FORM.

1. Considering their **form**, sentences are divided into three classes: simple, complex, and compound.

2. **A simple sentence** is a sentence that expresses but one proposition; as, *The stars are suns.*

<small>A **proposition** is the combination of one subject with one predicate making a complete sense. It is, as already defined, a thought or judgment expressed in words.</small>

3. **A complex sentence** is a sentence containing at least two propositions, one of which is principal and the other subordinate; as, *When the sun shines, the boys play.*

4. The **principal proposition** is called the **independent clause**; the **subordinate proposition** is called the **dependent clause**.

5. **A clause** is a component proposition of a compound or complex sentence.

6. A clause is **independent** when, taken by itself, it expresses complete sense; as, ***He** who labors faithfully **will be rewarded.*** *He will be rewarded* is the independent clause.

7. A clause is **dependent** when it modifies or completes the sense of another proposition; as, *They **who would govern others** must first govern themselves.* *Who would govern others* is the dependent clause.

8. In complex sentences one or other of the propositions may be contracted, by omission of the following parts.

> (1) **Of the subject**; as, (*He*) *Who has not virtue is not truly wise.*
>
> (2) **Of subject and predicate**; as, *Though* (*he was*) *famous for strength, he was a coward.*
>
> (3) **Of the object**; as, *He has the book* (*that*) *I presented.* These omissions are usual in comparison; as, *He is smaller than I* (*am small*). *He is not as well informed as I thought* (*he was informed*).

9. A compound sentence is a sentence composed of two or more independent propositions; as,

> "*In youth it sheltered me,*
> And *I'll protect it now.*"—GEORGE P. MORRIS.

10. In general, a sentence contains as many clauses as there are finite verbs expressed or understood; as, "[1] He | [2] *who does a good turn* | [1] should forget it; | [3] he | [4] *who receives one* | [3] should remember it."

11. Clauses are divided into **four** classes: substantive, adjective, adverbial, and explanatory.

> (1) **Substantive**; as, *How the accident occurred* is not known.
>
> (2) **Adjective**; as, I read of the glad year *which once had been*
>
> (3) **Adverbial**; as, He lives *wherever he can find a resting-place.*
>
> (4) **Explanatory**; as, Steamships, *which are a modern invention*, make quick voyages.

12. A substantive clause is a clause that takes the place of a noun.

13. A substantive clause may be:

> (1) The **subject** of a sentence: as, *That he could do no more* is clear.

(2) The **object** of a transitive verb or of a preposition; as, The law-student read *what was essential in Blackstone's Commentaries*.

(3) The **attribute** of an intransitive or neuter verb; as, My wish is *that you go immediately*.

14. An **adjective clause** is a clause that performs the functions of an adjective in qualifying a noun, a pronoun, or a substantive phrase or clause.

(1) A **noun**; as, This is the carriage *in which I travel*.
(2) A **pronoun**; as, He *that studies diligently* reaps his reward.
(3) A **substantive phrase**; as, In the frequent reading of the New Testament, *which he had reluctantly begun*, he found great consolation.
(4) A **substantive clause**; as, That he wrote an admirable essay, *which was no easy task*, is due to his painstaking industry.

15. An **adverbial clause** is a clause that performs the functions of an adverb in modifying a verb, an adjective, an adverb, or a phrase or clause that is adjective or adverbial.

(1) A **verb**; as, He found the watch *where he had left it*.
(2) An **adjective**; as, John is older than *his brother is*.
(3) An **adverb**; as, Mary recited as well as *had been expected*.
(4) An **adjective phrase**; as, Faithful to his promise, *which cost him something*, he came at the appointed time. *Faithful to his promise* is an adjective phrase, modified by the adverbial clause *which cost him something*.
(5) An **adverbial phrase**; as, He smote him with such force *that he died*. *With such force* is an adverbial phrase modified by the adverbial clause *that he died*.
(6) An **adjective clause**; as, This is the book that John lent his brother *when the latter was returning home*. *That*

John lent his brother is an adjective clause, modified by the adverbial clause *when the latter was returning home*.

(7) An **adverbial clause**; as, "*As the boy is*, so will be the man." *As the boy is*, is an adverbial clause performing the office of an adverb of manner. *How* will the man be? "*As the boy is.*" The clause *so will be the man* is also adverbial, **as-so** being correlative adverbs.

16. Adverbial clauses may express one or other of the following relations:

(1) **Time**, answering to the question *When?* as, I was present *when the lecture was delivered.*

(2) **Place**, answering to the question *Where?* as, Go *where duty calls thee.*

(3) **Manner**, answering to the question *How?* as, He hurt his knee *as he was ascending the ladder.*

(4) **Degree**, which is frequently introduced by the conjunction *than* or *as;* as, He is taller than *I am.*—Pecksniffs are as plentiful *as blackberries are.*

(5) **Cause** or **purpose**, answering to the question *Why?* as, He is beloved, for *he is good.*

(6) **Condition**, introduced by *if, though, although, unless, except;* as, He will be ruined *unless he reforms.*

(7) **Consequence**, generally introduced by *that;* as, He studied so hard *that he won the prize.*

17. An **explanatory clause** is a clause that explains some noun or pronoun in a sentence; as, It is evident *that he will be elected.*

18. Clauses may be connected by conjunctions, relative pronouns, or conjunctive adverbs:

(1) **Conjunctions**; as, Bring me your book *and* I will write your name in it.

(2) **Relative pronouns**; as, Here is your book, *which* I have read carefully.

(3) **Conjunctive adverbs**; as, He arrived *when* we were at dinner.

MODELS FOR THE ANALYZING OF COMPLEX AND COMPOUND SENTENCES.

I.

A man who employs his leisure moments well, will accomplish much during his life.

This is a complex declarative sentence.

The *principal* clause is, *A man will accomplish much during his life;* the dependent clause is, *who employs his leisure moments well.* The connective is *who.*

The subject of the principal clause is *man;* the predicate is *will accomplish;* the object is *much.*

The subject is limited by the article *a,* and modified by the dependent clause; the predicate is modified by the simple adverbial phrase *during his life;* the object is unmodified. The principal word of the phrase is *life,* which is modified by the adjective adjunct *his.*

The subject of the dependent clause is *who;* the predicate is *employs;* the object is *moments.*

The subject is unmodified; the predicate is modified by the adverbial adjunct *well;* the object is modified by the adjective adjuncts *his* and *leisure.*

II.

Prosperity gains friends, but adversity tries them.

This is a compound declarative sentence, consisting of the two independent clauses, *Prosperity gains friends* and *adversity tries them,* connected by *but.*

The subject of the first clause is *prosperity;* the predicate is *gains;* the object is *friends.*

The subject of the second clause is *adversity;* the predicate is *tries;* the object is *them.* Neither has any adjuncts.

III.

Men believe that reason is lord over their words; but it happens, too, that words exercise a great power over the human mind.

This is a compound declarative sentence. The connective between the two members is *but*.

The first member is complex, consisting of the independent clause *men believe* and the dependent clause *reason is lord over their words*. The connective is *that*.

The subject of the dependent clause is *reason;* the predicate is *is;* the attribute is *lord*. The attribute is modified by the adjective phrase *over their words*. The principal part of the phrase is *words*, which is modified by the adjective adjunct *their*.

The second member is also complex, consisting of the independent clause *it happens* and the dependent clause *that words . . . . human mind*. The connective is *that*.

The subject of the principal clause is *it;* the predicate is *happens*.

The subject is modified by the dependent clause, which is explanatory.

The predicate is modified by the adverbial adjunct *too*.

The subject of the dependent clause is *words;* the predicate is *exercise;* the object is *power*. The object is modified by the adjective adjuncts *a* and *great*, and the predicate is modified by the simple adverbial phrase *over the human mind*. The principal word of the phrase is *mind*, which is modified by the adjective adjuncts *the* and *human*.

EXERCISES.

I. Tell whether the sentence is simple or complex, and underline the predicates:

1. Faint hearts make feeble hands.—Do the spoils belong to him who gains the victory?—Do you appreciate Browning's great soul-studies?—I know that he is difficult to understand.—Every great poet is obscure to his contemporaries.

2. The man that has a taste for poetry has an inexhaustible source of amusement.—Ask him to teach you to appreciate the great masters

of song.—How nobly Wordsworth sings!—He who reads him diligently will learn to look upon Nature with a new sense.—Have you read his *Ode to Duty?*

II. Draw one line under the principal, and two lines under the dependent clause:

A person who speaks truth is always respected.—Them that honor me I will honor.—Byron, though he wrote with great force, lacks the qualities belonging to the highest order of art.—Persons who are easily vexed are unpleasant companions.—The key that is used is always bright.—Lines that are parallel never meet.—They who slander others break the divine commandment.

III. Analyze the following sentences:

1. Sir Walter Raleigh, when paying a visit to the poet Spenser, first planted the potato in Ireland.—2. All good books are interesting companions.—3. Emerson writes beautifully, but thinks badly.—4. No man can be happy who is not virtuous.—5. Brownson saw the truth and beauty of the Church; Emerson did not see it.—6. Hatred stirreth up strifes, but charity covereth all sins.—7. Give what you can spare to the poor.—8. Deeds are fruit, but words are only leaves.—9. How great is the reward of the martyrs, who preferred death to apostasy!—10. Have you regretted any act of charity that you ever performed?—11. Virtue is its own reward; vice brings its own punishment.—12. Ben Jonson, who was a great poet and a great student of his language, admired Shakespeare's genius.—13. Temperance and exercise strengthen the body and improve the mind.—14. He whose life is upright and pious preaches sublimely.—15. "Kind words are the music of the world. They have a power which seems to be beyond natural causes, as if they were some angel's song, which had lost its way, and come on earth, and sang on undyingly, smiting the hearts of men with sweetest wounds, and putting for the while an angel's nature into us. In truth, there is hardly a power on earth equal to them; it seems as if they could almost do what in reality God alone can do—namely, soften the hard and angry hearts of men."—FABER,—*Kind Words.*

IV. Analyze the following sentences:

1. I hear the reapers singing go
   Into God's harvest; I, that might
   With them have chosen, here below
   Grope shuddering at the gates of night.
   —Lowell,—*Extreme Unction.*

2. Lowell's *Extreme Unction* is a powerful poem illustrating the despair and disappointment of a wasted life at the threshold of death. Mr. W. T. Stead, the editor of *The Pall Mall Gazette,* says of its influence upon him: "It made a deeper dint on my life than any other printed matter I ever read, before or since."

3. Green be the turf above thee,
   Friend of my better days;
   None knew thee but to love thee,
   None named thee but to praise.
   —Fitz-Greene Halleck.

4. Thou who wearest that cunning, heaven-made organ, a tongue, think well of this. Speak not, I passionately entreat thee, till thy thought have silently matured itself, till thou have other than mad and mad-making noises to emit; hold thy tongue till some meaning lie behind, to set it wagging.—Carlyle.

CHAPTER XVI.

SENTENCE-BUILDING:—RULES.

1. Sentence-building not only consists in developing phrases and clauses and in multiplying sentences; it also consists in rejecting all unnecessary words, phrases, clauses, or sentences.

2. Where two or more **words** are employed to express the same thought, only the most fitting word should be retained.

SENTENCE-BUILDING :—RULES.

Example.—Suppose we write: None rejoice and are glad in the season of Easter less than those who have not sorrowed and grieved for their sins in the season of Lent. This sentence is diffuse, and may be recast as follows:
1. Instead of *rejoice and are glad*, write simply *rejoice*.
2. Instead of *the season of Easter*, write *Easter-tide*.
3. Instead of *sorrowed and grieved for their sins*, write *grieved*.

Making these corrections, the sentence reads as Cardinal Newman expressed it: "None rejoice in Easter-tide less than those who have not grieved in Lent."—*Parochial and Plain Sermons*, Selections, p. 191.

3. When two or more phrases are employed to express the same thought, only the most fitting phrase should be retained.

Example.—Some of you, I do not doubt for a moment, have seen and remember Genoa; you have seen that queenly city with its streets of palaces, rising tier above tier from the water, girdling with the long lines of its bright white houses the vast and immense circular sweep of its harbor, at the mouth of which lies a huge natural mole of rock, crowned on the top by its grand, noble, and magnificent light-house tower.

This sentence is also diffuse, and may be improved upon as follows:
1. Instead of *I do not doubt for a moment*, write *I doubt not*.
2. Instead of *have seen and remember*, write *remember*.
3. Instead of *vast and immense circular sweep*, write *vast sweep*. This expresses the extent and the circular feature of the harbor.
4. Instead of *crowned on the top*, write *crowned*.
5. Instead of *grand, noble, and magnificent*, write *magnificent*.

The sentence thus transformed will read as Dr. Thomas Arnold wrote it: "Some of you, I doubt not, remember Genoa; you have seen that queenly city with its streets of palaces, rising tier above tier from the water, girdling with the long lines of its bright white houses, the vast sweep of its harbor, the mouth of which is marked by a huge natural mole of rock, crowned by its magnificent light-house tower."
—*Lectures on Modern History.*

4. Where two or more **clauses** are employed to express the same thought, only the most fitting clause should be retained.

Example.—Every foe who had approached and had drawn sufficiently near him, had felt the might of that terrible axe, but his axe could not guard and defend him against this awful shower of arrows.

This sentence may be reduced as follows:

1. Instead of *had approached and had drawn sufficiently near*, write *had come near*. This expresses everything intended.
2. Instead of *guard and defend*, write *guard*.

The sentence will then read as Professor Freeman wrote it when describing the prowess of Harold in the battle of Senlac : "Every foe who had come near him had felt the might of that terrible axe, but his axe could not guard him against this awful shower of arrows."— *Old English History for Children.*

5. Sometimes the **repetition** of clauses or phrases adds to the force or beauty of a sentence.

Example.—"With what tenderness he sings, yet with what vehemence and entireness ! There is a piercing wail in his sorrow, the purest rapture in his joy ; he burns with the sternest ire, or laughs with the loudest or slyest mirth; and yet he is sweet and soft, '*sweet as the smile when fond lovers meet, and soft as their parting tears.*'" —CARLYLE,—*Essay on Burns.*

Here the phrase *soft and sweet* is repeated in a more developed form with great force and beauty.

6. Where two or more **sentences** are employed to express the same thought, only the most fitting sentence should be retained.

Example.—"The true gentleman does not cause pain to those in whose company he finds himself. The true gentleman is careful to avoid giving them annoyance. The true gentleman makes it a point to consider their feelings and not wound them."

All these sentences are simply putting the same idea in different words. Here is the same idea sketched with a master's hand:

"The true gentleman carefully avoids whatever may cause a jar or a jolt in the minds of those with whom he is cast:—all clashing of opinion, or collision of feeling, all restraint, or suspicion, or gloom, or resentment; his great concern being to make every one at his ease and at home. He has his eyes on all his company; he is tender towards the bashful, gentle towards the distant, and merciful towards the absurd; he can recollect to whom he is speaking; he guards against unseasonable allusions, or topics which may irritate; he is seldom prominent in conversation, and never wearisome."—CARDINAL NEWMAN,—*Idea of a University*, p. 209.

7. **No adjective or adverb should be employed that does not add to the sense, or complete the sense of a sentence.**

Example.—"Frederick the Great, King of Prussia, was rather low-sized—not tall—of stature; he was florid and highly colored in complexion; his face had the air of being authoritative, serious, earnest, frank, and sincere."

Here the words *low-sized* and *not tall* cannot stand together; neither can *florid* and *highly-colored*, nor *frank* and *sincere*. Now note how Carlyle paints this hero. He piles adjective upon adjective; but it is like the great painter placing the proper colors upon the canvas. The picture stands out a thing of life when the last touch is given.

"He was not tall of stature, this arbitrary king: a florid-complexioned, stout-built man; of serious, sincere, authoritative face. Man of short, firm stature; stands at his ease, and yet like a tower. Most solid; eyes steadfastly awake; cheeks slightly compressed, too, which fling the mouth rather forward .... Face, figure, and bearing, all in him is expressive of robust insight and direct determination; of healthy energy and authority, a certain air of royalty reduced to its simplest form."—CARLYLE,—*History of Frederick the Great.*

Copy this passage, supplying all words and phrases implied. Then parse the different words. The grammatical construction may be improved; but in doing so the expression is weakened.

8. Always use a short word in preference to a long word.

Children naturally use short words when speaking about matters that they understand. The short word is, therefore, the natural word. It is frequently the most expressive. Words of Old English origin are generally short and forcible. Thus, the word *daily* is preferable to *diurnal*, and the word *think* reaches the intelligence sooner than the word *cogitate*.

9. In writing a sentence, express it in words as **simple, natural,** and **direct** as those you employ in speaking. Remember that the object of all language is to reveal thought, and not to conceal it.

10. In order to get the **most fitting phrase** or form of expression in a sentence, the sentence should be written **several times,** until that form the most correct and most fitting is found.

The greatest writers, men who have given their whole lives to composing, cannot at first hit upon the best form of expression. It is only after repeated trials that they finally come upon the form that suits them best. An example will illustrate the usual difficulties under which one labors in attempting to write a composition:

Example.—Suppose we would write upon *Good Books*. The opening sentence would pass through the following various forms:

1. *Good books are very good things.*

Now, this is too indefinite; in fact, it says nothing. Another form:

2. *Good books are good companions.*

This is more definite; but there is still something wanting.

3. *Books are our solace in trouble, our instructors in difficulty, our companions in solitude. They speak to us in good language; they reprove us without giving offence; they strengthen our resolves for good; they interpret the vague sentiments of our nature; they instruct, edify, and improve.*

Here we have struck upon something like the proper form of expression. Still, some of the clauses might be better arranged; the opening sentence should be more introductory. And it occurs to us that, if we were to speak of *the good book*, instead of using the plural form *good books*, we could give our sentences a fuller form of expression. Let us try:

4. *The good book is a boon and a blessing. It becomes a solace in trouble, an instructor in difficulties, a companion in solitude. It entertains us in polished language; it reproves us without giving offence; it strengthens our resolves for good; it interprets the under-currents of our thought and the vague sentiments of our nature; it is an instrument of help, edification, and improvement.*

EXERCISES.

I. Condense the following three sentences to one, omitting all superfluous words:

1. A tree is adorned with green leaves.—2. Some trees are laden with ripe fruit.—3. A tree is a beautiful object under certain circumstances (as in 1 and 2).

II. Combine the sentences in each of the following three groups, omitting all superfluous words:

1. Knowledge elevates the mind.
    Knowledge improves the faculties of the mind.
    Knowledge procures for us the respect of others.
    Knowledge enables us to add to the pleasures of life.
    Knowledge enables us to fulfil our duties with greater facility.

2. The children were playing in a field.
    The field was near the river.
    The field was beautifully shaded.
    The field was a favorite spot for the children.

3. Sleep strengthens the mind and the body.
    Sleep prevents weariness of life.

Sleep brings to the unfortunate a temporary forgetfulness of their misery.
Sleep taken in excess causes a loss of time.
Sleep taken in excess enfeebles the body.
Sleep taken in excess stupifies the mind.

III. Construct a sentence upon EXPERIENCE, *from the following points.*

1. The knowledge that comes from experience is the most vivid.
2. Give an illustration within your own experience.
3. Cardinal Manning thus writes on the subject:

"There is no knowledge like the knowledge of experience. How hard it is to realize the look of any country by description in a book; or to know the spirit of a man from his written life; or to appreciate sweetness from illustration, or harmony from the written language of music. How the least personal experience by sight or hearing gives to all these a vividness and reality which make them at once part of our minds forever."—*Sermons*, vol. iii. 1847.

IV. Write a few short sentences on THE INFLUENCE OF NATURE. *Illustrate from your own experience, recounting your feelings when strolling through the country, or watching a sunset, or boating on the river.*

Wordsworth, in one of the noblest passages in English literature, has thus summed up the influence of Nature:

> ——" Nature never did betray
> The heart that loved her; 'tis her privilege
> Through all the years of this our life, to lead
> From joy to joy; for she can so inform
> The mind that is within us, so impress
> With quietness and beauty, and so feed
> With lofty thoughts, that neither evil tongues,
> Rash judgments, nor the sneers of selfish men
> Shall e'er prevail against us, or distrust
> Our cheerful faith that all which we behold
> Is full of blessings."—*The Excursion.*

Read and re-read this passage, till it is understood, and then write out the idea contained in it in your own words.

PART III.
SYNTAX.

1. **Syntax** treats of the relations of words in a sentence.

2. These relations are **threefold**; namely, relations of agreement, relations of government, and relations of connection.

3. **Relations of agreement** are the relations existing between

   (1) The verb and its subject.
   (2) The noun and its qualifying words, the article and adjective.
   (3) The noun and its pronouns.
   (4) The adverb and the words it modifies, be they verbs, adjectives, or other adverbs.

4. **Relations of government** are the relations existing between

   (1) The verb and its object.
   (2) The preposition and its object.
   (3) The possessive case and the name of the person or thing possessed.

5. **Relations of connection** are the relations of words expressed by the **conjunction**.

These various relations cover the whole ground of Syntax.

The interjection expressing no relations with other words has not, properly speaking, a syntax.

6. The following terms are employed in explaining the structure of a sentence :

(1) **Apposition.**—When one noun is used to explain another it is said to be in apposition with the noun it explains; as,

> Dickens, *the novelist*, is more than Dickens *the writer*.

(2) **Pleonasm.**—Superfluous words, such as the use of a pronoun in the same sentence with its noun, sometimes occur either through carelessness or for emphasis. This redundancy is called **pleonasm**:

> Yon silver *beams*,
> Sleep *they* less sweetly on the cottage-thatch
> Than on the dome of kings ?—SHELLEY.
> The world it is empty, the heart will die.—COLERIDGE.

(3) **Ellipsis.**—Words necessary to complete the grammatical construction of a sentence are often omitted. This omission is called **ellipsis**:

> "Whose is this image and superscription? They say unto him *Cæsar's.*" That is, *Cæsar's image and superscription.*

CHAPTER I.

SUBJECT AND VERB.

1. A verb agrees with its **subject** in **person** and **number**.

2. The subject of a verb may be,

(1) A noun; as, *God* is our fortress.—SHAKESPEARE.

(2) A pronoun; as, *He* comes, the herald of a noisy world.—COWPER.

(3) A root-infinitive; as,

> *To laugh* were want of goodness and of grace,
> And *to be grave* exceeds all power of face.—POPE.

(4) A participial infinitive; as, *Trembling* came upon me.--COLERIDGE.

(5) A phrase; as,

To have ideas is to gather flowers; to think is to weave them into garlands.—MADAM SWETCHINE.

(6) A sentence; as, *What one man owns* cannot belong to another.—CHANNING.

Dust thou art, to dust returnest,
Was not spoken of the soul.—LONGFELLOW.

3. **The subject of a verb in sentences of affirmation is generally placed before the verb; as,**

"The *mountains* look on Marathon,
And *Marathon* looks on the sea."—BYRON.

4. **The subject follows the verb or its auxiliary:**

(1) In emphatic or forcible expressions; as,

——Not to me *returns*
Day, or the sweet approach of even or morn.—MILTON.
Then *burst* this mighty *heart*.—SHAKESPEARE.
Flashed all their *sabres* bare.—TENNYSON.
Vanished the Saxon's struggling *spear;*
Vanished the *mountain-sword*.—SCOTT.

(2) When the verbs *say, reply, think*, and the like, are made part of a dialogue; as,

"Have you dined?" *asked* Mr. Wickfield. "Thank 'ee. I am going to dine," *said* Mr. Maldon.—DICKENS.

(3) In interrogative sentences; as,

O, when *will death*
This mouldering old partition-wall throw down?—YOUNG.

5. **When the subject of a verb is a noun or pronoun it is in the nominative case; as,**

"The *child* is father of the man."—WORDSWORTH.
"*They* also serve *who* only stand and wait."—MILTON.

6. When the noun or pronoun has **qualifying words,** its person and number are not affected; as,

"*The most laborious and successful student* is confined in his researches to a very few of God's works."—CHANNING.

7. When the noun or pronoun is connected with other nouns or pronouns by means of a **preposition,** it alone determines the person and number of the verb.

Thus we say:

"The steamer, with the crew and passengers, *was* lost;" not, "*were* lost."

"Day after day *passes* away;" not, "*pass* away."

"The second book of the Æneid is one of the greatest masterpieces that ever *were* executed by any hand·" not, "*was* executed."

8. Two or more nouns in the **singular** number connected by **and,** take a verb in the plural; as,

"Honor *and* shame from no condition *rise;*
Act well *your* part, there all the honor lies."—POPE.

9. Two or more nouns in the **singular** number, without any connecting word, take a verb in the plural; as,

"Art, empire, earth itself, to change *are* doomed."

"Patriotism, morality, every public and private consideration, demand our submission to lawful government."

10. When two or more nominatives stand for the **same** person or subject, the verb agrees with them in the **singular;** as,

"The philosopher and poet *was* banished from his country."

"A purpose, a design, an intention, is evident in everything."

"The truth, and the truth only, is worth seeking for its own sake."

11. Two or more singular **nominatives**, whether connected by *and*, or unconnected, when preceded by the words *each, every, either, no* and *not*, take the verb in the **singular**; as,

"*Every* man, woman, and child *knows* this to be so."
"*Not* a bird *and not* a beast, *not* a tree *and not* a shrub *was* to be seen."

12. Two or more singular nominatives grammatically connected by *or, nor, as well as*, or by any other **disjunctive**, take the verb in the **singular**; as,

There is *not* a word *nor* a thought that *has* not its bearing upon human character.
Poetry, *as well as* painting and music, *is* a fine art; not "*are* fine arts."

13. Where **either** of two or more nominatives connected by a disjunctive, is in the **plural**, the verb should also be in the **plural**; as,

Neither *riches* nor poverty *affect* a man's happiness.
An example or two *are* sufficient to illustrate the general observation.
Some grammarians say that the verb should agree with the nominative nearest to it. Others say that the verb should agree with the nominative that is the principal word.

"Not we, but God, *is* educating us."—KINGSLEY.

14. A **collective noun** takes the verb in the **singular** number when the **idea** conveyed by the noun is **singular**; as,

An army of many thousands *was* assembled.
The House of Lords *is* a brake upon the House of Commons.

15. A **collective noun** takes a verb in the **plural** number when the **idea** conveyed by the noun is **plural**; as,

The assembly *were* divided in *their* sentiments.

"An audience, even though ignorant *themselves* of the subjects of an examination, can comprehend when questions are answered and when they are not."—CARDINAL NEWMAN.

A collective noun conveys the idea of **unity** when the idea is of a whole taken simply as a whole. It conveys the idea of **plurality** when the idea is of a whole considered as made up of its respective parts.

16. The title of a book, a sum of money, or a period of time, in the **plural** form, is usually followed by a verb in the **singular**; as,

The *Annals* of Tacitus *is* the statesman's manual.

"Three hundred thousand dollars *is* to constitute the capital for the company." "*This* seven years *has* passed."

17. The word **whereabouts**, when a noun, takes a singular verb; as,

The *whereabouts* of the child *was* unknown to him.

CHAPTER II.

THE VERB.

1. The verb **be** takes the **same** case after as that which precedes it; as,

It is *I*; not, it is *me*. I believed it to be *him*; not, to be *he*.

Note that in the example, *It is I*, the word it is an expletive, and the real subject is I; still the verb agrees with it. This was not always so. In CHAUCER we read:

THE VERB.   171

> "Awake, my knight! Lo! *it am I*
> That to you speak."

> "It *are* such *folk* that loved idleness."—LATIMER.

So also in the old English the construction was : *ic sylf hit eom* = it am I myself.

2. When the verb **be** has a nominative **after** and **before**, and one nominative is plural, or consists of two or more singular nouns connected by *and*, the verb agrees with the nominative that **most naturally** forms its subject ; as,

"The wages of sin *is death*." Here *death* becomes the subject of the verb rather than *wages*.

His illness *was* pleurisy and rheumatism. The same rule holds true for clauses, phrases, and sentences ; as,

> "All my strength and all my art
> *Is to touch the gentle heart*."—SCOTT.

3. Intransitive and **passive** verbs also take the same case after as before, when both words refer to the same person or thing ; as,

> "*He* returned a *friend, who* came a *foe*."—POPE.
> "The child was named *John*."

4. A verb in the **subjunctive** mood has generally one of the following words before it :

(1) **If** ; as, *If* I go you cannot come.
(2) **Though** ; *Though* you hate me, I will still strive to do you good.
(3) **Unless** ; *Unless* you study, you cannot become learned.
(4) **Except** ; *Except* he ride, he cannot reach his destination.
(5) **Whether** ; I know not *whether* the sentence be correct.
(6) **That** ; "Would *that* charity reigned in every heart!"
(7) **Lest** ; "I kept guard over him, *lest* he do violence to himself."

5. While the verb is occasionally used in the **subjunctive** mood, the tendency of modern writers is to employ it exclusively in the **indicative** mood. The distinction in the employment of each of these moods may best be cleared up by the following definitions and rules:

(1) A sentence is said to be **hypothetical** when the truth of one proposition is dependent upon the truth of another proposition; as,

"*If thou read this*, O Cæsar, *thou mayest live.*"—SHAKESPEARE.

(2) The clause that contains the condition is called the **conditional** clause. In the example here given, *thou read this* is the conditional clause.

(3) The clause that contains the consequent of the supposition, is called the **consequent** clause. Here, *thou mayest live* is the consequent clause, because it follows as a consequence from the first clause, *if thou read this.*

(4) When the conditional clause expresses an action **past** or **present**, the verb should be in the **indicative** mood; as,

"If satire *charms*, strike faults, but spare the man."—SHAKESPEARE.

We know it for a fact that satire charms; hence the verb is in the indicative.

"If the creature *is* ever setting in motion an endless series of physical causes and effects, much more is the Creator."—CARDINAL NEWMAN.
"If a man *has* built a house, the house is his."
"Whether the translation was ever published I am not aware."

(5) When the conditional clause expresses a hope, a wish, or a thought containing the **idea of futurity**, the verb should be in the **subjunctive** mood; as,

"He will not be pardoned, *unless he repent.*"
"Would that *he were here.*"
"On condition *that he come*, I will consent to stay."
"I would learn my trade thoroughly *if I were you.*"

"What shall we do,
If he approach with a still greater army?"—LONGFELLOW.

(6) When the conditional clause expresses an **uncertainty**, the verb is used in the **subjunctive**; as,

"*If it were so*, it was a grievous fault."—SHAKESPEARE.

Here there is doubt that it is so.

"Yet if our heart *throb* higher at its sway,
The wizard note hath not been touched in vain."—SCOTT.

(7) When there are various connected clauses in a sentence, the verb in each should be used in the same mood. For this reason the following sentence is incorrect:

"If there *be* but one body of legislators, it *is* no better than a tyranny; if there *are* only two, there *will want* a casting vote."

The sentence should read as follows:

"If there *be* but one body of legislators, it *will be* no better than a tyranny; if there *be* only two, there *will want* a casting vote."

6. The subjunctive may be expressed without the particle if by placing the verb before its subject.

"*If I had* a book, I would read" = "*Had I* a book, I would read."
"*If I were* you, I would go" = "*Were I* you, I would go."

7. The words *may, can, could, would,* and *should* are employed in the potential mood.

8. The same distinction that obtains in the use of *shall* and *will* in the indicative, is observed in the use of should and would in the potential mood; namely, *would* refers to an exercise of the will, and *should* implies dependent action or obligation.

Would is used to express,

(1) A **wish**: "Would I had employed usefully all my spare hours!"
"Would God I had died for thee, O Absalom!"

(2) A **custom**: "She would weep all day."
"He would often talk about these things."

(3) **Determination**: "He would depart, I could not stop him."
"He would persist in his course in spite of all I could say."

Should is used to express,

(1) **Dependence**: "I should like to go to town, and would go if I could."
(2) **Duty or obligation**: "He should go by all means, but he will not."
"You should not allow such conduct in your house."

Should and would are used indifferently to express a conditional assertion:

"I should not do so, if I were in your place."
"I would not do so, if I were in your place."
"He would give, if he had the means."

9. When the **infinitive mood** comes after the following verbs, the particle **to** is omitted:

Dare: "I *dare do* all that may become a man."—SHAKESPEARE.
Let: "*Let* darkness *keep* her raven gloss."—TENNYSON.
Bid: "Nor *bid* a warrior *smile*, nor teach a maid to weep."—SCOTT.
Make: "The hope thereof *makes* Clifford *mourn* in steel."—SHAKESPEARE.
See: "I *saw* him *run* after a gilded butterfly."—IBID.
Hear: "I *hear* thee *speak* of the better land."—HEMANS.
Feel: "I *felt* the blackness *come* and *go*."—BYRON.
Need: "Her kindness and her worth to spy
You *need* but *gaze* on Ellen's eye."—SCOTT.
Have: "I should be delighted *to have* you *write* a preface."—LONGFELLOW.
Gin — begin, in poetry—

"Amid the copse *gan peep*
A narrow inlet still and deep."—SCOTT.

Durst: "Thou hast dared
To tell me what I *durst* not *tell* myself." PERCY

The particle *to* after the verb *dared* is here introduced for the sake of the metre.

10. When two or more verbs in the infinitive occur together in the same sentence, the particle is inserted before the *first* only ; as,

" *To* shake the head, relent, and sigh, and yield."
" Many authors expect the printer to point, spell, and digest their copy, so that it may be intelligible to the reader."

11. The particle **to** should not be separated from the verb by any intervening word ; as,

"The student must not expect *to always find* study agreeable." Read : " *Always to find.*"
Instead of *to incessantly think*, say, *to think incessantly*.

12. The infinitive verb should not be omitted at the end of a sentence, leaving the particle **to** ; as,

"I have not written, and I do not intend *to*." Read : "I do not intend *to write*."
"He has not done it, nor is he likely *to*." Read : " Nor is he likely *to do it*."

13. **Active transitive** verbs govern in the **objective** case ; as,

" We *carved* not a *line*, and we *raised* not a stone."—C. WOLFE.

14. The object of a transitive verb may be a **noun** or any of its equivalents.

(1) A noun : "The old man *shook* his *head*."—DICKENS.
(2) A pronoun :

" Where the enamoured sunny light
Brightened *her* that was so bright."—WORDSWORTH.

(3) An infinitive in -ing : " He loved *planting* and *building*."— EVELYN.

(4) An **infinitive** with **to**: "Learn *to labor* and *to wait*."—LONGFELLOW.

(5) An **infinitive** phrase:

"Ladies, you deserve
   To have a temple built you."—SHAKESPEARE.

(6) A **sentence**: "As we made our way through the crowd, I perceived *we brought good humour with us.*"—GOLDSMITH.

15. When a sentence is the object of a verb, it is generally introduced by **that**; as,

"The good woman saw at once *that her son was a genius and a poet.*"—WASHINGTON IRVING.

"Teach him *that states of native strength possest,
Though very poor may still be very blest.*"—GOLDSMITH.

16. An intransitive verb is sometimes found with an object **cognate** in meaning with the verb; as,

"I have *fought* a good *fight.*"—ST. PAUL.
"*Dreaming dreams* no mortals ever dared to dream before."—POE.

17. Certain transitive verbs take two objects, the **direct** and the **indirect**; as,

"Give *me* the *book*." Here *book* is the direct object, and *me* is the indirect object.

The principal verbs taking both objects are:

allow	cost	get	make	pay	promise	send	throw
bring	deny	give	offer	play	provide	show	write
buy	do	leave	order	pour	refuse	sing	
carry	draw	lend	pass	present	sell	tell	

18. Transitive verbs of making, appointing, creating, teaching, and the like, also take **two** objectives; one representing the **person**, the other the **office**; as,

"Nature had made *Mr. Churchill a poet;* but destiny had made him a schoolmaster."—LONGFELLOW.

"He was gathered under the wings of one of those good old motherly dames, found in every village, who cluck together the whole callow brood of the neighborhood, *to teach them their letters* and keep them out of harm's way."—WASHINGTON IRVING.

19. The object is usually placed **after** the verb; but it is placed before the verb—

(1) When **emphasis** requires it:

"*Honey* from out the gnarled hive I'll bring,
And *apples* wan with sweetness gather thee.—KEATS.

(2) When the object is a **relative** or **interrogative** pronoun:

"*Whom* hast thou, then, or *what*, to accuse,
But Heaven's free love dealt equally to all?"—MILTON.

20. The **imperfect** and the **preperfect participles** derived from transitive verbs, take an object; as,

"*Respecting ourselves*, we shall be respected by the world."—BURKE.

"He was finally sent off to bed *blowing little bubbles* with his mouth."—LONGFELLOW.

"*Having finished the work*, he withdrew to his home."

21. When the article is used **before** a participle, the participle should be followed by the preposition **of**; as,

"In *the* forming *of* his sentences he was very exact."

22. Sometimes the sentence is improved by the **omission** of both article and preposition; as,

"By *establishing* good laws we secure our peace." This is preferable to the form, "By *the establishing of* good laws."

23. The preposition *of* should not be used after the participle when the article is omitted before the participle.

Instead of: "From calling *of* names they proceeded to blows,' read, "From calling names they proceeded to blows."

24. A noun or pronoun before a participle should be in the possessive case, when the noun or pronoun represents an **active** agent; as,

"Much will depend on the *pupil's composing* frequently."
"*Lady Macbeth's walking* in her sleep is an incident full of tragic horror."

25. When the noun or pronoun represents a **passive** subject, the possessive case should not be used; as,

"The daily instance of *men dying* around us." Not, "*men's dying*."
"When they speak of *John having inherited* a fortune." Not, "*John's having inherited*."

26. The **imperfect active participle** is sometimes used in a passive sense; as,

"I hope your new book is *printing*."—JOHNSON.

27. There is also a **progressive passive participle**; as,

"For those who *are being educated* in our seminaries."—SOUTHEY
"It *was being uttered*."—COLERIDGE.
"It signifies properly, though in uncouth English, one who *is being beaten*."—WHATELY.

When we say: "I *saw one dragging into light*, as I passed by the ruins of a palace," the meaning is obscure; but, using the progressive passive form, the meaning becomes clear: "*I saw one being dragged into light*."

CHAPTER III.

THE NOUN.

1. A noun or pronoun, used to explain another noun or pronoun, is put by **apposition** in the same case ; as,

>—"So work the honey *bees*,
>*Creatures* that by a rule in nature teach
>The art of order to a peopled kingdom.—SHAKESPEARE.

2. A phrase or **a sentence** may be in **apposition** to a noun; as,

>"O let us still the *secret joy* partake,
>To follow virtue e'en for virtue's sake."—POPE.

"In the serene expression of her face he read *the divine beatitude,*
 '*Blessed are the pure in heart.*'"—LONGFELLOW.

3. Apposition may be expressed :

(1) By **direct union** of the words : "The *steamer Germania* arrived."

(2) By the word **as** : "*St. Francis de Sales* is no less esteemed *as a writer* than *he* is loved *as a man.*"

(3) By the word **or** : "The *puma*, or the *American lion*, is found in Brazil."

(4) By the word **that** when there is an **appositive sentence** :

>"I held *it truth*, with him who sings
>To one clear harp in divers tones,
>That men may rise on stepping-stones
>Of their dead selves to higher things."—TENNYSON.

(5) By transitive verbs of **naming, choosing**, and the like; "Congress named *Washington commander-in-chief* of the forces."

4. **A noun** or **pronoun** in the **possessive case** is governed by another noun with which the former generally stands in the relation of possession ; as,

"St. Paul recounts *his* sufferings for the faith."
"The *Church's* warfare with the world ends only with time."

5. The **term** belonging to the possessive word is sometimes **omitted** ; as,

James heard mass at *St. Monica's;* meaning *St. Monica's Church.*
The senator got his diamond pin at *Tiffany's;* meaning *Tiffany's jewelry store.*
Under this rule falls that peculiar construction in our language by which the possessive ending is retained after the preposition of; as, I have a volume of *his* among my books; that is, *a volume of his books.* A discovery of Franklin's; that is, *one of Franklin's discoveries.*
Here note the distinction between the expressions, *A bust of Horatio Seymour* and *A bust of Horatio Seymour's.*
A bust of Horatio Seymour=a representation of Horatio Seymour.
A bust of Horatio Seymour's=a bust belonging to Horatio Seymour.

6. When two or more nouns, connected by **and**, express **joint** ownership the possessive case-ending is attached only to the last ; as,

"William and Mary's reign."

7. When the possessive is a **compound word**, a complex term, or the like, the possessive sign is attached only to the **last** ; as,

The *Mayor of Boston's* address; my *father-in-law's* will.

8. When nouns in **apposition** are used in the possessive, the case-ending is attached to the **last** ; as,

For *David* my *servant's* sake.

9. But when both nouns refer to **distinct** and **separate** things, each retains the possessive case-ending; as, *Webster's* and *Worcester's* dictionary.

10. When two or more nouns are connected by a **disjunctive**, or by the phrase **as well as**, each retains the possessive case-ending; as,

"They relieve neither the *boy's* nor the *girl's* distress."
She had the *physician's*, the *surgeon's*, *as well as* the *apothecary's* assistance.

11. If the noun expressing possession is **antecedent** to a relative clause, the form in **of** is employed; as,

"This was the face *of a man whose* life was spent rather in a career of thought and literary effort, than in a career of active and laborious strife."—MASSON.

12. Sometimes the possessive case-ending is **omitted**; as,

"They arrived weary and fatigued after a twenty *miles* walk."

13. Where the addition of the **'s** would render the word awkward the **s** is omitted, and the apostrophe retained; thus, we say

For *conscience'* sake, and not for *conscience's* sake.
But not all nouns ending in **s** dispense with the **'s**. Thus custom says "*St. James's*," meaning the English Court, and not "*St. James'*." So also we speak of "*Willis's Rooms*," not *Willis' Rooms*."

14. A noun or pronoun, the object of an action or of a relation, is said to be in the **objective** case.

(1) Of an **action**; that is, of an **active transitive** verb; as, *Love your enemies.*
(2) Of a **relation**; that is, of a **preposition**; as, *Do good to them that persecute you.*

15. A noun or pronoun may also be the object of the **participle** of a transitive verb ; as,

William was seen *studying* his *lessons* in the evening.

16. A noun or pronoun addressed is said to be in the **nominative case addressed**; as,

"Rise, crowned with light, imperial *Salem*, rise!"—Pope.

17. A noun or pronoun limited by a participle, and depending on no other word in a sentence, is said to be in the **nominative case absolute**; as,

"*Spring* returning, the swallows reappear."

18. A noun or pronoun used by **pleonasm** is in the **nominative case independent**; as,

"Here *she* stood,
Engirt with many a florid maiden-cheek,
The *woman-conqueror*."—Tennyson.

CHAPTER IV.

THE PRONOUN.

1. A pronoun agrees with the noun which it represents in **person, number,** and **gender.**

2. To this rule occur the following **exceptions** in regard to **personal** pronouns :

(1) Neuter nouns, when personified, take the pronoun in the gender of personification; as,

"To him who in the love of Nature holds
Communion with *her* visible forms, *she*
Speaks a various language."—Bryant.

(2) Authors and editors use the pronoun **we** to represent a singular antecedent; as, *We regard the tornado as a visitation of Providence.*

(3) The plural **you** is used when addressing one person; as, *John, are you going out?*

(4) A noun in the **common gender** sometimes takes a masculine and sometimes a neuter pronoun; as, *The duty of the parent to educate his child cannot be transferred to the State.*
The baby sleeps in its cradle.

3. **Personal pronouns**, when those of different persons occur together, admit of a **certain order** in their use:

(1) In the **singular** number the **second** person has precedence over the others; as, *You and he and I are called upon to speak.* The third person has precedence over the first; as, *He and I must go.*

(2) In the plural number the first person has precedence; next comes the second, and lastly the third; as, *We and they sail to-morrow.*

4. The **case** of a personal pronoun depends upon its relation with the verb or the preposition.

(1) After **than** or **as** the pronoun may be in the nominative or the objective case; thus, *I loved none better than him;* that is, *than I loved him. He reads more than I;* that is, *than I read.* The following are therefore incorrect:

"Is she as tall as *me?*"—SHAKESPEARE.
"She suffers hourly more than *me.*"—SWIFT.
"The nations not so blessed as *they.*"—THOMSON.

(2) After **let** the pronoun should be in the objective case; as, *Let us study Shakespeare together.* The following sentence is incorrect:

"Let you and *I* endeavor to improve the enclosure."—SOUTHEY.

(3) Pronouns governed by **between** should be in the objective case; as, *Between **him** and **me**.* Hence the following is considered erroneous:

"All debts are cleared between you and *I*."—SHAKESPEARE.

(4) Pronouns following the word but may be in the objective or the nominative, according as this word has a **prepositional** or a **conjunctive** force. *He examined all but me.* Here *but* may be taken as a preposition governing the pronoun *me;* or it may be taken as a conjunction, in which case the sentence would read: *He examined all, but me he examined not;* when *me* would be the object of examined. Considering *but* a conjunction, the following examples are correct:

"Which none *but* Heaven and you and *I* shall hear."—SHAKESPEARE.
"Which none may hear *but she* and *thou*."—COLERIDGE.

Cardinal Newman and others among our most careful modern writers, incline to the use of *but* simply in a conjunctive sense.

5. When the antecedent of the pronoun is a **collective** noun used in a sense implying **unity**, the pronoun should be in the **singular** number, **neuter** gender; as,

"Congress holds *its* sessions in Washington."

6. When the antecedent is a collective noun, used in a sense implying **plurality**, the pronoun should be in the **plural** number; as,

"The party were quarreling among themselves."

"To this, our pathway gently-winding leads,
Where march a *train* with baskets on *their* heads."—POPE'S ILIAD.

7. The collectives **many, score, few,** and the like, when preceded by the article **a,** take a pronoun in the **plural** number; as,

"A great many are prepared to share *their* opinion; only a few can be found to share their purse."

8. An antecedent modified by the words **many a** takes **a singular** pronoun; as:

"Many a man tramples upon *his* nobler self."

"Full many a flower is born to blush unseen,
And waste *its* sweetness on the desert air."—GRAY.

9. When the pronoun is not in the same clause with the words **many a**, it may be in the **plural**; as,

"It has been the fate of many a genius, that *they* have been but ill-understood by their contemporaries."

"In Hawick twinkled *many a light*,
Behind him soon *they* set in night."—SCOTT.

10. A pronoun having two or more singular antecedents referring to **different persons or things** connected by **and**, should be in the **plural** number; as,

The lazy, the careless, and the vicious are hoarding regrets for *their* old age.

11. A pronoun having two or more singular antecedents, referring to the **same** person or thing, connected by **and**, should be in the **singular** number; as,

"This wit, orator, and statesman, left *his* impress on the age."

12. Two or more singular antecedents connected by **and**, and modified by the words **each, every, no**, or similar distributives, require the pronoun in the singular number; as,

"Every *plant* and *every tree* produces others after *its* own kind."
"It is the cause of *every reproach* and *distress* which *has attended* your government."—JUNIUS.

13. A pronoun having two or more singular antecedents connected by a **disjunctive** conjunction, should be in the **singular**; as,

"Neither *wealth* nor *honor* can secure the happiness of *its* votaries."

"What *virtue* or what mental *grace*,
But men unqualified and base
Will boast *it* their possession?"—COWPER.

14. A pronoun having **two** antecedents, one **singular** and one **plural**, connected by a disjunctive, should be in the **plural**; as,

"Neither the *teacher* nor his *pupils* can shirk *their* duty."

15. Two singular antecedents of different genders connected by **or** sometimes take a pronoun corresponding to the gender of each; as,

Every *man* or *woman* should examine *his* or *her* conscience.

16. Sometimes the pronoun is put in the **plural**; as,

"When a *man* or *woman* shall make a vow to be sanctified, and will consecrate *themselves* to the Lord."—NUMBERS vi. 2.

17. Sometimes when the antecedent is **indefinite** both pronouns are used; as,

"I make this comment and solicit the reader's attention to it in *his* or *her* consideration of this tale."—DICKENS.

18. Two or more pronouns expressing difference of person, connected by a **conjunction**, may be represented by a pronoun in the **first person** plural, if one of the antecedents is in the first person; and if one of the antecedents is not in the first person, by a pronoun in the **second person** plural.

"*John* and *I* are pleased with *our* presents."
"*You* and *James* study *your* lessons well."
"*Either you* or *I* will be in *our* place in due time."
"*Your* character, which *I, or any other writer* may now value *ourselves* by drawing."

19. The mingling of **thou** and **you** in the same sentence is inelegant and inaccurate. For instance:

"So, as *thy* sun rises over the humble house-top round about *your* home, shall you wake many a day to duty and labor."—THACKERAY
For *thy sun* read *your sun*.

20. The pronoun **it** has several peculiar functions in English:

(1) **It** stands for the name of child, animal, or living thing the sex of which is likely to be overlooked; as,

"The child lost *its* toy." "The mouse ran into *its* hole."

(2) It is used **indefinitely** in regard to persons or things; as,

"Who is *it?* *It* is I." "What is *it?* I do not know what *it* is."

(3) It is used as an **expletive**, introducing a sentence; as,

"'Tis the sunset of life gives me mystical lore,
And coming events cast their shadows before."—CAMPBELL.

In this instance it takes the place of the real subject, which comes after the verb.

(4) It is made to stand for an **antecedent** word, phrase, or sentence; as,

"Here is the book; to whom shall I give *it?*"
"*You have done him good*, and need not regret *it.*"

(5) It is made to stand for **a general** state of affairs; as,

"We roughed *it* in the woods."
"Think of me when *it* shall be well with thee"

(6) It is used **idiomatically** without reference to any antecedent word, phrase, or sentence; as,

> "Trip it as you go
> On the light fantastic toe."—MILTON.

(7) It is used **impersonally**; as, *It* snows. *It* rains.

21. The **compound personal pronouns** take the verb in the **same** person and number as the pronouns from which they are derived; as,

> "Which way I fly is hell; *myself am* hell."—MILTON.
> "Captain, *yourself are* the fittest."—DRYDEN.
> "*Ourself* to hoary Nestor *will repair*."—POPE's HOMER.

22. Sometimes the compound pronoun is used exclusively in the **third** person; as,

> "*Myself hath* been the whip."—CHAUCER.
> "*Myself knoweth* not where."—HEYWOOD.
> "Conversation is but carving:
> Carve for all, *yourself is starving*."—SWIFT.

This form grows out of the fact that, as early as the fourteenth century the word **self** began to lose its original **adjective** meaning, and came to be regarded as a noun.

23. **One**, when used pronominally, does not admit any other pronoun to represent it. Thus we say:

> *One speaks one's mind; not one speaks his mind.*

24. The **relative pronoun** may be either the subject or object of a verb, or the object of a preposition, or it may express the relation of possession.

> (1) **Subject of a verb:**
> "I see the golden helmet that shines far off like flame."—MACAULAY.
>
> (2) **Object of a verb:**
> "Shall he alone, *whom* rational we *call*,
> Be pleased with nothing, if not blessed with all?"—POPE.

(3) Object of a preposition:

"And Rome may bear the pride of him.
Of whom herself is proud."—MACAULAY.

(4) Relation of possession:

"There is a reaper *whose* name is Death."—LONGFELLOW.

25. The relative should be placed **near** its antecedent:

"The man *who* has charity for his neighbor, has more than riches."

26. When the antecedent is a pronoun of the **first** or of the **second** person, the relative takes the **person** of the antecedent; as,

"I, who *am* your friend, tell you so."

27. When the relative has antecedents **different** in person, it agrees with that which is **nearest**; as,

"You are an enemy *who is* fair in speech and foul in thought."
"You, *who are* fair in speech, are an enemy foul in thought."

28. When the antecedent is a **collective** noun taken in a **singular** sense, the relative is **which**; as,

"A board of managers, *which* is composed of sensible men, governs the institution."

29. When the antecedent is a **collective** noun taken in a **plural** sense, the relative is **who**; as,

"The poor, *who* had nothing to offer but their lives, seemed ready to devote them to his service."—SCOTT.

30. The relative **whose** has generally for antecedent rational beings; as,

"The man *whose* views of life are purely mercenary, knows not the meaning of his existence."

31. The relative **whose** has also for antecedent inanimate objects, especially in poetry; as,

> "That undiscovered country from *whose* bourne
> No traveller returns."—SHAKESPEARE.
> "He spoke of love, such love as spirits feel,
> In worlds *whose* course is equable and pure."
> —WORDSWORTH.

Whose is in this case the possessive of *which*. The tendency of the best modern writers is to break down all distinction between the forms **whose** and **of which**.

32. The relative **that** may take the place of **who** or **which**, subject to the following rules:

(1) **That** is employed after an adjective or an adverb in the superlative degree; as, "*Read the best books that you can procure.*"

(2) After the pronominal adjectives **all, every, same**: "*Others have the same difficulties to overcome that you have.*" "*I did for him all that I could.*"

(3) After the interrogative **who**: "*Who, that has slandered his neighbor, is not bound to restore his good name?*"

(4) After the pronoun it, used indefinitely: "*It was he that spoke about Brownson.*"

(5) After two or more antecedents which separately would require **who** and **which**; as, "*Such are the authors and the writings that I proposed discussing.*" Separately we would read *authors whom* and *writings which*.

33. The rules governing the use of **who, which,** and **that,** are as follows:

(1) **Who** relates to **persons**, and is used when a quality, or attribute, or circumstance is added to the meaning conveyed by the antecedent clause; as, "*I met the Earl of Denbigh,*

who showed me through the House of Lords." This sentence is equivalent to the following: "*I met the Earl of Denbigh,* **and** *he showed me through the House of Lords.*"

(2) **Which** relates to things, and is also used when a quality, or attribute, or circumstance is added to the meaning conveyed by the antecedent clause; as, "*He gave me a letter,* **which** *he requested me to read.*" That is, "*He gave me a letter,* **and it** *he requested me to read.*"

(3) **That** refers either to persons or things, and is used simply to qualify or restrict the sense of the antecedent; as,

"I read the book *that* I found on the table."
"Thoughts *that* breathe and words *that* burn."—WORDSWORTH.
"Music *that* brings sweet sleep down from the blissful skies."—TENNYSON.

To render the distinction clearer we will take the following instances:

1. When we say, "*The heirs,* **who** *have been notified, will be present,*" we mean that *all* the heirs will be present, *and* that they have been notified accordingly.

2. When we say, "*The heirs* **that** *have been notified will be present,*" we mean that *only the notified heirs* will be present, to the exclusion of all others. (See Ayres' edition of COBBETT'S ENGLISH GRAMMAR, Editor's note, pp. 5-10.)

34. The relative **what** represents things, names, or qualities, and has no antecedent expressed; as,

"Tell me *what* you want and I shall attend to it."
"I scarcely know *what* to call him."
"It desires *what* it has not, the beautiful."—SHELLEY.
"The world which credits *what* is done,
  Is cold to all that might have been."—TENNYSON.

In this last sentence, the clause *what is done* is the object of the verb *credits,* and *what* is the subject of *is done.* In some sentences *what* may be resolved into *that which,* but it is contrary to the genius of the English language to do so. It is simply a changing of English idiom into a foreign form of expression.

35. **What** is used in various functions:

(1) As an interrogative pronoun: *What are you doing?* This was the primitive use of what as a neuter of who.

(2) As a relative: "*What I do now, you know not.*"

(3) As an interrogative adjective: *What manner of man is this, that even the winds and the sea obey him.*—Matt. viii. 27.

(4) As a demonstrative adjective: *What books I read, I buy;* i. e., *Those books that I read, I buy.*

(5) As an adverb, in which case the word is repeated: "*He had so used the matter that what by force, what by policy, he had taken from the Christians thirty small castles.*"—*Knolles.* "*What by force, what by policy*" = "*partly by force, partly by policy.*" In such instances *what* is generally followed by *with*.

(6) As an interjection:

"*What!* can you lull the winged winds asleep?"—Campbell.

36. **What** should not be used for **that**:

"He would not believe but *what* I did it." Read: "He would not believe but *that* I did it."

The sentence, "*I have nothing but what you see,*" is correct.

37. The **demonstrative** pronoun must be in the same number as the noun that it points out; as,

This picture, *that* book.

38. A **plural** noun having a collective meaning in the singular number, takes a **singular** demonstrative; as,

"*This seven years* did not Talbot see his son."—Shakespeare.

'They could not speak; and so I left them both, To bear *this tidings* to the bloody King."—Ibid.,—*Richard III.*

39. When **this** and **that**, or their plural forms, are used in the same sentence, **this** points out the noun nearest as regards time or space; as,

"*This* book is more expensive than *that* engraving."

40. When standing for their nouns, **this** or **these** represents the **latter** antecedent, and **that** or **those**, the **former**; as,

"And reason raise o'er instinct as you can,
In *this* 'tis God directs, in that 'tis man."—POPE.
"Farewell my friends! farewell my foes!
My peace with these, my love with those."—BURNS.

CHAPTER V.

THE ARTICLE.

1. When several objects are **separately** specified the article is **repeated** before each; as,

"To *a* strong spirit, difficulty is *a* stimulus and *a* triumph."—FOSTER.
  "*The* flower-like woods most lovely in decay,
  The many clouds, *the* seas, *the* rocks, *the* sands,
  Lie in the silent moonshine."—COLERIDGE.

2. When several nouns describe the **same** person or thing, the article is placed only before the **first**; as,

"Gladstone excels as *a* statesman, orator, and scholar."
"He sent a letter to Mr. Larkin, *the* bribe-agent and broker on this occasion."—BURKE.

3. When several adjectives qualify the **same** noun, the article is usually employed only before the **first**; as,

"*The* wisest, brightest, meanest of mankind."—POPE.
"There is about the whole book *a* vehement, contentious, replying manner."—MACAULAY.

But sometimes the article is **repeated** for the sake of emphasis; as,

"*A* sadder and *a* wiser man."—COLERIDGE.

"*The* most wicked, *the* most atrocious, *the* boldest and most dexterous villain that that country ever produced."—BURKE.

4. When several adjectives, though qualifying the same noun, relate to **different** objects, the article should be placed before **each**; as,

A sweet and *a* sour apple; *the* Old and *the* New Testament.
Note that it is erroneous to say, "*The first and the second pages.*"
The sentence should read: "*The first and the second page.*"

5. The article is placed before the name of a well-known person to express one of the same type of character; as,

"Shakespeare was *the Homer*, or father, of our dramatists; Jonson was *the Virgil*, the pattern of elaborate writing."—DRYDEN.
"He may be *a Newton* or *a Herschell* in affairs of astronomy, but of the knowledge of affairs of the world he is quite ignorant."—BURKE.

6. The indefinite article **an, a,** is a weakened form of the numeral **one.** Traces of its numerical origin occur in the following expressions:

A hundred dollars. This is less emphatic than to say "*one hundred dollars.*"
"*A* thousand liveried angels lacquey her."—MILTON.

7. The article **a** should not be placed before a word used in its most general sense; as,

"What kind of *book* is this?" not, "What kind of *a* book."

8. There are a few peculiar forms of expression in which the article **a** stands between the noun and certain words:

(1) **Many**: "For *many an* April and *many a* May."—CHAUCER.
(2) **What**: "What *a* piece of work is man!"—SHAKESPEARE.
(3) **Such**: "Such *a* downy tip was on his callow chin."— DICKENS.
(4) **All**: *All the* difference between stubbornness and firmness is, that one is blinded by passion and the other yields to the dictates of reason.
(5) **Both**: *Both the* men trudged along their weary course.

9. When the adjective is **preceded** by certain other words, the article stands **between** it and the noun:

(1) **Too**: "You hold *too* heinous *a* respect of grief."—SHAKESPEARE.
(2) **So**: "'Tis a very hard calumny upon our soil to affirm that *so* excellent *a* fruit will not grow there."—TEMPLE.
(3) **As**: "We were introduced to *as* queer *an* exhibition as the eye has often looked on."—THACKERAY.
(4) **How**: See *how* short *a* letter he has written.

10. The insertion of **a** before the words **few** and **little** changes the meaning of the sentence:

(1) *Few* men were present = *not many* men were present.
 A few men were present = *some men* were present.
(2) He deserves *little* sympathy = he deserves *scarcely any* sympathy, *if any at all.*
 He deserves *a little* sympathy = he deserves *some* sympathy.

11. Where **corresponsive** conjunctions are used, embracing two or more nouns, if the article is used with **one** noun it should also be used with the **other**; as,

"*Both the* author *and the* publisher are deserving of censure."
"*Neither the* conscious receiver of stolen goods *nor the* willing listener to slanderous speech, is free from guilt."

The definite article the is a remnant of an old English form of the demonstrative **that**.

The expression *that book* is more precise—points out the object more clearly—than the expression *the book*.

12. The definite article is used:

(1) For the sake of **emphasis**: "Shakespeare is *the* poet of England."

Mountains and rivers are also emphasized by the use of **the**; thus we speak of **the** *Hudson,* **the** *Alps,* **the** *Rhine.*

13. When an adjective follows its noun as a special epithet, it is preceded by **the**; as,

Alfred *the* Great, Peter *the* Hermit.

14. **The**, before the comparative of adjectives and adverbs in certain forms of expression, has the force of an adverb; as,

The more he learns, *the* humbler he becomes. (See *Etymology*, Chap. xxiv. 25).

15. The article **a** is often used with nouns as a **distributive**; as,

"And passing rich with forty pounds *a* year."—GOLDSMITH. That is, "forty pounds *each* year." So, *Two dollars a day*, means *Two dollars each day*.

A-day, a-year, was written in an older stage of the language, on-day, on-year.

CHAPTER VI.

THE ADJECTIVE.

1. The **adjective** limits or describes the noun or pronoun to which it relates ; as,

   "An *honest* man's the *noblest* work of God."—POPE.

   (1) A **limiting** adjective defines or restricts the meaning of a noun; as, *Two* books, the *second* chapter.
   (2) A **descriptive** adjective expresses some quality or property belonging to the noun ; as, *A sour apple, green ribbons.*

2. An adjective is sometimes used as an abstract noun ; as,

   "This age still retains enough of *beautiful*, and *splendid*, and *bold*, to captivate an ardent, but untutored, imagination."—COLERIDGE.

3. An adjective is sometimes used instead of an adverb ; as,

   "The green trees whispered *low* and *mild*."—LONGFELLOW.

   This use of the adjective for the adverbial form is of frequent occurrence in poetry.

4. The adjective generally **precedes** the noun.

   Thus, it is more in accordance with the genius of the language to say, "*a black horse*," than to say, as the French do, "*a horse black.*"

5. There are cases in which the adjective is found after the noun :

   (1) In **poetry** the adjective frequently follows the noun ; as,

   "Once upon a midnight *dreary*."—POE.
   "And the spring arose on the garden *fair*."—SHELLEY.

(2) In **titles of French origin** the adjective follows the noun; as, *The heir* **apparent,** *the prince* **regent,** *the princess* **royal,** *the poet* **laureate.**

(3) Participles are sometimes placed after the noun; as, *The person* **named,** *the objects* **specified.**

(4) When other words depend upon the adjective, it follows the noun; as, "*A mind* **conscious of right** *and a heart* **free from guile.**"

(5) When **qualifying words** are prefixed to the adjective, it generally **follows** the noun; as,

"A sovereign whose temper, *never very gentle*, had been rendered morbidly irritable by age."—MACAULAY.
" A land *more bright*
Never did mortal eye behold."—MOORE.

6. When two or more adjectives are connected by **and**, it is of frequent occurrence, in poetry and in old English prose, for one to precede the noun, and the others to follow it; as,

" They the *holy* ones and *weakly*
Who the cross of suffering love."—LONGFELLOW.
"A *dark* prince and infinitely *suspicious*."—BACON.

7. The **comparative degree** is employed when one of two objects, or two sets of objects, is said to possess a quality or property in a greater degree than the other; as,

" It is *better* to write one word upon the rock, than a thousand on the water or the sand."—GLADSTONE.

8. When **more than two objects,** or two sets of objects, are compared, the comparative form should never be used.

It would be incorrect to say, " He is the *better* of the three."

THE ADJECTIVE.

9. Forms of speech implying comparison generally require **than** to introduce the second term of comparison; as,

"His own tastes would have led him *rather* to political *than* to commercial pursuits."—MACAULAY.

"Method is not less requisite in ordinary conversation *than* in writing, provided a man would talk to make himself understood."
—ADDISON.

The word *than* is a modern form of the adverb *then*. Shakespeare and his contemporaries wrote *then* where we now use *than*. Some writers regarded *than* as a preposition, and accordingly put the pronoun following it in the objective case:

"She suffers hourly more than *me*."—SWIFT.

We would consider it more correct to say: "*She suffers hourly more than I.*"

Of the two comparative forms, elder and older, *elder* is applied to persons of the same family, to denote priority of birth; as, *Patrick is the elder brother:* older is applied to length of time generally, as contrasted with *new* or *young;* as, *John is older than his sister Mary*. *Older* takes *than;* *elder* never does.

10. The terms of comparison should be placed as **near** each other as possible; as,

"Your plot of ground is *larger than* John's."
This construction is preferable to the following:
"Yours is a *larger* plot of ground *than* John's."

11. Double comparatives are not regarded as good forms of speech in modern English. They were employed by the old English writers in order to emphasize the comparison; as,

"He shall find
The unkindest beast *more kinder* than mankind."—SHAKESPEARE.

Custom recognizes the use of the double comparative *lesser* instead of *less*.

12. The **superlative** degree is employed when one of more than two objects, or sets of objects, possesses a quality in a greater degree than all the others :

"Longfellow is the *most popular* of the American poets."

13. When only two objects, or sets of objects, are compared, the superlative should not be used.

Thus, instead of saying, "*This is the **best** of the two*," say, "*This is the **better** of the two*."
"*Of two evils choose the **least**.*" This should read, "*Of two evils choose the **lesser**.*" Still, good writers use the superlative in comparing two things.

14. Double superlatives are not regarded as good forms of speech in modern English.

Like double comparatives, they were employed by our elder writers to render the expression more emphatic ; as,

"This was the *most unkindest* cut of all."—SHAKESPEARE.

Far from being regarded as incorrect, they were thought to add to the force and elegance of the language. Of the double superlative Ben Jonson says: "This is a certain kind of English Atticism, or eloquent phrase of speech, imitating the manner of the most ancientest and finest Grecians, who for more emphasis and vehemencies sake used to speak thus."

15. The **superlative** is often used when no comparison is intended, simply to express **excellence** or pre-eminence in some quality ; as,

"Yet in these ears till hearing dies,
  One set slow bell will seem to toll
  The passing of the *sweetest* soul
  That ever looked with human eyes."—TENNYSON.

16. When the comparative degree is used one term of comparison should **exclude** the other; as,

Iron is *more useful* than *all the other metals*—not, "than *all metals.*'

17. When the superlative degree is used one term of comparison should **include** the other; as,

Iron is the *most useful* of *all metals*—not, "of *all other metals.*"

The meaning of the positive is diminished by adding the suffix ish to the adjective; as, *white*, **whitish**; *gray*, **grayish**.

18. The words **farther** and **farthest** relate to distance; **further** and **furthest** to movement in advance, or increase in quality; as,

"One may go *farther* and fare worse." "Come *further*." "I have nothing *further* to say."

19. Where the idea of **collective** unity is conveyed a **singular** adjective may precede a **plural** one; as,

"*One* hundred men." "*Every* two months."

20. When a compound adjective is composed of a numeral and a noun, the noun is put in the **singular** number; as,

"A six-*foot* pole." "Two five-*dollar* notes."

21. The ordinal numbers **first, second**, also the words **next, last**, should qualify the cardinal numbers, rather than be qualified by them.

Thus, we are told that we should say, "*The last two letters,*" and "*The first two lines,*" rather than "*Two last letters*" and "*Two first lines.*"

This form may be in accord with the genius of our language, but the forms *two last, two first*, cannot express any absurdity since they are the only forms recognized in French idiom.

"The general rule seems to be that the word to which we wish to call special attention is placed first."—B. F. TWEED, *Grammar for Common Schools*, p. 110.

22. The pronominals **each, either,** and **neither,** as well as the adjective **every,** qualify in a **distributive** sense; that is, the noun to which they relate is always singular in form; as,

Each person, *either* book, *neither* side, *every* man.

(1) **Each** refers to one out of many, and is used with reference to the individuals taken separately and individually; as,

"*Each* in *his* narrow cell for ever laid,
The rude forefathers of the hamlet sleep."—GRAY.

(2) **Every** also refers to one out of many, but it is used with reference to the whole taken collectively; as,

"England expects *every* man to do *his* duty."—NELSON.

23. **Either** and **neither** are used to designate one of two objects; as,

"*Either* you or he must go; *neither* wind nor tide waits."
"Both may excite our wonder, but *neither* is entitled to our respect."—BACON.

(1) **Neither** is the negative of *either*.

(2) Some writers use the word *either* in the sense of *both;* as,

"On *either* side
Is level fen, a prospect wild and wide,
With dike on *either* hand."—CRABBE.

Wicliffe uses the compound *ever-either* for *both*.

(3) **Either** and **neither** are sometimes used in relation to any indefinite number of objects; as,

"Dryden, Pope, and Wordsworth have not scrupled to lay a profane hand upon Chaucer,—a mightier genius than *either*."—GEORGE P. MARSH.

"Neither of the ten was there."

24. The pronominals **such** and **other** qualify in a comparative sense:

(1) Such implies **resemblance**; as,

"*Such* harmony is in immortal souls."—SHAKESPEARE.

(2) Other implies **difference**; as,

"*Other* sheep I have, that are not of this fold."

(3) Such and other are also used as nouns; as,

"Mere strength of understanding would perhaps have made him *such* in any age."—DE QUINCEY.
"The one complained to the *other*."

As a noun other takes a plural others: "It is of all *others* that which most moves us."

Other takes **than** or **besides** as a corresponsive, but not but. The sentence, "*This is none other but the house of God*," should read, "*This is none other than the house of God.*"

When other takes **than**, the things to which it refers are **exclusive** of those mentioned; as, "*He has other views than those you mention;*" that is to say, "*He has views exclusive of those you mention.*"

When other takes **besides**, the things to which it refers are **inclusive** of those mentioned; as, "*He has other views besides those you mention;*" that is to say, "*He has views in addition to those you mention.*"

25. The pronominals **some, any, many, few, all, both, none**, whether as adjectives or as nouns, are to be taken in a **quantitative** sense; that is, they express number or quantity.

Some: "*Some* natural tears they dropt."—MILTON.
"*Some* of his skill he taught me."—SCOTT.

As an adjective, some takes other; as, "*Some time or other*," not, "*Some time or another.*"

Any: "It is not alleged that, to gratify *any* anger or revenge of my own, I have had a share in wronging or oppressing *any* description of men, or *any* one man of *any* description."—BURKE.

Any is **an** = one, with the old English diminutive **ig** = **y**.

Many: "Many speak fair to one's face."

"O thou fond[1] *many*."—SHAKESPEARE.

Few: "*Few, few* shall part where many meet."—CAMPBELL.

All: "*All* the contrivances which we are acquainted with are directed to beneficent purposes."—PALEY.

Both: "He had disobliged *both* the parties whom he wished to reconcile."—MACAULAY.

Both takes **and:** "He is *both* virtuous *and* learned;" not "*both* virtuous *as well as* learned."

None: "*None* knew thee but to love,

None named thee but to praise."

The word **none** is **n-one** = **ne-one** = **not-one**. It is used either with a singular or with a plural verb:

"In at this gate none pass the vigilance here placed."—MILTON.

26. The terms **each other** and **one another** are used to express **reciprocal** relations.

(1) **Each other** is used of two persons only; as, "Brother and sister love *each other*."

(2) **One another** is used of more than two persons; as, "If God so loved us we ought also to love *one another*."

CHAPTER VII.

THE ADVERB.

1. The **adverb** modifies the verb, adjective, or other adverb to which it relates; as,

"*Merrily, merrily*, shall I live *now*

Under the blossom that hangs on the bough."—SHAKESPEARE.

---

[1] The word *fond* here means *foolish*.

2. The adverb is generally placed as follows :

(1) Before the **adjective** which it modifies: "The student is *remarkably* diligent."
(2) Before the **adverb**: "He speaks *very* correctly."
(3) After the **verb** in the simple tenses:

"All hail him victor in both gifts of song,
Who sings so *loudly* and who sings so *long*."—POPE.

(4) After the first **auxiliary** in the compound tenses:

"I will *simply* set down what occurs to me to say on each side of the question."
—NEWMAN.

3. An adverb should not stand between the **infinitive** and its sign **to**; as,

To read *correctly* is a rare accomplishment; not, "to *correctly* read."

4. An adverb should be placed **as near as possible** to the word it limits.

A change in the position of the words **only, merely, solely, chiefly first, at least,** and other adverbs or adverbial phrases, changes the meaning of the sentence.

Only: *He **only** reads French;* he does not speak it. *He reads **only** French;* not German.

Merely: *He is **merely** a student;* that is, nothing more than a student. *He **merely** is a student;* none of the others are students. In an earlier stage of the language the word *merely* was used in the sense of *entirely, purely;* as,

"Ulysses was to force forth his access though *merely* naked."—CHAPMAN.

Solely: *Live that you may do good **solely**;* that is, nothing but good. *Live that you **solely** may do good;* that is, no other person than you.

Chiefly: *He writes poetry **chiefly**;* that is, rather than prose. *He **chiefly** writes poetry;* that is, rather than doing anything else.

First: ***First** he wrote a poem;* that is, before anybody else. *He wrote a poem **first**;* that is, before doing anything else.

At least: *William is at least as good as John;* if not better. *William at least is as good as John;* no matter who else may be.

5. Adverbial **phrases** and **clauses** should also be placed **as near as possible** to the words they limit; as,

"He read *with great care* the book that I gave him;" not, "He read the book that I gave him *with great care.*"

6. An **adverb** should not be used instead of an **adjective** to express **quality**; as,

The rose smells *sweet;* not, the rose smells *sweetly.* The word *sweet* expresses a *quality* of the rose, and not the *manner* of smelling. Hence it should be an *adjective.*

7. An **adjective** should not be used instead of an **adverb** to express time, degree, or manner.

Time: He came *recently;* not *recent.*
Degree: The work goes on *more slowly* than we had expected; not *slower.*
Manner: He ran very *swiftly;* not *swift.* It is *more easily* said than done; not *easier.*

8. Two negatives are not employed in modern English to express a negation.

Do not say, "I *don't* know *nothing* about it." Say, "I *don't* know *anything* about it;" or, "I know *nothing* about it."

The vulgar form of using two negatives is a remnant of old English usage.

Until the middle of the seventeenth century an accumulation of negatives was employed in order to strengthen the negation; as,

"Thou *never* didst them wrong, *nor no* man wrong."—SHAKESPEARE.
"Therefore saith the King Solomon,
Be *not* idle *never more.*"—ROBERT OF BRUNNE.

The adverb **ever** should not be used for **never**; as, "He seldom or *never* writes;" not, "He seldom or *ever* writes."

The words **scarcely, hardly,** and the like, conveying a negative sense, do not admit of another negative; as, "*I can hardly understand;*" not, "*I cannot hardly understand.*" "*He scarcely ever reads;*" not, "*He scarcely never reads.*"

9. A word having a **negative** prefix or suffix, may take a negative in order to express an **affirmative** thought; as,

The case is *not hopeless* = There is hope for the case.
He is *never unprepared* = He is always prepared.

10. The word **not** is sometimes used with **but** to express an affirmative thought in an emphatic manner; as,

"He *cannot but* succeed;" that is, "He is certain to succeed."

11. The adverbs **not** and **no** are corresponsive to **whether** in disjunctive clauses or phrases; as,

"We may choose *whether* we will take the hint or *not*."—SHERIDAN.
"An exclusive line of study has led him, *whether* he will or *no*, to run counter to the principles of religion."—CARDINAL NEWMAN.
"When English grammarians declare **not** in this case to be more correct than **no**, they disregard the historical foundation of the use of **no**."—MAETZNER, *Eng. Gram.*, iii. p. 140. They also ignore the practice of our most classic writers.

12. An **affirmative** adverb is sometimes used **independently**; as,

"*Certainly*, to an enthusiast in behalf of any science whatever, the temptation is great to meet an objection against its dignity and worth."—NEWMAN.

13. The affirmative adverb, when taken absolutely, is employed to express a **whole sentence**; as,

"She is all that we can desire."—*Exactly.*—TROLLOPE.
"Is not this true?"—"*Ay*, sir."—SHAKESPEARE.

14. Negative adverbs either form parts of a sentence, or, when taken absolutely, represent a whole sentence:

(1) **Parts of a sentence:** "Shall I be your play-fellow?" "*No;* I'll none of you."—SHAKESPEARE.
(2) **Represent a whole sentence:** "Think you he will relent?" "*Never.*"

15. The adverb **there** is sometimes used to introduce a sentence without expressing any relation of place. It is then called an expletive; as,

"*There* is a pleasure in the pathless woods,
There is a rapture on the lonely shore;
There is society where none intrudes
By the deep sea, and music in its roar."—BYRON.

The adverb there, when used as an expletive, generally accompanies the verb **be**.

16. After verbs of motion, the adverbs of place **here, there,** and **where,** generally assume either of two forms:

(1) Motion **towards** a place is expressed by the forms **hither, thither, whither;** as,

"For scarce my life with fancy played—
Still *hither thither* idly swayed."—TENNYSON.
"*Whither* I go, you cannot come."—ST. JOHN xiv. 33.

The same motion may also be expressed by the simpler forms **here, there,** and **where;** as,

"Go *where* duty calls you."—COLERIDGE.
"Thou led'st me *here* perchance to kill."—BYRON.
"*There* he led him."—PARNELL.

(2) Motion **from** a place is expressed by the forms **hence, whence,** and **thence;** as,

"*Whence* should I have flesh to give unto all this people."—NUMB. xi. 3.
"The good man went into his garden . . . . to supply another with something he wanted *thence.*"—FIELDING.
"Get thee *hence.*"

Some writers use the forms *from hence, from thence, from whence.* The word *from* is tautological.

"And sailing *from thence,* the following day we came over against Chios."—Acts xx. 15.

CHAPTER VIII.

THE PREPOSITION.

1. A **preposition** governs a noun or pronoun in the objective case, and expresses a relation between its object and some other word, or words, in a sentence.

2. The preposition generally **precedes** its object; as,

"They came to a land *in* which they could recognize nothing."—MACAULAY.

Here *in* expresses the relation between *which* and *land*, and precedes its object *which*.

3. When a preposition is removed from the **pronoun** which it governs, the pronoun should still have the **objective** form; as,

"*Whom* did you play *with;*" not, "*Who* did you play *with.*"

4. In **poetry** the preposition is often made to **follow** its object; as,

"From peak to peak the rattling crags *among.*"—BYRON.

5. In prose the relative **that** usually precedes its governing preposition; as,

Every writer expresses himself most clearly in the language *that* he thinks *in.*

6. In all styles of English, the **object** of a sentence is frequently placed **before** the verb in the sentence, while the preposition comes **after** it; as,

"The *world* he lived in made him and used him."—NEWMAN.

Here, the expression, "*The world he lived in*" = "*The world that he lived in.*" Such forms have been called inelegant and incorrect; but they are in accord with the genius of our language.

7. Prepositions should *correctly* express the relations intended. Thus:

At—in : At is used before the names of houses and villages; in before the names of countries and large cities. In is taken in a broader sense. Thus, we say, "He is *at* a hotel *in* Washington."

Again, one may be an expert *at* surgery, and very expert *in* dressing wounds. Here at is used before the noun and in before the active participle.

In—into : In expresses rest; into expresses motion; as, "He went *into* a carriage and rode *in* it through the park."

In—of: One is disappointed *in* a thing obtained, and *of* a thing not obtained.

From—to : One thing is different *from* another; not "*to* another."

From—after : The artist copies *from* the model and *after* his master.

From—with : William differs *from* James in his whole behavior; Thomas differs *with* John in opinion.

With—to : One agrees *with* a person, and *to* a proposal. One reconciles an act *with* one's conscience, and a person *to* one's opinion.

> We compare one thing *with* another in regard to quality, and one thing *to* another for the sake of illustration.
>
> The farmer unites *with* his neighbor in building a wall; he unites one stone *to* another with mortar.
>
> One person may correspond *with* another; one thing may correspond *to* another.

With—by : By is used of a conscious agent; with, when an instrument is implied. The statue was engraved *by* an artist, and *with* a chisel.

Between—among : Between is used in respect to *two;* among, to *more than two.* A man may divide his property *among* his four sons; not *between* them.

8. A relative clause introduced by **what** may be the object of a preposition ; as,

Place no confidence in *what he tells you*. Here, the clause, *what he tells you*, is the object of the preposition *in*.

9. The preposition **of** expresses various relations :

(1) **Possession**; as, The crown *of* the king.
(2) **Relation of part to the whole**; as, The doors *of* a house.
(3) **An attribute**; as, The sweetness *of* his disposition.
(4) **Reference**; as, The Book *of* Proverbs.
(5) **Quality**; as, A crown *of* gold.
(6) **Apposition**; as, The sin *of* slander; the city *of* Utica.
(7) **Objectivity**; as, The love *of* our neighbor. This does not mean our neighbor's love, but love *for* our neighbor.

10. Where the preposition **for** was formerly used with the infinitive, it is now omitted ; as,

"What went ye out *for to* see ?"—LUKE, vii. 26. Omit the word *for*.

In the older English forms, the expression for to had a meaning of destination and purpose.

CHAPTER IX.

THE CONJUNCTION.

1. A conjunction connects sentences, or the elements of a sentence, between which it is placed :

(1) **Sentences :** "While an author is yet living we estimate his powers by his worst performances, *and* when he is dead we rate them by his best."—JOHNSON.

(2) **Elements of a sentence:** "The dawn on the mountain was misty *and* gray."—SCOTT.

The adjectives *misty, gray*, which are elements of this sentence, are connected by *and*.

2. **Co-ordinate** conjunctions connect words of the same form; for instance, verbs in the same mood and tense, or nouns in the same case; as,

"Up *rose* the sun, *and* up *rose* Emily."—CHAUCER.
Oxygen *and* hydrogen are the elements of water.

3. **Subordinate** conjunctions connect dependent phrases or clauses with the phrases or clauses on which they depend; as,

"Men may come, and men may go,
But I go on for ever."—TENNYSON.

4. **Correlative** conjunctions should always be placed nearest the words to which they refer; as,

"John the Baptist came *neither* eating bread *nor* drinking wine."

(1) Care should be taken to use the proper correlatives; as, "*Neither* one *nor* the other has the least chance of success;" not "*neither* one *or* the other."

(2) In like manner, the words **than** and **as** cannot be used indifferently. Thus, we cannot say correctly, "He is taller, but not *so* old *as* his brother." This sentence should read: "He is taller *than* his brother, but not *so* old."

(3) Do not use **but that** or **but what** for **that**; other-but for other-than; if for whether.

5. Conjunctions sometimes **introduce** a sentence.

The principal conjunctions introducing a sentence, are **and** but, that, if, and though.

Some grammarians object to **and** and **but** as introducing sentences; but the best writers so employ these words.

6. Conjunctions are sometimes **omitted** between words or clauses.

The omission frequently adds life and energy to the sentence. This omission has been admired in the following quotation:

> ——" Through many a dark and dreary vale
> They passed, and many a region dolorous;
> O'er many a frozen, many a fiery Alp,
> *Rocks, caves, lakes, fens, bogs, dens, and shades of death—*
> *A universe of death.*"—MILTON.

7. Conjunctions are sometimes **repeated** between words or clauses.

The repetition renders emphatic the forms before which the conjunction is repeated; as,

> " Seasons return ; but not to me returns
> Day, *or* the sweet approach of even *or* morn,
> *Or* sight of vernal bloom, *or* summer's rose,
> *Or* flock, *or* herds, or human face divine."—MILTON.

8. Sometimes the conjunction **though** or **if** is omitted and the verb placed before the subject ; as,

> "*Were* I a common laugher."—SHAKESPEARE.

This is equivalent to the form, "*If I were* a common laugher."

9. The words **reason** and **because** should not be used together ; as,

"The *reason* I ask you to do this, is *because* you can do it so much better than I."

This sentence should read: "The *reason* I ask you to do this is *that* you can do it so much better than I."

"*Because* Newton was a great mathematician is no *reason* why he should be a great theologian." Read: "*That* Newton was a great mathematician is no *reason* why he should be a great theologian."

10. Conjunctions should not be used instead of prepositions or other parts of speech ; as,

"Try *and* do right," for "Try *to* do right."

11. Other parts of speech should not be used instead of conjunctions; as,

"He reads *like* his teacher does." This should be, "He reads as his teacher does."

"He looks *like* me;" not, "He looks *like* I." Like is a preposition in this sentence.

CHAPTER X.

THE INTERJECTION.

1. The **interjection** has no grammatical relation to the other parts of a sentence; as,

"*O* then began the tempest to my soul."—SHAKESPEARE.

2. In expressing a **wish**, the verb is frequently **omitted** after an interjection; as,

"O for the touch of a vanished hand,
And the sound of a voice that is still."—TENNYSON.

"O for the touch" = "O how I wish for the touch."

3. When the verb is omitted, **that** is frequently found after the interjection; as,

"*O that* the desert were my dwelling-place!"—BYRON.

4. When the emotion is one of **desire** expressed in a phrase or sentence, or when the person or thing is **addressed**, the form of exclamation is **O** ; as,

"Give judgment, *O* king !"

5. When the emotion is **apart** from any proposition or word, and expresses grief, joy, pain, pleasure, and the like, the form of exclamation is **Oh !**; as,

"*Oh !* deep enchanting prelude to repose."

CHAPTER XI.

IDIOM.

1. **Idiom** is a form of expression peculiar to the language.

Many idiomatic forms are apparently irregular, and will not bear analysis according to the ordinary rules of syntax. Still these forms are of general use, and are understood by every person employing them.

2. **English idiom** should not be overlooked, or set aside; nor should its form be changed.

It is customary to discourage the use of English idiom, and even to attempt to change idiomatic expressions to others more regular in structure and more easily accounted for. The practice is of a nature to do great injury to our language.

3. Idiom is an **essential part** of every language. It cannot be dispensed with.

4. Every **good writer** makes frequent use of idiom. All of our literature that is classical abounds in idiomatic forms of expression.

5. Idiom **strengthens** language.

Idiom moulds an expression into the form that most easily takes hold of the popular mind. It gives directness to the expression. Directness of expression aids directness of thought. "If men," says Coleridge, "would only say what they had to say in plain terms, how much more eloquent would they be!"

6. Idiom primarily expresses the **popular mode of thought**.

Idiom is generally a condensed and forcible form of expression. The people are not given to reflection and self-analysis. They think directly, and are content to use, without reference to grammatical propriety, such forms of speech as will express a great deal in a few words.

7. Idiom is not prepared according to preconceived notions; nor can it be imposed upon a language at will.

The scholar and the scientist may invent technical terms to express new mechanical inventions or new scientific discoveries; but they cannot impose upon a language new phrases or new idioms. New phrases and new idioms are rather the outcome of popular thinking.

8. Idiom has **four** distinct sources:

(1) There are idioms which are **remnants** of older forms of expression that had been used not unfrequently in a different sense in other stages of the language. Thus, we still use the expression, "**without let or hindrance,**" even though the word **let** has now a meaning the opposite of the word **hindrance**. But in a previous stage of our language **let** had the same meaning as **hindrance**. They were synonymous. The phrase survived after the primitive meaning of the words had passed, and it now belongs to the idiom of the language.

(2) There are idioms which have grown out of what once might be considered **slang**.

Every living language has a constant growth of expressions that are peculiarly appropriate to the sense they would convey. They condense whole sentences into a few words, and there is no mistaking their meaning. Periodically a new growth of such expressions springs up. This perishes to give place to another. The slang of London or New York twenty years ago is not the slang of those cities to-day. But, out of all the slang phrases that appear, an occasional expression survives and becomes part of the language, and is henceforth to be regarded as idiom. At times it becomes current upon the authority of a great writer; at times it becomes current because of the neatness and accuracy with which it expresses what in more regular form would take many words. Thus does the slang of one generation become the idiom of the next.

Sometimes the process is reversed, and what was once good English idiom, for a time degenerates to slang. Such was the fate of the expression **hardly ever** through its peculiar employment by Mr. Gilbert in the popular comic opera, *Pinafore.*

(3) There are idioms that grow out of **special occasions.** A certain combination of circumstances gives rise to a certain expression; it becomes part of popular speech, and long after the occasion is forgotten the expression remains as an idiom. Thus, the idiom, **in the long run,** grew out of the practice of racing or coursing. Out of the wonderful stories told of the two celebrated peers of Charlemagne, Roland and Oliver, grew the expression, **to give a Roland for an Oliver,** applied to two persons well matched in argument or witticism.

(4) There are idioms that arise from **figurative language,** especially from analogy with other things. Thus, one who makes every effort to attain an object is said to strive **tooth and nail**; one deeply in debt is said to be **over head and ears** in debt.

9. As a rule particular idioms can seldom be traced to their source.

They are deeply-rooted in the language. They begin we know not where; but once they have taken possession of the popular mind they become recognized forms of expression.

10. Many forms of expression, not permitted in good writing, are employed in conversation. They are known as slang, vulgarisms, and colloquialisms.

Slang: Every profession and trade has, besides its recognized technical language, a certain amount of slang expression. The pupils of college and convent have their own peculiar slang. The army, the navy, the law, the club-house, has each its respective slang.

Vulgarisms: Vulgarisms are sometimes identified with slang, but they differ in that they originate exclusively with the rude and illiterate element of society. Many of our purest English idioms are set down as vulgarisms.

Colloquialisms: Colloquialisms are familiar forms of speech always permissible in conversation.

11. Only those idioms that have **survived** the changes of language, should be employed in formal composition.

12. Idioms are of verbs, of nouns, or of prepositional phrases.

13. Verbal idioms are idioms based upon some peculiar construction of the verb, not accounted for by the ordinary rules of syntax. Of these are:

(1) Idioms formed by combining the verb with certain **particles**:

By: "Compositions which *go by* the name of essays."—ADDISON.

"Hath God a name *to swear by?*" ... "Hath God a name *to curse by?*" ... "And hath God no name *to pray by?*"—DONNE.

For: "What we earnestly desire we earnestly *toil for.*"—GEORGE W. CURTIS.

"I could perceive he was out of humor at being *sent for*."—GOLDSMITH.

"Knowledge must be *worked for, studied for, thought for;* and more than all *it must be prayed for.*"—ARNOLD, *of Rugby.*

In, on, upon: "Houses are made *to live in* and not *to look on.*"— BACON.

"I saw her just above the horizon, decorating and cheering the elevated sphere she just began *to move in.*"—BURKE.

"The way in which the discoveries of Adam Smith *fitted in* with the great mechanical inventions that were made at the same time is too obvious to need *dwelling upon.*"—JOHN MORLEY.

At, of: "He was a most satisfactory object, from the thorough healthfulness and wholesomeness of his system, and his capacity, at that extreme age, to enjoy all, or nearly all, the delights which he had ever *aimed at*, or *conceived of.*"—HAWTHORNE.

"It is not by logic, certainly not by logic alone, that the faculty *I speak of* is acquired."—CARDINAL NEWMAN.

About: "I am far from denying that some among them know what they *are talking about.*"—CARDINAL NEWMAN.

With: "I was no more than a stripling boy, noting little as boys do, except for their present purpose, and even that soon *done with.*"— BLACKMORE.

Other constructions are frequently preferred to those in which the particle ends a sentence; but they are not always English, whereas these forms are good and forcible English. "The false fastidiousness," says Henry Reed, "which shuns a short particle at the end of a sentence, is fatal often to a force which belongs to the language in its primal character. The superiority of the idioms I am referring to, could be proved beyond question by examples of the best writing in all the eras of the language."

(2) Idioms formed by the verb **had**:

Had as lief: "I *had as lief* not be as live to be
    In awe of such a thing as I myself."—SHAKESPEARE.

Had rather: "I *had much rather* be myself the slave,
    And wear the bonds, than fasten them on him."
         —COWPER.

Had better: "Some things the State *had better* leave alone; others it *had better* not."—MATTHEW ARNOLD.

"But if I like the gay equipage so well as to go out of my road, I *had better* have gone afoot."—EMERSON.

(3) Idioms formed by the verb **get**:

Get on: "If I *get on* with this story."—BLACKMORE.

Get up: "As the school-boy *gets up* his Euclid."—CARDINAL NEWMAN.

"Or because he has been *getting up* a little architecture on the road from Florence."—LOWELL.

Get rid of: "*To get rid of* fools and scoundrels."—POPE.

Get by heart: "It being harder with him *to get* one sermon *by heart* than to pen twenty."—FELL.

(4) Idioms formed by the verb **do**:

Do: "Now, this will never *do*."—JEFFREY.

Do do: How *do you do?*

The auxiliary *do* is of different origin from the principal verb **do**. The latter is from the old English *dugan* = *to avail*.

(5) Idioms formed by the verb **matter**:

"It *matters* not at what college it may be celebrated."—GEORGE WM. CURTIS.

14. Idioms of nouns are expressions depending upon a peculiar sense of the nouns used. Among these may be mentioned:

(1) Idioms formed by the noun **matter**:

"What is the *matter*?"

"In the *matter* of payment."

"There are indeed persons who prefer a different view of the *matter*."—CARDINAL NEWMAN.

(2) Idioms formed by the following nouns expressive of emphatic negation:

Iota: "They never depart *one iota* from the authentic formulas of tyranny and usurpation."—BURKE.

Jot: "Neither will they bate *one jot* of ceremony."—SHAKESPEARE.
"I argue not
Against Heaven's hand or will, nor *bate a jot*
Of heart or hope, but still bear up, and steer
Right onwards."—MILTON.

Tittle: "*Every tittle* of this prophecy is most exactly fulfilled."—SOUTH.
"'Till heaven and earth pass, *one jot or one tittle* shall not pass from the law till all be fulfilled.—MATT. v. 18.

Whit: "I am *no whit* sorry."—DODSLEY'S OLD PLAYS, ii. 84.
"*A whit* more probable."—HUME.
"So shall I *no whit* be behind."—SHAKESPEARE.

Bit: "Your case is *not a bit* better than it was seven years ago."—ARBUTHNOT.

15. Idioms formed by **prepositional phrases** are peculiar expressions the popular sense of which is distinct from the literal sense. The following are of this class:

To the quick: "I am struck *to the quick*."—SHAKESPEARE.
"A tory *to the quick*."—TENNYSON.

On all hands: "When we are speaking of what is obvious and allowed *on all hands*."—CARDINAL NEWMAN.

For the nonce: "We do name thee, however, *for the nonce*."—CARLYLE.

In point: "One more remark is *in point*."—NEWMAN.

Of late: "Such *of late* Columbus found the American."—MILTON.
"Various valuable collections of ancient ballad-poetry have appeared *of late years*."—SCOTT.

Of mine: "This heart *of mine*." There is here question of only one heart, and yet, taking the phrase literally, it would seem to imply that there was more than one.

Of it: "A little flower, apprehended in the very plain and leafy fact *of it*."—RUSKIN.
"I think to make a long sleep *of it*."—COLERIDGE.

To it: "Poor Christian was hard put *to it*."—BUNYAN.

At all: "If .... he condescends to reflect, whether it has any meaning *at all*."—CARDINAL NEWMAN.

The following phrases are idiomatic: *At least; at the least; at first; at last; at all events; at present; at random; by far; in vain; for good and all; by and by; by the way; by the by; little by little; step by step; through and through; out and out; heart and soul; to all intents and purposes; root and branch; neck and crop; head and shoulders; part and parcel.*

16. The preposition **of** is used idiomatically for **by**; as,

"This dreaded sight twice seen *of* us."—SHAKESPEARE.
"He is loved *of* the distracted multitude."—IBID.
"Well loved *of* me."—TENNYSON.
"Shall I be tempted *of* the devil thus?"—SHAKESPEARE.
"And was driven *of* the devil into the wilderness."—LUKE viii. 29.

17. The expletives **there is, it is,** and the like, are idiomatic.

"*There came* to the beach a poor exile of Erin."—CAMPBELL.
"*It is I*, Hamlet the Dane."—SHAKESPEARE.

18. The forms **methinks, meseems,** are idiomatic.

"*Methought* my request was heard."—LAMB.
"*Methought* that I had broken from the tower."—SHAKESPEARE.
"I passed, *methought*, the melancholy flood."—IBID.
"*Methinks* he seems no better than a girl."—TENNYSON.

19. There are certain idiomatic forms of speech which are used to emphasize **equality of action** or **purpose.** Such are:

Arm in arm: "When *arm in arm* we went along."—TENNYSON.
Cheek by jowl: "Here was a doctor who never had a patient, *cheek by jowl* with an attorney who never had a client."—THACKERAY.

Day by day: "As she spake to Joseph *day by day*."—GEN. xxxix. 10.

Brow to brow:

"And frowning *brow to brow*, ourselves will hear
Th' accuser and th' accused freely speak."—SHAKESPEARE.

Hand in hand:

"They, *hand in hand*, with wandering steps, and slow,
Through Eden took their solitary way."—MILTON.

Of like import are the forms *shoulder to shoulder* and *face to face*.

PART IV.
PROSODY.

CHAPTER I.

DEFINITIONS.

1. **Prosody** treats of the rhythm and harmony of words in prose and verse.

Its object is to determine the mechanical construction of lines in **poetry** and of sentences in **higher prose**.

2. **Prose** is written discourse in which the ordinary arrangement of words is followed.

3. The chief **object** of prose is to convey in a clear and forcible manner the author's meaning.

4. Prose in its **highest form** may also please and move.

5. **Verse** is discourse consisting of lines of given length written in language metrically arranged. Its chief object is to please and to move.

"The term **verse** denotes a set of specially related sounds."— SYDNEY LANIER.

6. Two consecutive verses rhyming are called a **couplet**; as,

"Nor God alone in the still calm we find,
He mounts the storm, and walks upon the wind."—POPE.

7. Three consecutive verses rhyming are called a **triplet**; as,

" To search thro' all I felt or saw,
The springs of life, the depths of awe,
And reach the law within the law."—TENNYSON.

8. A **stanza** is a number of lines forming a division of a poem.

The form of the stanza and the character of the metre depend upon the nature of the subject and the taste of the writer. Every poetical subject has a musical swing which is natural to it and this musical swing determines the form the poem should take. A lyrical subject should not be treated in the heroic couplet, nor should a narrative poem be put in a lyrical dress. The true poet always suits the form to the subject.

9. A stanza usually consists of four, six, seven, eight, nine, or fourteen lines :

(1) A four-lined stanza, or a quatrain:

" One by one the sands are flowing,
One by one the moments fall:
Some are coming, some are going;
Do not strive to grasp them all."
—ADELAIDE PROCTER.

(2) A six-lined stanza, or a sestett:

" 'Tis not to cry God mercy, or to sit
And droop, or to confess that thou hast failed;
'Tis to bewail the sins thou didst commit,
And not commit those sins thou hast bewailed.
He that bewails and not forsakes them, too,
Confesses rather what he means to do."—QUARLES.

(3) A seven-lined stanza, called the rhythm-royal:

"To see sad sights moves more than hear them told;
  For then the eye interprets to the ear
The heavy motion that it doth behold,
  When every part a part of woe doth bear;
'Tis but a part of sorrow that we hear:
    Deep sounds make lesser noise than shallow fords,
    And sorrow ebbs, being blown with wind of words."
—SHAKESPEARE.

(4) An eight-lined stanza, known as the *ottava rima*:

" Then rose from sea to sky the wild farewell,—
    Then shrieked the timid, and stood still the brave,—
  Then some leaped overboard, with dreadful yell,
    As eager to anticipate their grave;
  And the sea yawned round her like a hell,
    And down she sucked with her the whirling wave,
  Like one who grapples with his enemy,
  And strives to strangle him before he die."—BYRON.

(5) A nine-lined stanza, known as the Spenserian stanza:

" Last noon beheld them full of lusty life,
    Last eve in Beauty's circle proudly gay,
  The midnight brought the signal sound of strife,
    The morn the marshalling in arms,—the day
  Battle's magnificently-stern array!
    The thunder-clouds close o'er it, which when rent,
  The earth is covered thick with other clay,
    Which her own clay shall cover, heap'd and pent,
    Rider and horse—friend, foe—in one red burial blent!"
—BYRON.

(6) The stanza of fourteen lines is called a sonnet. The sonnet is a complete poem. The sonnet is variously constructed. Its normal structure is as follows:

DEFINITIONS.

```
                   MAJOR QUATRAIN.
          ┌      ─────────── 1
          │      ─────────── 2
          │      ─────────── 2
          │      ─────────── 1
 OCTAVE. ─┤       MINOR QUATRAIN.
          │      ─────────── 1
          │      ─────────── 2
          │      ─────────── 2
          └      ─────────── 1

          ┌      ─────────── 3
          │      ─────────── 4
          │      ─────────── 3
 SESTETT.─┤      ─────────── 4
          │      ─────────── 5
          └      ─────────── 5
```

"Count each affliction, whether light or grave,
    God's messenger sent down to thee: do thou
    With courtesy receive him; rise and bow,
And ere his shadow pass thy threshold, crave
Permission first his heavenly feet to lave;
    Then lay before him all thou hast: allow
    No cloud of passion to usurp thy brow,
Or mar thy hospitality; no wave
Of mortal tumult to obliterate
    The soul's marmoreal calmness; grief should be
Like joy, majestic, equable, sedate,
    Confirming, cleansing, raising, making free;
Strong to consume small trouble, to command
Great thoughts, grave thoughts, thoughts lasting to the end."
                              —AUBREY DE VERE.

The first four lines of the **octave** are called the **major quatrain**; the second four, the **minor quatrain**; the last six, the **sestett**. The sestett generally expresses the point and purpose of the sonnet.

10. The **sense** of sentences in verse or prose is generally determined by punctuation.

CHAPTER II.

PUNCTUATION.

1. **Punctuation** is the art of dividing a sentence into its component parts by certain marks, or points.

2. The principal **marks of punctuation** are:

<table>
<tr><td>The period (.)</td><td>The exclamation (!)</td></tr>
<tr><td>The colon (:)</td><td>The dash (—)</td></tr>
<tr><td>The semicolon (;)</td><td>The hyphen (-)</td></tr>
<tr><td>The comma (,)</td><td>The parentheses ( )</td></tr>
<tr><td>The interrogation (?)</td><td>The brackets [ ]</td></tr>
</table>

The quotation points (" ")

I.—THE PERIOD.

3. The **period** is placed at the end of every complete sentence; as,

"Above all things our Blessed Lord is beautiful in His Mother. If we love Him we must love her. We must know her in order to know Him."—FABER.

4. The period is employed to mark **abbreviations**; as,

"A. D., for *Anno Domini*";—"*pro tem.*, for *pro tempore*";— "*ult.*, for *ultimo*";—"*inst.*, for *instanter*, instant";—"*Dr.*, for *Doctor* or *debtor.*"

5. The period, in this case, merely indicating the abbreviation, does not take the place of other marks; as,

"Baltimore, Md., Jan., 1889."

6. The period is usually placed after **Roman numerals**; as,

"Ps. lxv., 2."—"*Childe Harold*, III., xxviii."—"Henry of Richmond, under the name of Henry VII., began the Tudor dynasty."

7. Names of persons, **familiarly shortened**, do not require the period; as,

"Phil, Ned, and Tom are the names of his brothers."

8. The period is put after **headings** and **indications**; as,

"Church and State."—"Composition."—"For Sale."

It is now customary to print titles, page-headings and chapters of books without any punctuation mark.

II.—THE COLON.

9. The **colon** is used to introduce a direct quotation when referred to by the words *thus, following, as follows, this, these,* and the like; as,

Shakespeare's words are these:
"Let all the ends thou aim'st at be thy country's,
Thy God's, and truth's."—HENRY VIII., iii., 2.

10. The colon is placed after a clause **complete** in itself, but which is followed by some additional remarks or illustrations, especially if no conjunction is used; as,

"Study to acquire a habit of thinking: no study is more important."

"Life is a burden: bear it;
Life is a duty: dare it;
Life is a thorn-crown: wear it."
—ABRAM J. RYAN.

11. The colon is introduced after a **general statement** followed by two or more specific statements; as,

"Three elements enter into history: person, place, and time."

12. The colon is placed between the **greater divisions** of a sentence, when minor subdivisions are separated by semicolons; as,

"We perceive the shadow to have moved along the dial, but we did not see it moving; we observe that the grass has grown, though it was impossible to see it grow: so the advances we make in knowledge, consisting of minute and gradual steps, are perceivable only after intervals of time."

III.—THE SEMICOLON.

13. The **semicolon** is used between the similar parts of a sentence, when those parts are already subdivided by the comma; as,

"Mirth should be the embroidery of conversation, not the web; and wit the ornament of the mind, not the furniture."

14. The semicolon is placed before the clause in a sentence giving a **reason**; as,

"Economy is no disgrace; for it is better to live on a little than to outlive a great deal."

15. The semicolon is placed between clauses that are **loosely connected**; as,

"Be a man; do' your duty; let people talk."

16. The semicolon is placed after the words *Yes* and *No*, when they **begin** a sentence; as,

"Yes; we have come to stay."

17. The semicolon is placed before the words *as, namely, viz., that is,* when they **introduce** an example or a specification of particulars; as,

"There are six races of men; namely, the Caucasian, the Mongolian, the Malayan, the Australian, the American, and the Ethiopian."

IV.—THE COMMA.

18. The **comma** is used to separate the similar parts of a proposition : subjects, predicates, objects, attributes, adjuncts, phrases :

1. **Subjects.**—"Riches, honors, and pleasures are fleeting."
2. **Predicates.**—"Religion purifies, fortifies, and tranquilizes the mind."
3. **Objects.**—"Learn patience, calmness, self-command, disinterestedness."
4. **Attributes.**—"Alfred the Great was brave, pious, and patriotic."
5. **Adjuncts.**—"The work was neither dexterously, quickly, nor well done."
6. **Phrases.**—"To be wise in our own eyes, to be wise in the opinion of the world, and to be wise in the sight of our Creator, are three things so very different as rarely to coincide."

19. When the subject of a sentence consists of several terms, and the last two are not joined by a conjunction, a comma is placed **before** the verb, in order that it may not seem to relate to the last subject only ; as,

"English, French, German, Italian, are the languages most extensively used in Europe."

20. When words are joined **in pairs** by conjunctions, the pairs should be separated by the comma ; as,

"The rich *and* the poor, the weak *and* the strong, have one common Father."—"The dying man cares not for pomp *or* luxury, palace *or* estate, silver *or* gold."

21. The name of a person or thing **addressed** is separated from the rest of the sentence by the comma ; as,

"My son, give me thy heart."

22. The comma is usually inserted in place of a finite verb that is understood ; as,

"Reading maketh a full man; conference, a ready man; and writing, an exact man."—BACON.

23. A clause, a phrase, or a word, that **breaks** the connection of the sentence, and that can be omitted without altering the meaning, must be separated from the rest of the sentence by the comma ; as,

"Industry, *which is a law of nature*, is a source of happiness."—"Man, *created in the image of God*, has an immortal soul."—"Napoleon, *unquestionably*, was a man of genius."—"The butterfly, *child of the summer*, flutters in the sun."

24. A **restrictive** clause, phrase, or word, immediately following the word that it restricts, should not be preceded by the comma ; as,

"The things *that are seen*, are temporal; but the things *that are not seen*, are eternal."—"The chief misfortunes that befall us in life, may be traced to our own vices and follies."

25. When part of a sentence is **transposed**, it is usually separated from the rest of the sentence by the comma ; as,

"*To those who labor*, sleep is doubly pleasant."—"*Of all our senses*, sight is the most important."

26. A **short quotation**, or one introduced by the verbs *say, reply, cry*, is generally separated from the rest of the sentence by the comma ; as,

"There is much in the proverb, *No pains, no gains*."—"If wishes were horses," says the proverb, "beggars might ride."

27. The comma is generally used between the **simple** members of compound sentences, when they are very short; as,

"Man proposes, but God disposes."

" We carved not a line, and we raised not a stone,
But we left him alone with his glory."—C. WOLFE.

The comma is used after the adverbs *nay, indeed, finally, at least, however, lastly,* and the like ; as,

"Lastly, he was driven from the city."

V.—THE INTERROGATION AND EXCLAMATION POINTS.

28. The **point of interrogation** is used after every interrogative sentence, clause, or word; as,

" When shall we three meet again,
In thunder, lightning, or in rain ?"—SHAKESPEARE.

29. The **exclamation** is placed after every exclamatory sentence, clause, or word; as,

" Up, guards, and at 'em!"

" And He that doth the ravens feed,
Yea, providently caters for the sparrow,
Be comfort to my age!"

The point of exclamation should be sparingly used. It is out of place in all prose narratives and plain statements.

VI.—DASH, HYPHEN, PARENTHESIS, BRACKETS, QUOTATION POINTS.

30. The **dash** is used to mark a sudden interruption or transition; as,

" Here lies the great—false marble where ?
Nothing but sordid dust lies here."—YOUNG.

"'My pretty boy,' said he, 'has your father a grindstone?'—'Yes, sir,' said I.—'You are a fine little fellow,' said he, 'will you let me grind an ax on it?'"—FRANKLIN.

31. The **dash** is also used:

1. To set off a parenthetical expression; as,

> "Lord Marmion returned—well was his need—
> And dashed the rowels in his steed."—SCOTT.

2. Before a repetition made for effect or with a view of further explanation; as, "Never is virtue left without sympathy—a sympathy dearer and tenderer for the misfortune that has tried it and proved its fidelity."

3. To mark a more considerable pause than the structure of the sentence would seem to require; as, "Now they part—to meet no more."

4. To mark an omission or an unfinished statement; as, "K—g for king."—"In the village of C——."—"He is active, but—."

5. Between a title and the subject-matter and between the subject-matter and the author or work; as,

> "There's a wideness in God's mercy
> Like the wideness of the sea."—FABER.

32. The **hyphen** is used:

1. At the end of a line when part of a word is transferred to the next line.

2. To connect compound words; as,

> "Then must the *pennant-bearer* slacken sail."—BYRON.

33. The **parenthesis** is used to enclose a remark, a quotation, or a date, that may be omitted without breaking the construction or injuring the sense of the sentence; as,

> "I have seen charity (if charity it may be called) insult with an air of pity."
>
> "Know, then, this truth (enough for man to know):
> Virtue alone is happiness below."—POPE.

34. The **brackets** are used to enclose what one person puts into the writings of another, as a correction, an explanation, or an omission; as,

> "He [Brownson] wielded a vigorous pen in defence of the Church." --"He [the speaker] thought otherwise."—"The letter is dated May 12th, [1890]."

35. The **quotation points** are used to distinguish words that are repeated **literally** from their author; as,

> When Fenelon's library was on fire, "*God be praised*," said he, "*that it is not the dwelling of a poor man.*"
>
> Quotation points are also used when the **exact words** of a book are transcribed; as Cobbett says: "The dash is a cover for ignorance as to the use of points."

36. A quotation within a quotation or an example, is usually marked with **single** points; as,

> "Patrick Henry said: 'It is natural for man to indulge the illusions of hope.'"

37. Other **marks** are the following:

1. The **index** [☞] is occasionally used to point out a passage that is strongly emphasized.

2. Marks of **reference** are used to direct attention to foot notes. They are:

The asterisk [*]	The section [§]
The dagger [†]	The parallels [‖]
The double-dagger [‡]	The paragraph [¶]

In books recently printed these marks of reference are frequently supplanted by the simpler method of figures.

A line of **stars** [* * *] or **dots** [· · ·] indicates that part of a quotation is omitted.

38. Contractions.—Certain universally recognized contractions are to be met with in books. The following are of most frequent application:

1. **e. g.** for *exempli gratia* = for example's sake, to illustrate.
2. **i. e.** for *id est* = that is to say, to explain.
3. **viz.** for *videlicet* = to wit, to give an instance, or to enumerate the parts before referred to generally.
4. **&c.** for *et cetera* = and the rest, and so on, and so forth. This is used when it would be considered waste of time to enumerate further or quote at greater length.
5. A for *insert*. It is called a caret. Cobbett calls it the blundermark.
6. The **apostrophe** ['] is not only used before the possessive s, but also to mark contractions or elisions. This latter use is principally confined to poetry and to dialect in novels.

CHAPTER III.

VERSIFICATION.

1. **Versification** is the art of constructing verse.
2. All verse is written with or without rhyme.
3. **Rhyme** is a correspondence of sound in the last syllables of two or more lines succeeding each other immediately or at no great distance; as,

> " How sleep the brave who sink to *rest*,
> By all their country's wishes *blest* /"..Collins.

4. Rhymes are:

>Single; as, *wall, fall*.
>Double; as, *weary, dreary*.
>Triple; as, *readily, steadily*.

VERSIFICATION.

5. Rhymes are perfect or allowable.

6. A **perfect** rhyme is subject to the following conditions:

   (1) The **vowel sounds** should be exactly the **same**; as, *whole, soul.*

   (2) The **rhyming syllables** should be **accented**; as, *appears, her tears.*

   (3) The **consonants** preceding the vowel sounds should be different; as,

      "Honor and shame from no condition *rise*,
      Act well your part, there all the honor *lies*."—POPE.

7. An **allowable** rhyme is one in which the sounds are nearly alike; as,

   "Those hearts of ours—how warm! how *warm!*
   Like the sun's bright rays, like the summer's *charm.*"
                              —ABRAM J. RYAN.

8. **Alliteration** is the beginning of two or more words with the same letter; as,

   "But see! 'mid the *fast-flashing* lightnings of war,
   What steed to the desert *flies frantic and far?*"—CAMPBELL.

Old English metre was based to a great extent upon alliteration.

9. Verses are classified according to the kind and the number of feet they contain.

10. A **foot** is the metrical unit by which a line is measured. It is composed of two or three syllables, one of which is generally accented.

11. The **kind** of feet generally used in English verse are:

   (1) The **iambus**: a short syllable and a long ($\smile\ -$), as in *awake.*
   (2) The **trochee**: a long syllable and a short ($-\ \smile$), as in *hopeless.*

(3) The **anapest**: two short syllables and a long (⌣ ⌣ —), as in *entertain*.

(4) The **dactyl**: one long syllable and two short (— ⌣⌣), as in *loneliness*.

12. The **number** of feet varies from one to seven.

   (1) A line of one foot is called a **monometer**.
   (2) A line of two feet is called a **dimeter**.
   (3) A line of three feet is called a **trimeter**.
   (4) A line of four feet is called a **tetrameter**.
   (5) A line of five feet is called a **pentameter**.
   (6) A line of six feet is called a **hexameter**.
   (7) A line of seven feet is called a **heptameter**.

13. Verses are deficient, complete, or redundant.

   (1) A verse in which a syllable is wanting, is called **catalectic**.
   (2) A verse in which the measure is complete, is called **acatalectic**.
   (3) A verse in which there is a syllable too much, is called **hypermetrical**.

14. Iambic verse is commonly used in long English poems. It is that metre with which the ear is most familiar. It may be divided as follows:

Monometer: How bright
            The light.

Dimeter: "Awake and sing,
          And be all wing!"—CRASHAW.

Trimeter: "Blow, blow, thou winter wind
          Thou art not so unkind
              As man's ingratitude."—SHAKESPEARE.

Tetrameter:
$$\smile\ -\ |\smile\ -\ |\smile\ -\ |\smile\ -$$
"The smiles of joy, the tears of woe,
Deceitful shine, deceitful flow."—MOORE.

Tennyson's *In Memoriam*, portions of Moore's *Lalla Rookh*, and most of Scott's poetry are written in this metre. The *tetrameter* alternating with the *trimeter* forms the most common measure of lyric poetry; as,

$$\smile\ -\ |\smile\ -\ |\smile\ -\ |\smile\ -$$
$$\smile\ -\ |\smile\ -\ |\smile\ -$$

"With gentle swiftness lead me on,
Dear God! to see Thy face;
And meanwhile in my narrow heart
Oh make Thyself more space!"—FABER.

Pentameter; as,

$$\smile\ -\ |\smile\ -\ |\smile\ -\ |\smile\ -\ |\smile\ -$$

"True ease in writing comes from art, not chance,
As those move easiest who have learned to dance."—POPE.

Iambic pentameter is called the heroic metre. In its rhymed form it is the metre in which Chaucer and Dryden and Pope wrote a great deal of their poetry. Pope perfected the iambic pentameter couplet. In its unrhymed form, it is the usual metre of blank verse. Milton, Wordsworth, Tennyson, and Browning have employed it with great power.

Hexameter:

$$\smile\ -\ |\smile\ -\ |\smile\ -\ |\smile\ -\ |\smile\ -\ |\smile\ -$$

"That like a wounded snake drags its slow length along."—POPE.
This *iambic hexameter* is called the Alexandrine measure.

Heptameter:

$$\smile\ -\ |\smile\ -\ |\smile\ -\ |\smile\ -\ |\smile\ -\ |\smile\ -\ |\smile\ -$$

"For right is right, since God is God; and right the day must win;
To doubt would be disloyalty, to falter would be sin."—FABER.

This metre is generally divided up into four lines, two being *iambic tetrameters* and two *iambic trimeters* alternately. Stanzas so formed are known as *common metre* stanzas.

15. **Trochaic verse** gives a rapid movement to the line. It may be divided as follows:

Monometer: "Tūrnĭng,
   Bŭrning."—ADDISON,—*Rosamond.*

Dimeter: "Wīshĕs | rīsĭng!
   Thoughts surprising!"—IBID.

Trimeter: — ◡ | — ◡ | — ◡
"Go where glory waits thee,
   But while fame elates thee
   Oh! still remember me."—MOORE.

The last line is in *iambic trimeter* measure.

Tetrameter: — ◡ | — ◡ | — ◡ | — ◡
   "Farewell hours that late did measure
   Sunshine days of joy and pleasure."—BURNS.

The tetrameter is the trochaic form most employed in English Longfellow's *Hiawatha* is in this metre.

Pentameter: — ◡ | — ◡ | — ◡ | — ◡ | —
   "Then methought I heard a hollow sound
   Gath'ring up from all the lower ground."
                                        —TENNYSON.

Hexameter: — ◡ | — ◡ | — ◡ | — ◡ | — ◡ | — ◡ |
   "Holy, holy, holy! all the Saints adore thee."
                                        —HEBER.

Heptameter:

— ◡ | — ◡ | — ◡ | — ◡ | — ◡ | — ◡ | — ◡ | —
"In the spring a fuller crimson comes upon the robin's breast,
In the spring the wanton lapwing gets himself another crest."
                                        —TENNYSON.

These lines are *heptameter hypermeter*.

Octometer:

— ◡ | — ◡ | — ◡ | — ◡ | — ◡ | — ◡ | — ◡ | — ◡ |
"Once upon a midnight dreary, while I pondered weak and weary,
   Over many a quaint and curious volume of forgotten lore."—POE.

VERSIFICATION.

16. In anapestic verse the accent is placed upon every third syllable. It may be divided as follows:

Monometer: ⏑ ⏑ —
      Then again
      Came the rain.

Dimeter: ⏑ ⏑ — | ⏑ ⏑ — | —
    "He is gone on the mountain,
      He is lost to the forest,
      Like a summer-dried fountain
        When our need was the sorest."—Scott.

These lines are hypermetrical.

Trimeter: ⏑ ⏑ — | ⏑ ⏑ — | ⏑ ⏑ —
    "Not a pine in my grove is there seen,
      But with tendrils of woodbine is bound;
      Not a beech's more beautiful green,
      But a sweet briar twines it around."—Shenstone.

Tetrameter: ⏑ ⏑ —|⏑ ⏑ —| ⏑ ⏑ —|⏑ ⏑ —|
    "'Tis the sunset of life gives me mystical lore
      And coming events cast their shadows before."
                      —Campbell.

17. In dactylic verse the accent is placed upon the first syllable, the fourth, and so on. It is seldom found unmixed with other meters.

Monometer: — ⏑ ⏑
      Fearfully
      Tearfully.

Dimeter: — ⏑ ⏑ | — ⏑ ⏑ |
    "Touch her not scornfully,
      Think of her mournfully,
      Gently and humanly."—Hood.

Trimeter: — ⏑ ⏑ | — ⏑ ⏑ | — ⏑ ⏑ | —
    "Merrily, merrily, shall I live now."

This line is hypermetrical.

Tetrameter: − ᴗ ᴗ | − ᴗ ᴗ | − ᴗ ᴗ | − ᴗ ᴗ ;

"Sorely thy little one drags by thee barefooted;
Cold is the baby that hangs at thy bending back,
Meagre and livid and screaming for misery."

—SOUTHEY.

Hexameter:

− ᴗ ᴗ | − ᴗ ᴗ | − ᴗ ᴗ | − ᴗ ᴗ | − ᴗ ᴗ | − ᴗ

"This is the forest primeval: but where are the hearts that beneath it
Leap'd like the roe, when he hears in the woodland the voice of the huntsman?
Where is the thatched-roofed village, the home of Acadian farmers?"

—LONGFELLOW.

The **dactylic hexameter** was the heroic verse of Greek and Latin poetry. Both Homer and Virgil made use of it. In the ancient classical poetry a spondee, or two long syllables, could take the place of a dactyl, except in the fifth foot, which was usually a dactyl. The sixth foot was always a spondee.

18. There are four other species of feet, occasionally to be found in verses. They are called **secondary** feet:

The **spondee**: two long syllables, − −.
The **pyrrhic**: two short syllables, ᴗ ᴗ.
The **amphibrach**: a short, a long, and a short syllable, ᴗ − ᴗ.
The **tribrach**: three short syllables, ᴗ ᴗ ᴗ.

19. Verses are rarely constructed upon any one species of measure exclusively. They are generally **mixed**.

20. In addition to the usual pauses marked by the punctuation, there are also the final and the cæsural pause.

(1) The **final pause** is a slight suspension of the voice at the end of each line, even when the grammatical sense does not require it.

(2) The **cæsural pause** is a slight suspension of the voice within the line, and generally about the middle of it. This

pause is preceded by a syllable more strongly accented than any other in the verse; as,

"But look | the morn in russet mantle clad."—SHAKESPEARE.

"The quality of mercy | is not strained."—IBID.

21. The rhythm of a line depends mainly on the **position of the cæsural pause.**

22. Verse without rhyme is called **blank verse**; as,

"O many are the poets that are sown
By nature, men endowed with highest gifts,
The vision and the faculty divine;
Yet wanting the accomplishment of verse,
Which, in the docile season of their youth,
It was denied them to acquire, through lack
Of culture, and the inspiring aid of books."—WORDSWORTH.

23. Blank verse is generally written in **iambic pentameter** measure.

24. Blank verse is divided into weak endings and strong endings.

25. Weak endings are those in which the line ends in an unaccented syllable; as,

"On their sustaining garments not a *blemish.*"—THE TEMPEST, Act I. Scene 2.

26. Strong endings are those in which the metre is full and the line ends in an accented syllable; as,

"Methinks thou art more honest now than wise."—TIMON OF ATHENS, Act iv. Scene 1.

27. The **early** plays of Shakespeare abound in rhyming couplets and strong endings; his **later** plays have few rhymes and abound in **weak** endings.

Thus, in *Love's Labor's Lost,* one of his earliest plays, there are one thousand rhyming lines. As he advanced in his art he dropped the practice of rhyming. In his latter plays there are few or none. For instance, *A Winter's Tale* is among his latest plays, and has not a single rhyming couplet. Again, as the employment of rhyme diminished, the use of double or weak endings increased. In *Love's Labor's Lost* there are nine lines with weak endings, while in *A Winter's Tale* there are six hundred and thirty-nine lines.

This test helps to determine the genuineness and to approximate the order of priority of Shakespeare's plays.

CHAPTER IV.

RHYTHM IN PROSE.

1. **Rhythm** is a recurrence of stress upon certain words at intervals more or less regular.

Rhythm is a series of **sounds** and **silences** with primary reference to their **duration.**

2. Rhythm belongs both to **prose** and to **verse.**

Every series of English words, both in prose and verse, is primarily **rhythmical.**

3. The rhythm of **verse** depends upon **accent** and **pause.**

Rhythm in verse is frequently identified with accent; but it differs from accent. Rhythm belongs to words alone; accent belongs to words and syllables. Rhythm includes accent. There may be many accents where only a single rhythmic word exists. Thus in the line—

"The vision and the faculty divine"—

there are five accents and only two rhythmic words—*vision* and *faculty.*

4. The rhythm of **prose** is determined by **emphasis** and **pause**.

When the pauses occur at intervals equally apart, or increasing or diminishing according to a regular scale, and when the emphatic words follow in the same order of regularity, the prose is said to be rhythmic. The rhythm of prose is less definite and more subtle than the rhythm of verse. But it is none the less a reality. "Prose," says Sydney Lanier, "has its rhythms, its tones, and its tone-colors, like verse; and while the extreme forms of prose and verse are sufficiently unlike each other, there are such near grades of intermediate forms that they may be said to run into each other, and any line claiming to be distinctive must necessarily be more or less arbitrary."[1]

5. Prose rhythm as an art was cultivated in early stages of our language.

It abounds in the sermons and homilies of the tenth and eleventh centuries. In the *Anglo-Saxon Chronicle* we find rhyming prose (A. D. 1036).

In the fourteenth century prose rhythm received great attention. It was then called **cadence**. Thus Chaucer makes the distinction between *rhyme* and *cadence*:

> "To maken[2] books, songs, and ditties
> In ryme, *or else in cadence*,
> As those best can."[3]—House of Fame.

The prose in his *Canterbury Tales* is written in this rhythmic manner.

6. Prose works intended to be read aloud were **rhythmically** arranged.

The Brethren of the Common Life were experts in transcribing books with rhythmic notation.

Thomas à Kempis, one of their most distinguished members, has followed a special system of notation in his *Imitation of Christ*. This

---

[1] *Science of Verse*, p. 57.   [2] Maken = make.   [3] Can = know.

book, on account of its rhythmical notation, was called in his own day, a "metrical volume," and later on was known as "ecclesiastical music." His system of notation is as follows:

(1) The **period** followed by a **large** capital;
(2) The **period** followed by a **small** capital;
(3) The **colon** followed by a **small** letter;
(4) The **clivis** or **flexa** (𝄋) used in the musical notation of that time.

These signs are used according to a well-conceived method. "They serve in his writings the same purpose as do in music the signs which indicate the modulations of the voice; they mark the pauses which the reader must observe in order that he may recite the sentence in accordance with the intention of the author, and give it that effect, that cadence, that charm which speech requires to make it penetrate into the hearer's soul."[1] An extract will best illustrate the use of this rhythmic notation. We take a passage from Dr. Challoner's English version of *The Imitation:*

"If all were perfect, what then should we have to bear with from others for the love of God ? But now God hath thus ordered it, that we may learn to bear one another's burdens ; for no one is without defect, no one without his burden ; no one is sufficient for himself, no one is wise enough for himself ; but we must support one another, comfort one another, help, instruct, and admonish one another. But the measure of each man's virtue is best seen in occasions of adversity. For occasions do not make a man frail, but they show what he is."

According to the notation of Thomas à Kempis, the passage reads as follows:

Si essent omnes perfecti 𝄋	Were all men perfect |
Quid tunc haberemus ab aliis,	What would be left for us to bear with, |
pro Deo pati ?	one from the other, for God's sake ? |
Nunc autem Deus sic ordinavit,	But now hath God so ordained,

---

[1] Charles Reulens: Introduction to the fac-simile of the autograph manuscript of *The Imitation*, in the Royal Library of Brussels, p. 18.

ut discamus alter alterius onera portare ⁋	that we learn each to bear the other's burden |
quia nemo sine defectu,	for no man is without his failings,|
nemo sine onere:	none without his burden: ❙
nemo sibi sufficiens,	none self-sufficing,|
nemo sibi satis sapiens ⁋	none for himself wise enough. ❙
sed oportet nos invicem portare	But it behoveth each in turn to support the other,|
invicem consolari:	to comfort and console: ❙
pariter adjuvare,	likewise to help,|
instruere et admonere.	to instruct and to admonish. ❙
Quantæ autem virtutis quisque fuerit,	But what measure of virtue each may have,|
melius patet occasione adversitatis.	best appeareth in adversity. ❙
Occasiones namque hominem fragilem non faciunt:	Occasion never maketh a man frail: ❙
sed qualis sit,	but what he is, |
ostendunt.[1]	that it showeth. ❙

Lib. I. cap. 16 (Edition of Hirsche, p. 39).

7. The rhythm of modern prose has a **twofold** dependence :

(1) Upon the **nature** of the idea expressed ;
(2) Upon the **mental tone** of the speaker or writer expressing the idea.

8. Prose rhythm is an expression of the ever-present **rhythms of Nature.**

Every atom in Nature has a recurrent motion. Every continuous motion or sound is made up of elementary pulsations. Every expression of human thought has underlying it, in a manner more or less

---

[1] The perfect rhythm of the book can only be appreciated in the original Latin in which it was written. We cannot make too careful a study of a book so rich in spiritual thought and so universal a favorite.

distinct, varying with the force and intensity of the expression, these recurrent pulsations. This is what is meant by rhythm.

9. **Rhythm accompanies the sense and meaning of the expression as well as the expression itself.**

Where the rhythm exists in an original form of thought, it will be found in any translation of that form. The rhythm of the Old Testament and the New—especially the solemn music of the Hebrew—is found more or less in every translation of the Bible. Men felt the rhythmic flow of *The Imitation* in its weakest translations, long before its rhythmic structure was discovered.

10. **The rhythm of nature becomes embodied in language whenever the brain of the speaker or writer is at a certain tension of emotion caused by some passion.**

"Deeper than all the rhythms of art is the rhythm of nature, for the rhythm of nature is the rhythm of life itself. We mean the living metre of that energy of the spirit which surges within the bosom of him who speaks. Being rhythm, it is of course governed by law as surely as the rhythm of art, but it is a law which transcends in subtlety the conscious art of the metrecist; a law which, being part of nature's own sanctions, can, of course, never be formulated, but only expressed—expressed, for instance, in the melody of the bird, in the inscrutable harmony of the entire bird-chorus of the thicket, in the whispers of the leaves of the trees, and in the songs or wails of the winds and seas."—*Athenæum*, No. 2969.

11. **Every great writer or speaker has a distinct keynote running through the rhythm of his composition.**

This follows from the fact that the rhythm is determined both by the nature of the subject-matter and the temperament of the speaker or writer. Edmund Burke's magnificent passage on Marie Antoinette is in a far different key-note from Webster's Bunker Hill speech, or John Bright's peroration on the American war, or Macaulay's celebrated eulogy on the Catholic Church.

12. Rhythmic recurrence varies according to the nature of the idea the author would express.

This may best be illustrated by analyzing some passages according to their rhythm.

L.

This begins in the natural conversational tone and gently ascends to a more elevated form of expression in the last clause.	"I have of late (but wherefore I know not) lost all my mirth, | foregone all custom of exercises; |
Here the poetic glow vibrates still more clearly.	and indeed it goes so heavily with my disposition, | that this goodly frame, the earth, seems to me a sterile promontory; |
Rhythmic recurrence is here apparent: *this goodly frame* . . . *this most excellent canopy* . . . *this brave o'er-hanging firmament* . . . *this majestical roof*.	this most excellent canopy, the air,| look you, this brave o'er-hanging firmament, | this majestical roof, fretted with golden fire—|
Here is the anti-climax giving expression to despondency in a minor key.	why, it appears no other thing to me, but a foul and pestilent congregation of vapors. |
Here the emotion deepens. Every exclamation is heavily laden with thought. The form is changed in order to avoid monotony: *how noble . . . how infinite . . . in form.* Note also the double rhythm—*form . . . moving—express . . . admirable*—where the construction is changed.	What a piece of work is a man !| How noble in reason !| How infinite in faculty !| in form and moving how express and admirable !| in action, how like an angel !| in apprehension, how like a god !| the beauty of the world!| the paragon of animals !|
Note the solemn tone in which the despondency of Hamlet is expressed.	And yet, to me, what is this quintessence of dust ?| Man delights not me.—SHAKESPEARE,— *Hamlet*, Act ii, Sc. 2.

The concluding short sentence contains as many rhythmic words as the longer sentence preceding. In the long sentence are the three rhythmic words, *me, quintessence, dust;* in the short, are the three words, *man, delights, me.*

II.

CARDINAL NEWMAN ON MUSIC.

This is a plain statement, in few and simple words, of the point the author would develop. The rhythm arises from the contrasts mentioned.

There are seven notes in the scale; | make them fourteen; | yet what a slender outfit for so vast an enterprise! | What science brings so much out of so little? | Out of what poor elements does some great master in it create his new world! |

Here the sentences become more complex, as the author seeks a solution, and replies to objections. The rhythm is also of a more complex character.

Shall we say that all this exuberant inventiveness is a mere ingenuity or trick of art, | like some game or fashion of the day, | without reality, | without meaning? | We may do so; | and then, perhaps, we shall also account the science of theology to be a matter of words; | yet, as there is a divinity in the theology of the Church | which those who feel cannot communicate, | so is there also | in the wonderful creation of sublimity and beauty | of which I am speaking. |

The author again makes a simple statement regarding the technicalities of music.

To many men the very names which the science employs are utterly incomprehensible. |

Note how well balanced these two clauses are. The author wishes to say that we cannot speak of musical composition as we would speak of literary composition.	To speak of an idea or a subject seems to be fanciful or trifling, | to speak of the views which it opens upon us to be childish extravagance; |
Here the author's language glows. Note the balance of every rhythmic phrase and the music of the whole.	yet is it possible that that inexhaustible evolution and disposition of notes, | so rich yet so simple, | so intricate yet so regulated, | so various yet so majestic, | should be a mere sound, which is gone and perishes? |
Here note the variety in length, in these phrases or clauses, the recurrence of expressions, the effect of the repetition of the word *and*, and the regularity of rhythmic words in each phrase or clause.	Can it be that those mysterious stirrings of heart, | and keen emotions, | and strange yearnings after we know not what, | and awful impressions from we know not whence, | should be wrought in us by what is unsubstantial, | and comes and goes, | and begins | and ends | in itself? |
Note the perfect balance of these two solemn denials.	It is not so; | it cannot be. |
Read and re-read this sentence. It is a magnificent outburst of eloquence. And yet, the speaker, while his soul is vibrating in rhythmic harmony with his sub-	No; | they have escaped from some higher sphere; | they are the outpourings of eternal harmony | in the medium of created sound; | they are echoes from our Home; | they are the voice of Angels, | or the Magnificat of Saints, |

ject, holds in check his imagination and uses only simple words. The whole passage is one of the most beautiful in the English language.

{ or the living laws of Divine governance, |
or the Divine attributes; |
something are they besides themselves, |
which we cannot compass, |
which we cannot utter,— |
—though mortal man, | and he perhaps not otherwise distinguished above his fellows, | has the gift of eliciting them.

—*Oxford University Sermons*, pp. 346, 347.

EXTRACTS FOR RHYTHMIC ANALYSIS.

I.

AMBITION AND DEATH.

O eloquent, just, and mighty death! whom none could advise, thou hast persuaded; what none hath dared, thou hast done; and whom all the world hath flattered, thou only hast cast out of the world and despised; thou hast drawn together all the far-stretched greatness, all the pride, cruelty, and ambition of man, and covered it all over with these two narrow words, *Hic jacet!*[1]—SIR WALTER RALEIGH—*History of the World.*

II.

THE EVERLASTING CHURCH.

There is not, and there never was on this earth, a work of human policy[2] so well deserving of examination as the Roman Catholic Church. The history of that Church joins together the two great ages of human civilization. No other institution is left standing which carries the mind back to the times when the smoke of sacrifice rose from the Pantheon, and when camelopards and tigers bounded in the Flavian amphitheatre. The proudest royal houses are but of yesterday when compared with the line of the Supreme Pontiffs. That line we trace back, in an unbroken series, from the Pope who crowned

---

[1] *Hic jacet* = here lies, the words with which it was customary to begin epitaphs on tombstones.

[2] Macaulay, not being a Catholic, regarded the Church as a purely human institution. The Church is divine in her origin and her teaching.

Napoleon in the nineteenth century, to the Pope who crowned Pepin in the eighth; and far beyond the time of Pepin the august dynasty extends. . . . The republic of Venice came next in antiquity. But the republic of Venice was modern when compared with the Papacy; and the republic of Venice is gone, and the Papacy remains. The Papacy remains,[1] not in decay, not a mere antique, but full of life and useful vigor. The Catholic Church is still sending forth to the farthest ends of the world, missionaries as zealous as those who landed in Kent with Augustin, and still confronting hostile kings with the same spirit with which she confronted Attila. The number of her children is greater than in any former age. Her acquisitions in the New World have more than compensated her for what she has lost in the Old. Her spiritual ascendancy extends over the vast countries which lie between the plains of Missouri and Cape Horn; countries which, a century hence, may not improbably contain a population as large as that which now inhabits Europe. The members of her communion are certainly not fewer than one hundred and fifty millions.[2] . . . Nor do we see any sign which indicates that the term of her long dominion is approaching. She saw the commencement of all the governments and of all the ecclesiastical establishments that now exist in the world, and we feel no assurance that she is not destined to see the end of them all. She was great and respected before the Saxon had set foot on Britain, before the Frank had passed the Rhine, when Grecian eloquence still flourished in Antioch, when idols were still worshipped in the temple of Mecca. And she may still exist in undiminished vigor, when some traveller from New Zealand shall, in the midst of a vast solitude, take his stand on a broken arch of London Bridge, to sketch the ruins of St. Paul's.

III.

CIVILIZING INFLUENCE OF THE BLESSED VIRGIN MARY.

For the first time woman was elevated to her rightful position, and the sanctity of weakness was recognized as well as the sanctity of

---

[1] Note the effect with which these words, *the Papacy remains*, are repeated.
[2] At present they are estimated at over two hundred and seventy-five millions.

sorrow. No longer the slave or toy of man, no longer associated only with ideas of degradation and of sensuality, woman rose in the person of the Virgin mother into a new sphere, and became the object of a reverential homage of which antiquity had had no conception. Love was idealized. The moral charm and beauty of female excellence was for the first time felt. A new type of character was called into being; a new kind of admiration was fostered. Into a harsh and ignorant and benighted age, this ideal type infused a conception of gentleness and of purity unknown to the proudest civilizations of the past. In the pages of living tenderness which many a monkish writer has left in honor of his celestial patron; in the millions who, in many lands and in many ages, have sought with no barren desire to mould their characters into her image; in those holy maidens who for the love of Mary have separated themselves from all the glories and pleasures of the world, to seek in fastings and vigils and humble charity to render themselves worthy of her benediction; in the new sense of honor, in the chivalrous respect, in the softening of manners, in the refinement of tastes displayed in all the walks of society; in these and many other ways we detect its influence. All that was best in Europe clustered around it, and it is the origin of many of the purest elements of our civilization.—LECKY.

INDEX.

(The numbers refer to the pages.)

A, an, 14.
Adieu, 144.
Above, 144.
Absence of limitations, 15.
Acatalectic verse, 238.
Accent, 10.
Active voice, 77.
Adieu, 144.
Adjective, defined, 12.
    classes of, 34, 35.
    comparison of, 39.
    its modifiers, 19.
    syntax of, 197-204.
Adjective adjunct, 55.
    clause, 153.
    phrase, 57.
Adjuncts, 55.
Adverb, defined, 13.
    its modifiers, 59.
    how formed, 128.
    classification of, 124-127.
    modification of, 127-129.
    functions of, 129.
    syntax of, 197-204.
Adverbial adjunct, 55.
    clause, 153.
        its functions, 154.
    phrase, 57, 124.
Addison, 133, 199, 218, 240.
After, 144.
Affirmative conjugation, 83.
Agreement, 165.
All, 144.
Alliteration, 237.
Allowable rhyme, 237.
Amphibrach, 244.
Analysis, 51, 151.
Anapest, 238.

Anapæstic verse, 241.
Antecedent, 45.
Any, 144.
Apostrophe, 236.
Apposition, 166.
Arnold, Matthew, 220.
Arnold, of Rugby, 219.
Article, defined, 12.
    classes of, 34, 35.
    syntax of, 193-197.
As, 144.
Asterisk, 235.
Attribute, defined, 54.
    what it may be, 54, 55.
Aubrey de Vere, 227.
Auxiliary verb, 82.

BACON, 133, 198, 202, 232.
Beaumont and Fletcher, 150.
Be, conjugated, 88.
Behave, 107.
Before, 145.
Better, 41.
Beware, 114.
Blackmore, 220.
Blank verse, 242.
Blow, 108.
Brackets, 235.
Bret Harte, 142.
Brethren of the Common Life, 245.
Browning, 73.
Bryant, 182.
Built, 113.
Burke, 193, 194, 203, 219, 220.
Burns, 98, 240.
But, 145.
By, 146.
Byron, 27, 113, 167, 208, 210, 214, 226.

INDEX.

CADENCE, 245.
Cæsural pause, 242.
Campbell, 135, 187, 192, 204, 222, 237, 241.
Capitals, rules for, 6, 7.
Carlyle, 115, 231.
Cases, 28.
Catalectic verse, 238.
Change of form in tenses, 80.
Channing, 167, 168, 194.
Chapman, 205.
Chaucer, 171, 188, 195, 212, 245.
Child, Lydia Maria, 142.
Clause, 151.
Clomb, 113.
Cobbett, 235.
Coleridge, 81, 166, 167, 178, 193, 194, 197, 208, 221.
Collier, 133.
Colon, 229.
Comma, 231.
Common adjective, 36.
  noun, 15, 16.
Common metre, 239.
Comparative degree, 39.
Comparison, of adjectives, 39.
  degrees of, 39,
  regular, 39.
  by adverbs, 39.
  of adverbs, 127, 129.
Complex sentence, 151, 152.
Compound personal pronouns, 44.
  relative pronouns, 47.
Compound sentence, 152.
Compound word, 10.
Connection, relations of, 165
Conjunction, defined, 13.
  classification of, 135-139.
  syntax of, 213.
Consonants, 4.
Contractions, 236.
Co-ordinate conjunction, 212.
Correlative conjunction, 213.
Correct pronunciation, 10.
Couplet, 224.
Cowper, 11, 166, 186, 219.
Crabbe, 202.
Crawford, F. Marion, 130.
Curtis, George W., 218, 220.

DACTYL, 238.
Dactylic hexameter, 242.
Dagger, 235.

Dash, 233.
Declarative sentence, 51.
Declension, 31.
Defective verb, 82, 114.
Demonstrative pronoun, 47.
Dentals, 3.
Derivative word, 10.
Dependent clause, 151.
De Quincey, 203.
Dickens, 27, 167, 175, 186.
Dimeter, 238.
Diminution, degrees of, 40.
Diphthongs, 4.
Direct affirmative form, 83.
Dissyllable, 9.
Donne, 218.
Double-dagger, 235.
Dryden, 132, 146, 174, 188, 194.
Durst, 116.
Dwight, J. S., 54.

Eat, 108.
Elementary forms of language, 1.
Eliot, George, 188.
Ellipsis, 166.
Else, 146.
Emerson, 113, 220.
Etymology, defined, 1.
  its office, 12.
Except, 146.
Exclamation point, 233.
Exclamatory sentence, 52.
Explanatory adjuncts, 56.
  clause, 154.
  phrase, 57.
Exercises: In parsing, 14; in nouns, 16, 17; in formation of plural, 22-25; in genders, 28; in cases, 31-34; on the article, 35; in adjectives, 36-39; in comparison, 42, 43; in pronouns, 48-51; in analysis, 60-67; in sentence-building, 67-74; in verbs, 101-107, 117-119; in the infinitive, 120, 121; in participles, 122, 123; in adverbs, 130, 131; in prepositions, 135; in conjunctions, 135; in interjections, 141-143; in analysis, 156-158; in sentence building, 163, 164.

FABER, 157, 234, 239.
Fielding, 208.
Final pause, 242.
Finite forms, 76.
Fitz-Greene Halleck, 152.

INDEX. 257

Foot (poetic), 237.
For, 147.
    former use of, 212.
Ford, 146.
Forms of conjugation, 62.
Franklin, 138, 234.
Freeman, 104.
Full, 147.
Fuller, 146.
Future perfect tense, 80.
Future tense, 80.

GRAMMATICAL SUBJECT, 52.
Gray, 185, 202.
Gutturals, 8.
Gender, defined, 25.
    how distinguished, 26, 27.
    how distinguished in Old English, 27.
Gladstone, 198.
Goldsmith, 150, 176, 196.
Government, 165.
Grammar, 1, 2.
    Cardinal Newman on, 2.

Have, conjugation of, 85
Hawthorne, 219.
Hazlitt, 149.
Heber, 240.
Heptameter, 238.
Heroic metre, 239.
Hexameter, 238.
Heywood, 188.
Holland, 101.
Hood, 54, 142, 241.
Hume, 221.
Hung, 113.
Hypermetrical verse, 238.
Hyphen, 234.

IAMBUS, 237.
Iambic pentameter, 243.
Iambic verse, 238.
Idioms, 218-221.
If, 214, 215.
Ill, 147.
Imperative mood, 99.
    sentence, 51-53.
Imperfect participle, 75.
    tense, 80.
Impersonal verbs, 77.
Independent clause, 151.
    phrase, 57.

Indicative mood, 78, 98.
Interrogative conjugation, 84.
    pronoun, 47, 48.
    sentence, 52.
Interjection, defined, 18, 140.
    lists of, 140, 141.
    syntax of, 165.
Intransitive verb, defined, 76.
Irregular verbs, defined, 76.
    principal parts, 107.
Irving, 55, 108, 176, 177.
Infinitive forms, 75.
    mood, 99.
    forms of, 119.
    phrases, 119.
Italics, rules for, 8, 9.

JEFFREY, 220.
Johnson, 178, 212.
Jonson, Ben, 182.
Junius, 185.

KEATS, 177.
Kingsley, 79.

LABIALS, 8.
Lade, 109.
Lamb, 222.
Langland, 48.
Language, 1.
Lanier, Sydney, 224.
Late, last, latter, later, latest, 40.
Lecky, 253.
Letters, 3-7.
Less, 41.
Lien, 109.
Like, 147.
Lingard, 105.
Logical subject, 52.
Longfellow, 28, 72, 78, 167, 172, 177, 178, 189, 197, 198, 220, 242.
Losen, lorn, 111.
Love, conjugated, 90.
Lowell, 33, 74, 158.

MACAULAY, 134, 188, 189, 198, 199, 204, 210.
Maetzner, 207.
Marsh, George P., 202.
Masson, 181.
Methinks, 77.
Milton, 46, 109, 112, 132, 133, 134, 167, 177, 188, 194, 208, 204, 213, 214, 221, 223.
Mixed verse, 242.

INDEX.

Models in analysis, 155, 156.
Monometer, 238.
Monosyllable, 9.
Mood, 78.
Moore, 198, 240.
Morley, John, 219.
Morris, George P., 152.
Much, 41.
Mun, 82.
Must, 82, 116.

NASALS, 3.
Near, 41.
Need, 117.
Needs, 118.
Negative form of a verb, 84.
    imperative, 85.
    interrogative, 85.
Nelson, 202.
Newman, Cardinal, 2, 8, 53, 69, 73, 117, 172, 205, 207, 210, 219, 220, 221, 222, 250.
Nil, 82, 115.
Nominative case, 20.
Noun, defined, 12.
    classes of, 15.
    its modifiers, 58.
    syntax of, 179-182.
Now, 148.
Number, 18-21.
    in verbs, 81.
    of feet, 238.
Numeral adjectives, 36.

OBJECTIVE CASE, 30.
Object of a sentence, 58.
Organs of speech, 3.
Orthography, 1-3.
Ottava rima, 226.
Ought, 115.

PALATALS, 3.
Paley, 204.
Paragraph, 235.
Parallels, 235.
Parenthesis, 234.
Parnell, 242.
Parsing, 13.
Participles, defined, 121.
    object of, 58.
    modifiers of, 59.
    forms of, 121.
    used as prepositions, 122.
Participial adjective, 36.

Participial infinitive, 122.
Parts of speech, 12.
Passive voice, 77, 78.
Pentameter, 238.
Period, 228.
Perfect infinitive, 119, 120.
    tense, 80.
    rhyme, 237.
Persons, 18; in verbs, 81.
Personal pronouns, 43, 44.
Personification, 27.
Phrase, definition, 56.
    classes of, 56-58.
Piers Plowman, Vision of, 150.
Pleonasm, 166.
Pluperfect tense, 80.
Poe, Edgar Allan, 116, 240.
Polysyllable, 9.
Pope, 11, 133, 149, 166, 167, 171, 176, 179, 182, 184, 188, 193, 197, 205, 220, 224, 234, 239.
Positive degree, 39.
Possessive case, 30.
Potential mood, 78, 98.
Predicate, defined, 53.
    grammatical, 53.
    compound, 53.
Prefix, 10.
Preperfect participle, 122.
Preposition, defined, 13, 131.
    object of, 58.
    functions, 131.
    lists of, 132-134.
    syntax of, 200.
Present tense, 80.
Primary adjuncts, 56.
Primitive word, 10.
Principal words, 58.
Principal proposition, 151.
Procter, Adelaide, 225.
Pronominal adjective, 36.
Pronoun, defined, 12, 43.
    classes of, 43.
    syntax of, 182-193.
Pronunciation, correct, 10.
Proper nouns, 15.
    adjectives, 36.
Prose, 224.
Prosody, 224.
Punctuation, 228-236.

QUARLES, 225.
Quatrain, 225.

INDEX. 259

Quotation, 235.
Quoth, 115.

REGULAR VERBS, 76.
Relations, of agreement, 165.
  of government, 165.
  of connection, 165.
Relative pronoun, 45.
  its syntax, 188.
Robert of Brunne, 206.
Rome, 11.
Robinson Crusoe, 71.
Root-infinitive, 75.
Rhyme, 236, 237.
Rhythm in prose, 244-254.
  in verse, 244.
Rhythms of nature, 247-251.

Save, 148.
Scott, 54, 116, 167, 173, 174, 185, 189, 203, 213, 221, 234, 241.
Sea, 11.
Secondary feet, 42.
  adjuncts, 56.
Section, 235.
Self, 44.
Sentence, defined, 13.
  classes as to meaning, 51.
  classes as to form, 151.
  -building, 67-74; 158-163.
Sestett, 225.
Shakespeare, 11, 41, 46, 51, 52, 74, 78, 109, 115, 132, 133, 134, 143, 166, 167, 172, 173, 174, 176, 179, 183, 184, 190, 192, 195, 199, 200, 204, 206, 207, 210, 219, 221, 222, 223, 226, 229, 233, 238, 243, 249.
Shakespeare's Plays, 243; note on, 244.
Shelley, 166, 191, 197.
Shenstone, 241.
Sheridan, 207.
Shook, 109.
Shope, 113.
Sibilants, 4.
Sidney, 133, 148.
Simple sentence, 52, 151.
  personal pronouns, 44, 45.
  subject, 51.
Smote, 109.
So, 148.
Sonnet, 220, 227.
Southey, 182, 242.
Spelling, correct, 11.
Spenser, 111, 116.

Spenserian stanza, 226.
Spondee, 242.
Stanza, 225.
Strong endings, 243.
Strong verbs, 107.
Study, conjugated, 96.
Subject, 52, 168-170.
Subjunctive mood, 79, 98, 99.
Subordinate proposition, 151.
Substantive phrase, 56, 57.
  clause, 152.
Suffix, 10.
Swetchine, Madam, 167.
Swift, 142, 183, 188, 189.
Syllable, 9.
Syntax, 1, 165.

TATLER, 134.
Taylor, 121.
Tea, 10.
Temple, Sir W., 134, 195.
Tennyson, 30, 73, 79, 133, 167, 179, 182, 191, 200, 208, 213, 214, 221, 222, 225, 240.
Tense, 80.
Tetrameter, 238.
Thackeray, 187, 195, 222.
That, 45, 47.
The, 140.
This, 47.
Thomas à Kempis, 245.
Thou, 53.
Though, 214.
Thomson, 183.
Till, 149.
Transitive verb, 54, 76.
Tribrach, 242.
Trimeter, 238.
Triplet, 225.
Trisyllable, 9.
Trochaic verse, 240.
Trochee, 237.
Trollope, 207.

UNIPERSONAL VERB, 76.

VERB, defined, 13.
  its modifiers, 59, 74.
  classification as to form, 75, 76.
  classification as to meaning, 76.
  modifications of, 77.
  principal parts of, 81.
  conjugation of, 82.

Verb, agreement of, 168.
    syntax of, 170.
Verbal nouns, 120, 121.
Verse, 224.
Versification, 226.
Vocal sounds, 3.
Voice, 77.
Vowels, 4.

W, when a consonant, 5.
Weak verbs, 107.
Welcome, 107.
Well, 149.
Went, 109.
What, 45, 46, 47.
Whately, 178.
Where and its compounds, 46.
Whether, 48.

Which, 45, 46, 47.
While, 150.
Whittier, 55, 84, 142.
Who, 45, 46, 47.
Will, 82.
Willy nilly, 115.
Wit, 116.
Wot, 115.
Wolfe, 175, 232.
Won't, 115.
Words, 1, 5, 9, 10, 148.
Wordsworth, 164, 167. 175, 190, 242.
Worth, 114, 150.
Would, 115.

Ymade, 150.
Yon, yond, yonder, 196.
Young, 167, 233.